CORPORATE-SPEAK

Corporate-Speak

The Use of Language in Business

Fiona Czerniawska

First published 1997 by
MACMILLAN PRESS LTD
Houndmills, Basingstoke, Hampshire RG21 6XS
and London
Companies and representatives
throughout the world

ISBN 0–333–67477–4

A catalogue record for this book is available
from the British Library.

This book is printed on paper suitable for recycling and made from fully managed and sustained forest sources.

10 9 8 7 6 5 4 3 2 1
06 05 04 03 02 01 00 99 98 97

Copy-edited and typeset by Povey–Edmondson
Tavistock and Rochdale, England

Printed and bound in Great Britain by
Creative Print and Design (Wales), Ebbw Vale

For Stefan

'Then you should say what you mean,' the March Hare went on. 'I do,' Alice hastily replied; 'at least I mean what I say – that's the same thing you know.' 'Not the same thing a bit!' said the Hatter. 'Why, you might just as well say that "I see what I eat" is the same thing as "I eat what I see!"'

(Lewis Carroll, *Alice in Wonderland*)

'From the world of business and management come many powerful words which have been developed to describe the line processes that go on in that world. In contrast to the academic world which is a world of description, the business world is a world of action'.

(Edward de Bono, *Wordpower*)

Contents

Introduction: The Daughters of Earth

> Roger . . . has a speech problem. One which prevents him from speaking intelligently in the presence of his business peers. Here is something Roger said recently to a colleague: 'The client has an overly high expectation, market penetration wise.'
>
> What does it mean? Nothing, I'm afraid. Roger is talking nonsense. But did his colleague turn round and say: 'What is that meant to mean, for heaven's sake?' No, I'm afraid he did not. What he said was: 'Well, when you're in a customer-focused situation, you need more product awareness than their sort of low-profile image is going to generate.'
>
> Yes, when Roger talks nonsense, his colleague talks nonsense back to him.[1]

This book is about that nonsense.

Why do we use business jargon? When does jargon cease to be jargon, and when does it start being everyday language? Why do particular companies use particular words? Why is a group discussion a 'meeting' for most companies, but an 'event' for some? Where does 'business language' come from? What impact does it have on the way we work?

These are not new questions – the jargon of business is as old as business itself – but they are ones which are becoming increasingly important.

In a world where the information age is more *ancien régime* than revolution, businesses succeed or fail on the extent to which they can share knowledge, overcome organisational boundaries and coordinate global resources. All these activities rely on better and more frequent communication, whether it is in terms of technology firing digitised data across the world in fractions of a second, or multifunctional – even multilingual – teams working together to resolve a common problem.

FROM NUMBERS TO WORDS

Traditionally, our preferred mode of communication has been figures: a simple balance sheet, after all, requires no translation. Like any language in use for thousands of years, the use of figures in business has evolved to a high level of sophistication, as a glance at any set of accounting standards shows.

But figures only get us so far. Look at the international financial services company which judged its national subsidiaries in terms of year-on-year profits and thus gave them no chance to make short-term sacrifices to achieve longer-term goals. Look at the retailer whose store managers were measured by their capacity to minimise stock loss and who therefore had no incentive to exploit local opportunities to increase sales. More and more companies are finding that some of their most important assets – people, knowledge, commitment – are non-quantifiable. And they are realising that, if they cannot express these assets in terms of figures, then they cannot use financial metrics to manage them. It is therefore not surprising that they are turning to something other than figures to fill the gap – words: mission statements, commitments to quality, customer charters, corporate advertising – the list is growing exponentially.

And it is not just the importance of words which is changing, so too are the words we use. Charles Handy noted this when he described the way in which organisations will need to change to meet the challenges of an uncertain environment:

> The softer words of leadership and vision and common purpose will replace the tougher words of control and authority because the tough words won't bite any more.[2]

But this cultural shift presents us with several problems. Western business – and anglophone businesses in particular – has always been very 'anti-language'. It is a prejudice which is frequently disguised as an appeal for straight-talking, plain English and the eradication of technical jargon, but its implications are more far-reaching and profound. We distrust people who are too good with words: hence the comparably low public opinion of politicians and advertising agencies. New words, glib words appear to be without substance:

> Consider the substance of the case in favour of embracing empowerment. It is put most vocally by that breed of business evangelists

and their missionary converts who seek some form of indelibility in business scriptures. For those familiar with modern management jargon and double-speak: empowerment is something that, if deeply understood and internalised by both executive management and the workforce, can unleash the synergistic creative energy of everyone in the organisation. De-jargonised, the message is simple: if you understand what it is all about, there is a pretty good chance that you'll get more out of it, than you put in.[3]

Take for example the way in which we talk and write about the management of change in organisations:

> The role of the traditional researcher has arguably been usurped by the wordsmith . . . who has mastery of the pithy phrase and who can fashion a colourful metaphor. In a remarkably short time the language used by practising managers, by many management trainers and by many researchers has coalesced into a diorama of metaphor.[4]

'MBA-speak', as it has been termed, suggests whiz-kids who take industries by storm with the latest management fads and buzz-words but who fail to add anything of lasting practical value. Worse still, MBA-speak smacks of hypocrisy:

> Unluckily a certain amount of claptrap is already being talked about methods of communication. The phrase 'work participation' is being used here as if it were some sort of psychological *abracadabra*. In the United States the idea of 'group thinking' in committee is being blown up into a panacea. The phrase 'industrial democracy' again may mean anything – or it may mean nothing. That favourite retort 'my door is always open' is loathed and generally ridiculed by our own trade union leaders. In fact, communication, like market research, public relations and industrial psychology before it, is already attracting its quota of racketeers in America.[5]

These comments were written in 1955, but sentiments continue to echo today, for example:

> Culture is a word that is common enough, just a touch high falutin', and perfect for the kind of oversimplification that television and

> video cassettes require. The serious business manager, however, will lose nothing by ignoring it . . . his brain may be clearer if he expunges the term from his consciousness altogether.[6]

At the heart of this is a belief that business is about action, not words. In fact, words and actions often seem mutually exclusive: how many times have we complained that a meeting has become a 'talking shop'?

Take a look at General Electric's 1995 annual report. Here is a company reporting record results: revenues increased by 17 per cent to $70bn, net earnings up by 11 per cent. Beside the figures, much of the thrust of the report is aimed at promoting the company's continued growth strategy and at defending it against the arguments for demerger:

> Our dream, and our plan, well over a decade ago, was simple. We set out to shape a global enterprise that preserved the classic big-company advantages – while eliminating the classic big-company drawbacks. What we wanted to build was a hybrid, an enterprise with the reach and resources of a big company – the body of a big company – but the thirst to learn, the compulsion to share and the bias for action – the soul – of a small company.

This is a report, therefore, which is about cultural change as much as financial performance; it is also about language. Big companies are too verbose: what GE wanted was to empower individuals to manage the resources of a big company but with 'small company' flexibility – it wanted to make them say less and do more:

> Self-confident people don't need to wrap themselves in complexity, 'businessese' speech, and all that clutter that passes for sophistication in business – especially big business. Self-confident leaders produce simple plans, speak simply and propose big, clear targets.

It was an approach which was mirrored at the strategic level. Senior executives whose personal style did not match the values GE was trying to grow were removed: the company had to 'walk the talk' – prove that its own statements were not just words, but were backed with action. Reading the report, we might in fact infer that words and action were in inverse proportion to each other: as the levels of 'stifling' verbiage fell, new life was breathed into the corporation:

> Meetings around the Company that used to consist of self-serving 'reports' and windy speeches became interactive forums for disseminating new ideas and the sharing of experiences. A whole new behavior has invigorated and freshened this century-old company.

Of course, this opposition between words and action has resonance far beyond GE's immediate corporate history and, indeed, beyond the wider prejudices of our business environment. It taps into a deeper cultural seam which has surfaced again and again over the centuries: a young boy in Shakespeare's *Henry V* opines that 'men of few words are the best men'.[7] 'Life's but a walking shadow', says Macbeth,

> a poor player,
> That struts and frets his hour upon the stage,
> And then is heard no more; it is a tale
> Told by an idiot, full of sound and fury,
> Signifying nothing.[8]

Even Samuel Johnson, when he had finished his Herculean labour over *A Dictionary of the English Language* in 1755, felt the need to reassure his readers:

> I am not yet so lost in lexicography as to forget that words are the daughters of earth, and that things are the sons of heaven. Language is only the instrument of science, and words are but the signs of ideas.[9]

Given this context, we should not be surprised that so many of the mission statements we encounter sound bland: if you do not trust words, you are hardly likely to produce anything memorable. But these are the horns of the particular dilemma on which we find ourselves caught. On the one hand, we do not like having to use words – they defer action – but on the other hand, we need words more than ever because we have to communicate more quickly and more effectively, and on subjects for which simple numbers will not be sufficient.

It is worse than this, in fact. As technology changes the way in which we work and as competition becomes sharper, the 'word-free' content of our lives is declining.

After the Second World War, a man making ball-bearings did just that: demand for steel outstripped its supply, so the majority of his customers came to him, rather than vice versa; interaction with those customers was limited as there was little facility to change the specification of manufactured goods to order; post-sales support was non-existent. Today, the same manufacturer faces over-capacity and global competition: to sell his products he needs to market them and to build up long-term customer relationships; to differentiate himself from his competitors, he has to offer added-value services; to keep his prices down, he must form strategic partnerships with his suppliers. Each of these new activities involves communication – with customers, with employees, with suppliers; before, doing was enough, now he has to talk as well. Some social scientists, like Elton Mayo, foresaw this. Writing on organisational communications in general, he noted in 1945 the way in which the traditional structures within businesses were starting to decay. 'Little of the old establishment survives in modern industry', he wrote,

> the emphasis is upon change and adaptability; the rate of change mounts to an increasing tempo. We have in fact passed beyond that stage of human organization in which effective communication and collaboration were secured by established routines of relationship.[10]

Thus, while we may, in cultural terms, be accustomed to words and action being mutually exclusive, practical experience is changing around us all the time – actions and words are constantly intermixed. We have just not admitted it yet.

LANGUAGE AND BUSINESS

Our prejudice against language is the reason why we have been slow to acknowledge in business just how central a role language plays: as a result, the study of language has remained the preserve solely of psychologists and scholars. Why, after all, should the business world be interested in what is such an esoteric academic subject?

A few years ago, we might well have asked the same question of chaos theory, and yet there is now a widespread acceptance that at least some of our assumptions about long-term planning and the extent to which the evolution of organisations obeys any sort of microeconomic natural law are misplaced. We increasingly recognise that what we thought was a straightfoward relationship between cause and effect may, in fact, be the result of a much wider and more complex system. Understanding the variability and unpredictability of weather patterns may teach us a lot about our business climates, just as new ways of thinking about the evolution of species may be starting to change the way we look at competition.[11]

I predict that the same will be true of language. It takes only a casual glance through the business press to highlight a couple of articles on language – often (like those quoted earlier) diatribes against the onslaught of jargon – yet there has been remarkably little attempt to draw out the patterns of this trend or to discuss its implications. But think how much money is being spent by businesses, either directly or indirectly, on language: internal and external communications, advertising, public relations, market research, building relationships with customers, transforming management styles, developing new organisational and reporting structures. If we think now that we used to make some broad assumptions when it came to future planning (the state of the economy, the needs of customers and so on), these are nothing compared to the scale of assumptions we are making today about the nature of language. We assume that if we issue a company-wide statement, everyone will understand it in the same way; that when we draw up a strategic plan, everyone will know how to act. But we have all seen instances where this is not the case: the corporate statement is interpreted differently by different groups; the relationship between strategy and action is not as straightforward as our plans might suggest.

We carry on doing what we have always done – in spite of the mounting evidence to the contrary because we do not know what else to do: we have no other way of thinking about corporate communications or strategic planning. All of management theory is based upon the notion that language is invisible and irrelevant to business. It therefore has neither the conceptual framework nor the analytical tools to enable us to understand the complex and increasingly prominent role which language is now playing in business. But plenty of theories and approaches do exist, although outside what is commonly supposed to be the confines of business writing: we need to start borrowing from these if we are to begin to understand the current role which language plays in business. Of the plethora of academic writing on language and its role in society – a subject which has evolved rapidly since the late 1970s – there are two aspects which are particularly relevant in a business context.

The first of these treats language – whether in *War and Peace* or in a 30-second television advertisement – as a coherent system of signs. It is an approach which has its roots in social anthropology and philosophy: every society or organisation has its own language system and that language, in its turn, determines the perception which that society or organisation has of reality. Thus, while we are used to thinking that we use language to represent what we see, it may rather be that what we see is determined by what we can say.

Military jargon is a good example of the way in which the meaning of words is used to determine the outlook and behaviour of a given organisation. The navy for example attaches a specific word to something – thus, the sides of a ship become 'port' and 'starboard'. This means that the relationship between the word and what it signifies is a very close one: its meaning is unlikely to be misinterpreted by people within the same organisation (although it is likely to be incomprehensible to those outside it). However, the most important thing about such words is not that they have a specific literal definition, but that their meaning is part of a greater systemic whole. Within organisations, this type of meaning appears in the way in which certain words or phrases acquire greater resonance – they become symbolic of ideas or values, rather then simple receptacles of literal meaning. Again, military organisations are particularly clear illustrations of this. The peculiar terms for ratings and ranks in the navy and the jargon in its rules and regulations helps to create and maintain the rigid structure of the organisation: everyone and everything has its place. If such an organisation is to change, it needs to change its language too.[12]

The second relevant strand of thinking about language takes this a step further: while language (and, indeed, the whole world) may be a system of signs, these systems may be chaotic: 'meaning' is neither as consistent or coherent as is commonly assumed. Thoroughly unpicked, the knitting of any piece of speech or writing becomes nothing more than pieces of wool – different colours, different lengths and unconnected.

The implications for business of this way of thinking are enormous. As we noted earlier, in a world where management by numbers is no longer enough, words are increasingly the heavy guns in the management armoury. Words are the means by which we get things done: we translate our desired action into words so that the person we talk to can translate what we say back into action.

Action → Language → Action

In doing this, we are making the assumption that the relationship between language and action is a straightforward one: in fact, there has to be a bridge between them – meaning.

Action → Meaning → Language → Meaning → Action

A colleague cannot do what we ask unless he or she understands what we mean. Like the Mad Hatter at Alice's tea-party, we assume that it is possible to mean what we say, and say what we mean.

Like us, the organisations in which we work are also built on the assumption that we can communicate, and that any communication has a single meaning – or resulting action – for all those involved. How else could we operate as a collective whole? We believe that we can improve communications, that if we give people the facts, the meaning will be clear: 'truth will prevail if there is ready access to all the relevant information'.[13] We also – fundamentally – believe that we can control meaning. But saying that the language that we use has no stable or consistent meaning is tantamount to admitting that organisational communications – mission statements, for instance – have no objective basis and that if similar actions result from them, then this is as much luck as management judgement. We might as well say that the organisation is outside our control.

It is tempting to apply the brakes to this particular line of argument, before it careers off the road. After all, when we look around us in everyday life, the language-action process does not seem unduly problematic. Of course, from time to time misunderstandings may arise, but these are (we believe) isolated incidents – occasions when we have not understood the meaning correctly: we are at fault, not the meaning. Unless we are very unlucky, if we ask for a glass of water, we get a glass of water. But we only need to move a little way outside our immediate working environment, or ask for something slightly more complex, and we can run into problems. Ask for a glass of cold water, and you may get water from the cold tap when you expected chilled water: 'cold' can mean different things to different people.

In fact, when we start looking for it, we are surrounded by evidence that the meaning of words – even in business – is an unreliable and unpredictable matter. How many IT projects (actions, for these purposes) turn out in the way we intended (described)? Or take one of those 'MBA-speak' terms so derided by business people: Michael Hammer is credited with first coining the phrase 'business process re-engineering' in 1990. His well-known imperative – 'don't automate, obliterate' – promised huge improvements in operational efficiency as organisations removed the barriers to cross-functional working in order to focus on a process 'end to end'. There was always a suspicion that BPR (as it has become known) was just old consultancy wine poured into new billing bottles, and certainly it seems to have been impossible to preserve the more radical aspects of Hammer's approach in practice: a report funded by the European Union in 1995 concluded that 'innovative' BPR has effectively become synonymous with traditional cost-cutting.[14]

A company which does not live up to its reputation is seen as hypocritical, but we should not, argues a leading Swedish sociologist, Nils Brunsson, assume any degree of consistency in organisational meaning at all:

> On the contrary we can expect to find inconsistencies between them: in order to reflect inconsistencies in the environment the political organization can employ inconsistencies, not only within separate areas of talk or decisions or products but also between them. In other words hypocrisy is a fundamental type of behaviour in the political organization: to talk in a way that satisfies one demand, to decide in a way that satisfies another, and to supply products in a way that satisfies a third.[15]

He cites the example of a scandal in Sweden in 1987 when the car manufacturer, Volvo, announced it was going to transport some of its body parts between plants by road not rail – a decision which seemed to fly in the face of the company's environmentally friendly profile.[16] Brunson's argument is that where its external environment is highly uncertain, an organisation has to develop certain strategies for dealing with the resulting internal conflict, and these may take the form of double-talk as much as formal restructuring.[17]

The analogy here is with chaos theory. Using very sophisticated computer-modelling techniques, we can now produce very accurate short-range forecasts. Longer-range forecasts are a different matter:

we are quite used to the notion that five-day forecasts are less reliable, but we do not often appreciate that the level of unpredictability grows exponentially. Thus, because weather is an inherently chaotic system, every minute we forecast into the future, the level of certainty is reduced. The same is true of the relationship between language and action: talk about a glass of water, and people will know what you mean; talk about a glass of cold water, and several possibilities (different meanings) emerge. Now transpose this trend to the specification of a massive IT project: we should not be surprised that so many of them fail so much as that any of them manage to succeed.

LANGUAGE AS A COMPETITIVE WEAPON

So where does this leave us? Just admitting that the relationship between language and action is fraught with difficulties is academic if we cannot do anything about it.

At first sight, it seems to suggest that our inbred suspicions about language are entirely justified: we are right to distrust it. But, as we have already noted, this is no longer an option which is available to us, because language and communication are becoming so fundamental to the way in which our organisations operate internally and compete externally. However much we distrust it, we are much more dependent on language in business than we used to be.

The first thing we can do is recognise that we are wrong to assume that the link between language and action is a simple and direct one. There will, of course, be many occasions when such an assumption would be perfectly valid, but we should not presuppose that just because, when we ask for a glass of water, we get a glass of water, that when we commission an IT project, we will get what we want.

A much more interesting and productive way of thinking about language is to analyse its 'symbolic' meaning.

For example, one company trying to acquire another will usually establish a team of people (some internal, some external) to manage the project. The work is intensive and the team members have to learn how to work together quickly and effectively: the best teams develop a strong sense of camaraderie and it is not uncommon for this to be accompanied by 'in' jokes and jargon. Language provides some of the most important glue in the standard forming–storming–norming–performing cycle of team-work. In 'Ambushes, Shootouts, and Knights of the Roundtable', P. Hirsch and J. Andrews studied how the team-specific jargon which typically develops in these situations actually helps the participants function more effectively. Not surprisingly under the circumstances, much of the imagery used was drawn from battle scenes and heroic myths. This imagery, they found, has four principal functions: it transposes the conflict onto a fictional basis where much of the physical aggression can be dissipated; it specifies how the different actors relate to one another (who is in charge, who is the enemy); it allows the action to be evaluated (against an archetype) and appeals to the value of the participants (people are encouraged to be 'brave').[18] As this illustrates, the meaning of the words used helps to create a different 'symbolic' reality which enables the participants to work more effectively.

For organisations, symbolic meaning is as important – if not more so – as literal meaning in language:

> Human organizations are informational as well as energic systems . . . Information exchange is itself energic, of course, but its energic aspects are of minor significance compared to its symbolic aspects. In other words, information transmission is significant for what it implies, triggers or controls. In general, the closer one gets to the center of organizational control and decision-making, the greater is the emphasis on information exchange and transmittal.[19]

Unlike literal language (the glass of water), symbolic language is unconstrained by physical reality. It therefore presents more possibilities to us than would be possible in 'reality', in fact it allows us to create an alternative reality, not necessarily bound by linear – literal – meaning:

> A linear perspective compels us to use language in a rigid and dehumanising way; the purpose of language in this approach is to *describe* reality. But when a complex open-ended perspective is seen as the source of our language, there is room for expression, creativity and freedom; the role of language in this approach is to *bring forth* reality.[20]

As such, symbolic language is an immensely powerful weapon. Merger and acquisition teams work more effectively because they have a mythic framework which provides both a structure and a meaning for their actions: their work ceases to be mechanistic.

Analysing management myths was one of the academic growth industries of the late 1980s. While fascinating, the drawback with the way in which it was approached is that it was carried out on the assumption that the 'patterned set of meanings' is coherent and stable, that the relationship between language and action – however remotely channelled through a variety of organisational myths – was still a viable one. But, in order to understand how language functions in an organisation, we need to go beyond this framework. We also need to understand the points at which management myths break down or cease to be effective; we need to look for discontinuities and ambiguities. After all, not all M&A teams can win all the time, and we have to understand the weaknesses as well as the strengths of symbolic actions.

To turn language into a truly competitive weapon in practical business, we need to start being more aware of the language we, our colleagues and our competitors use and see it for what it really is – visionary myths, power struggles, group boundaries, discontinuities, auguries of changes to come or relics of changes past. And, when we understand more about the limitations of organisational language, we will be better positioned to exploit its potential.

This book also puts forward the case that language can be a weapon of competitive advantage for organisations. At the moment, most businesses are making what may turn out to be a fatal mistake: they are assuming that the language they use has a straightforward connection to the actions which it is intended to precipitate. In order to get their organisations to do more – to rise to the linguistic-based challenges of the next decade – they are writing mission statements, initiating huge internal communication programmes, launching corporate advertising campaigns: 'one of the ideological outputs of organizations is *talk*'.[21] For all the billions spent on such activities, few companies have thought to look at how language actually functions in their organisations; few are therefore in a position to judge whether the language they use will have the actions they intended.

What this book is not is an exhaustive linguistic analysis of business language: a degree of academic sophistication has been waived in order to discuss the issues raised in a clear, accessible and – hopefully – thought-provoking fashion. What this book also is not is a 'how-to-do-it' guide to business communication: you will not discover how to write a better memo here. What it might make you do, however, is make you think about how and why we define 'better' as we do and why you choose to communicate certain – but by no means all – information in writing.

The overall objective of this book is to raise our awareness of the powerful role that language plays in business. If it makes people think about the words they use in their business lives, and the words they hear others using, it will have succeeded in this aim. As we become inured to the exponential growth of communication, we are in danger of anaesthetising ourselves about its impact.

Notes

1. Miles Kingston, *The Independent* (13 April 1992), quoted by Barsoux, 1993: 185.
2. Handy, 1996: 7.
3. *The Australian Financial Review*, 20 January 1995.
4. Wilson, 1992: 79
5. Chisholm, 1955: 20.
6. Thackery, 1986: 69.
7. Act III, scene 2.
8. Act V, scene 5.
9. Preface.
10. Mayo, 1945: 13.
11. Moore, 1996.
12. Evered, 1983: 125–43.
13. Katz and Kahn, 1966: 224.
14. From a recent report by the Cobra programme which was funded by the EU to look at the use of BPR (*Computing*, 6 July 1995).
15. Brunsson, 1989: 27.
16. Ibid. 28–9.
17. Ibid. 1–12.
18. Hirsch and Andrews, 1983: 145–55.
19. Katz and Kahn, 1966: 257.
20. McMaster, 1996: 32.
21. Brunsson, 1989: 26.

Part I

Putting the Moose on the Table: The Rise of Corporate-Speak

I said I would market a software package into which you fed people's management jargon and out of which you got a prediction as to how rapidly they would absorb the company's money and effort into themselves, forever organising how the company should do its job and forever avoiding the hard bit, which is actually doing it.

Mr Frith [a management consultant] was pleased. 'Thank you. I'll use that.'

(*The Sunday Telegraph*, 9 June 1996)

1 Talking the Talk

When John Grady was made redundant from his IS management position in the early 1990s, he compiled his own 'thesaurus of modern business language' containing many of the examples of corporate-speak he had encountered during his tenure. In it, he translated the phrase 'you don't act like a businessman' into 'you don't use pseudo-jargon such as mission-critical, vision statement, window of opportunity, behind the game-ball, go for it, brand awareness, closer to my customer'.[1]

His comments illustrate just how schizophrenic we are about management jargon. On the one hand, we believe in 'walking the talk': we recognise that it is not enough to have a bold mission statement without backing it up with action – putting our money where our corporate mouths are. But on the other hand, we also appear to subscribe to a contradictory view – that the actions are not enough if we are not using the right words. We need to talk, as well as walk, the talk. It is true that we often do this with a show of great reluctance and scepticism, but we do it nevertheless. And it only takes a brief review of the business papers we commonly read, or the meetings we attend, to see just how common this variant of political correctness is.

It is therefore not enough simply to be sceptical. We need to understand how such terms have become so prominent and to assess the impact they have on our working environments and our co-workers. Not to do this is to run the risk of underestimating something which has potentially tremendous influence (positive and negative) on our lives. As Susan Corby, a lecturer at Manchester Metropolitan University, has recently argued:

> Empowerment, globalisation, de-layering, flexibilisation, competencies, down-sizing, total quality, the learning organisation: such words trip lightly off managers' tongues . . . Many will shrug. After all, what's in a name? To shrug, however, is to ignore the importance of language. Words shape our values, colour our thinking and so influence our actions, as linguistic specialists have pointed out . . . Amusing as it may be, language has an underlying

significance, and the new management language is no exception . . . In his novel *1984*, George Orwell showed how the rulers employed 'newspeak' to condition people's thoughts. In 1994, with not quite such sinister overtones, management is using language to set the agenda.[2]

THE ORIGINS AND ECONOMICS OF CORPORATE-SPEAK

Management is, perhaps, the youngest science (some would dispute whether it constitutes a science at all). It is not possible to put a precise date on the moment it first appeared, but convention puts it in the second decade of the twentieth century with the publication of Frederick Taylor's *Principles of Scientific Management* in 1911, in which he argued that the traditional antagonism between managers and workers could be neutralised by systematic study of both the work involved and the management required. An often quoted example is his 'science of shovelling', which states that it is unlikely that a worker whose job is shovelling will independently identify the most efficient method because the factors involved are complex. Only a scientific study of shovelling can calculate the optimum shovel size and load. The role of management must be to provide the necessary shovels, direct the labourers accordingly and establish an appropriate incentive scheme. The year 1916 saw the publication of Henri Fayol's *Administration industrielle et générale* (translated into English in 1949), which promoted the idea that management could be analysed from a theoretical standpoint, and his definition of management as five activities (planning, organising, commanding, coordinating and controlling) became – as it continues to be – an influential framework. When the first edition of the *Harvard Business Review* appeared in 1922, its lead article by Wallace Donham, then dean of the Harvard Business School, was a call to arms to the business and academic community to create a new body of scientific knowledge for use by business.

Common to all these publications, and still a principle which underlies all management theory, is the idea that it is both possible and worthwhile to codify management into a series of universal principles or business 'rules'. The market for business books in the USA alone is now worth around $750m: if one expands this market to include activities which feed off management theory, such as consultancies and business schools, it grows to $15bn.[3]

It is a tendency to which, as Charles Hampden-Turner and Fons Trompenaars have pointed out in *The Seven Cultures of Capitalism*, the English-speaking world is peculiarly prone: 'only a nation with a history of codifying successfully would believe it possible'.[4] In the USA, and to a slightly lesser extent in the UK, faith in codification shores up far more than our management outlook:

> 'Parenting' and 'wellness' are among the latest subjects for which formulas are on sale, while the trend toward 'political correctness' on the nation's campuses is but the latest in a long line of moral preformulations . . . We are not so much alarmed that this tendency will oppress us, as intrigued by the assumption behind political correctness, that altering the language will reform the speakers, that the word comes before the deed.[5]

This notion – that the word precedes the deed – is at the heart of the discussion about the relationship between language and action in business: it also reveals our ambiguity on the subject. On the one hand, as this quotation suggests, the only possible value in management phraseology is that it can have an impact on those speaking or listening to it – it is designed to affect their actions and, the more effective the language, the more quickly and directly it will do this. But, on the other hand, the words should not become so effective that they take precedence over the action. This is the criticism which American academic Henry Mintzberg levels at management theory: 'a narrow, stylized process that, according to my research, has surprisingly little connection with what effective managers actually do'.[6] The standard division between the two forms of language is theoretically a clear one: using language to change actions is allowable; using it for its own sake is jargon. It is a distinction – as we will see – which is fundamental to our perception and use of 'corporate-speak', but it is also one which is becoming considerably more complex in practice as the economics which underlie management theory change.

Technical vocabulary – whether it relates to nuclear fusion or management – occurs when we graduate from describing a situation to formulating a scientific understanding of it. Describing something implies that we have no tools with which to analyse it: we therefore cannot discuss it, merely observe it. A technical vocabulary suggests that we have analysed the issue and can act on our findings.

Any type of scientific terminology is evidence that we have (or at least think we have) inferred something from a physical description which tells us more about an object or an action than the original description does. For example, we can describe symptoms, but we probably cannot treat them effectively until we have referred them to a doctor for diagnosis. The act of diagnosis converts our description into a medical term – a recognised disease, for instance – and is a precursor to treatment. The fact that the doctor can attach a name to the disease indicates that he or she understands more about the situation than the physical evidence itself (the symptoms) suggests. The fact that he or she can act on that knowledge lifts the medical term out of the realm of jargon, it legitimises it in the patient's eyes.

To this extent, the process of evolving from description to analysis has been no different for management theory than it has been for other sciences:

> As a discipline, marketing is in the process of transition from an art which is practised to a profession with strong theoretical foundations. In doing so it is following closely the precedents set by professions such as medicine, architecture and engineering.[7]

The advent of management terminology, therefore, is a sign of codified knowledge (it is no accident that corporate recovery specialists are called 'company doctors'). Similarly, when the world's management consultancies moved away from carrying out a host of important but ultimately amorphous cost-reduction and operational research projects, and into 'business process re-engineering', they were signalling that they had codified the work to date into a more effective and comprehensive 'science' which could be applied to any company anywhere in the world. Codification – and, by extension, the terminology of management which accompanies it – implies that the rules are understood; that we can write methodologies and draw up blueprints; that we understand and can control the situation. As with the doctor, it suggests we have the cure.

But the key point here is that that knowledge – encapsulated in a technical management term – is supposed to be a stepping-stone to practical action, not to further theoretical research, as the *Guidelines to Authors* issued by the Harvard Business Review make clear: 'HBR articles share certain characteristics . . . Their ideas . . . can be translated into management action.' Unlike some disciplines, management science cannot evolve in the controlled conditions of a laboratory or the rarefied atmosphere of a university: it needs 'real life' to thrive. This is catch-22. Management science cannot withdraw from business in order to develop its own academic credentials without endangering its *raison d'être*, but, equally, it cannot become a fully-fledged and respected discipline without these credentials.

It is not surprising, therefore, that the language of management science is rarely home-grown. Whereas the life sciences have a wealth of complex taxonomies to call on, and astronomy an array of impressive-sounding terms, from quark to quantum, management's terms are second-hand. Business theory is the thrift shop of science. This is not a new trend: when the American industrialist John D. Rockefeller said (at the turn of the century) that 'the growth of a large business is merely a survival of the fittest',[8] he was recalling Charles Darwin's *On the Origin of Species* (1859). Similarly, the emergence today of new theories of competition (biostrategies and business ecosystems) owes much to writers such as Stephen Jay Gould who have opened up to public debate the changing theories of evolution – that it does not represent a linear progression, but is determined by luck as much as logic. The application of chaos theory is perhaps the most recent scion of this line, as when David Freedman queried 'is management still a science?' in the *Harvard Business Review*

> What most mangers think of as scientific management is based on a conception of science that few current scientists would defend. What's more, just as managers have become preoccupied with the volatility of the business environment, scientists have also become preoccupied with the inherent volatility of nature and with the dynamics of unpredictable and unstable systems in the natural world . . . And therein lies an opportunity for fruitful dialogue between the world of management and the world of science.[9]

Management theory dons the clothes of other sciences because it does not have either the opportunity or the remit to make clothes of its own. The time allowed between gathering practical evidence and evangelising the lessons learned to others is shorter than for other sciences: an academic book can take two years to write; the average time for a business book is six months. To use its own phraseology, management theory has opted for the 'buy', not 'make', strategy and has outsourced its R&D function. It has therefore become a reflection of the businesses it describes: it is a 'lean machine', the output of which is increasingly delivered on a 'just-in-time' basis.

But this is where the paradox of management theory lies. Its market is both a growing one (with which its rates of production can scarcely keep pace) and a changing one.

Faced with a uncertain future and rapidly escalating rates of change, business leaders are constantly on the lookout for new ideas, and many of these new ideas – as we noted in the Introduction – are becoming increasingly language-centred.

The recognition that language plays an influential role in organisations has come from several sources: the need of management for information, and analysis of organisational communications and corporate culture. But it is a trend which has only become at all visible relatively recently. In *The Fifth Discipline* (1990), Peter Senge looks at the way in which project teams, brought together to solve complex problems, are inhibited by the simple, linear structure of language:

> The problems compound in a diverse, cross-functional team such as a management team. Each team member carries his or her own predominantly linear mental models. Each person's mental model focuses on different parts of the system. Each emphasizes different cause–effect chains. This makes it virtually impossible for a shared picture of the system as a whole to emerge in normal conversation.[10]

The solution, Senge suggests, lies in complex and dynamic tools such as systems thinking. *The Intelligence Advantage* (1996), by Michael McMaster, looks at the application of complexity theory to organisational design. For McMaster, language is one of the principal facilitators of change:

> To begin to change anything, we must change the way we speak about it . . . If we had to change the ideas, beliefs, values, or personal attributes of every person taking part in an initiative, we would be faced with an impossible task. But all we need to do is change the language, grammar and structure of interpretation that is used and we have provided everyone with an accessible, malleable and effective tool for any transformation effort.[11]

This trend contradicts the standard distinction between legitimate management terminology and jargon. Where, traditionally, the former was used to make people act differently, it is now being used to make them speak differently. Clearly, it would be overly simplistic to say that action has disappeared altogether from the equation, but the ratio of action to language has significantly shrunk. Language is now an action in its own right: the distinction between the two types of language has become irrelevant.

This has two primary implications.

In the first place, it has become genuinely difficult to tell what the value of a new management term is. Previously, we might have evaluated its worth by referring to the research methodology or the credentials of the author: now, the theory propounded may be questionable, but the term used to describe it may capture our imaginations. There is the story of a politician who came into his office announcing that he was planning on using the phrase 'change management' in a forthcoming speech, but who was concerned that 'business process re-engineering' might be the more fashionable term (this being 1995). One of his staff picked up the phone to ring his wife (a management consultant). 'Is business process re-engineering the right term?' he asked. 'No,' replied his wife, 'it's corporate transformation'. Her husband relayed this to his boss and 'corporate transformation' duly appeared in the speech. Does the phrase 'corporate transformation' represent any genuine departure in management thinking? Actually, the question is an irrelevant one: the point is that the term itself may have some use in changing the way companies reinvent themselves.

We will all have instances of this around us. For example, sitting in a meeting, we will sometimes find that a single word occurs several times. I was at a meeting recently where the word in question was 'disconnect' ('there is a disconnect between senior management and the business' was how it started). The word clearly touched a raw nerve among those present and thereafter every problem became one of disconnection. When this kind of domino effect takes place, it becomes impossible to know whether the 'disconnections' cited are real, or whether the word has become a label which can be attached to any problem irrespective of its real nature. Sometimes such a term can be helpful because, like the diagnosis of a disease, it attaches a clear meaning to an issue; at others, it can be a hindrance because it conceals the true nature of an issue.

The second implication of the loss of the distinction between allowable management terms and jargon is that generating words becomes an important process in its own right. One defence department has been credited with the invention of a 'buzz-word generator' in which any word from each of three columns could be combined at random to create new defence terms. The first column had words like 'integrated', 'parallel' and 'functional'; the second, 'logistical', 'management', or 'digital'; and the third, 'concept', 'mobility' and 'projection'. This is – at most – only partly a joke: what is alarming is the extent to which some of these combinations sound plausible ('parallel organisational capability', 'integrated reciprocal concept').

To summarise, management theory faces several threats, all of which can be analysed in its own terms. First, it is a relatively new science with little intellectual capital at its disposal; its portfolio of products is still evolving. It has tended to focus on serving its customers (producing material which can be adopted by managers in practice) rather than building up its own core competencies (producing in-house theories). However, its markets and its customers' needs are now changing: its traditional products (management actions) are being overtaken by new products (ideas and language) and management theory is poorly positioned to compete effectively in this situation; as a result, it cannot keep pace with growing demand in this area. Because demand has been outstripping supply and because the entry barriers to this market are low (who really checks the credentials of a management guru?), new entrants are springing up constantly.

'Corporate-speak', therefore, is not simply jargon and buzz-words. Corporate-speak is about the use of language for its own sake, not as a substitute for actions. It turns the old adage 'actions speak louder than words' on its head: in this case, it is the words which speak the loudest.

THE IMPACT OF CORPORATE SPEAK

'Putting the moose on the table' – described as 'arguably the most baffling management slogan of all time'[12] – was AT&T's phrase for de-layering management. It is an example of one of the most frequently cited impacts of corporate-speak – abdication of responsibility. The case against corporate-speak is that it allows those in positions of authority to duck the responsibilities their positions entail by providing them with a host of convenient excuses, none of which imply failure by the management team. When you stop to think about it, this is a curious line of attack. Is the implication that the act of making people redundant is all right as long as we 'tell it as it is'? That employees do not mind being fired if their managers own up to their part in the process? That the economic impact of being laid off is less important than the honesty with which it is done?

Actually, what is important about this argument is that it is a circular one. Euphemisms are seen as a symptom of a wider failure by managers – to face up to problems and find solutions, to act rather than talk. But the implication that if managers fixed their language they could fix their problems reinforces the idea that language is more important than action. In fact, it is the articles which we often see attacking the growth of corporate-speak which have helped to establish its existence and importance. It is like saying that the argument 'there is no God' establishes that God exists, at least as an idea.

What this implies is that the impact of corporate-speak is exponential. It may start with just a single word which suddenly gains wide currency within an organisation – much as the word 'disconnect' did in the meeting described above. But as soon as the influence of that one word is acknowledged, the floodgates open: one word grows into many words, because the whole idea that words are important has become established. A corporate language is easy to start, but difficult to stop. Language is like any other resource at the disposal of an organisation: it presents opportunities and threats which need to be managed.

To some extent, this is what businesses have always done: the myths of an organisation, its heroes and role models are all evidence of the way in which a company attempts to meld a common meaning and sense of purpose for itself out of disparate events. What is changing now – and this is evidence of the practical impact of the changing emphasis in management thinking outlined earlier – is that words (for example, corporate transformation) and not their meanings have become important, and that organisations are actively trying to manage their use.

Disneyworld is one of the best examples of the latter. To underscore the idea that Disneyworld is like show business, the personnel department has been replaced by 'central casting'. Employees are a 'cast member' who work 'on stage'. In looking at how corporate language has influenced employee behaviour, US academic Jeffrey Pfeffer cited the example of Lakeway Resort, Texas:

> Others have learned from Disney . . . One of the things the center did was to 'fix the language'. When employees leave private areas . . . there is a sign saying 'On Stage' to remind them that they will be in view . . . The strategy was successful, and Lakeway enjoyed a remarkable turnaround.[13]

In the UK, the National & Provincial Building Society stopped holding 'meetings' and started holding 'events'. At the supermarket chain Asda, staff members have become colleagues.

But corporate-speak contains internal contradictions which means that it is a complex process to exploit its potential effectively. As we have already seen, it is neither legitimate management terminology nor jargon, but a combination of the two: it is management language used for its own sake, as a substitute for action. Making it work in practice – as Disney does – involves making sure that people accept that it works: they may not like it or even believe in it entirely, but they have to acknowledge that it serves a useful purpose. If this is not the case, then the organisation opens itself up to a charge of hypocrisy.

Take the use of the word 'empowerment', for example. The term implies giving responsibility to all levels within an organisation, so that everyone 'owns' their immediate problems and has an incentive to resolve them (quality circles in manufacturing are a good example). But how can a management team *tell* its employees to be empowered? The idea is a contradiction in terms: *telling* people they are empowered negates any sense of individual ownership: '[some] would say that it enables management to cut costs while imposing additional stress on workers without giving them proportional financial recompense'.[14]

Corporate-speak – as I have said – poses both an opportunity and a threat for business. It is an opportunity because it provides a new tool by which to influence collective culture and individual behaviour. Language – as Disney has found – is a powerful way of instilling a common outlook and ideology (literally the idea of 'singing from the same hymn-sheet'). However, it poses a threat in the sense that absolute control of it is neither achievable or desirable.

It is not achievable for two reasons. First, because every organisation contains a multiplicity of communication channels, some official, some unofficial. Today, as the Internet effectively deregulates knowledge, there are too many possible sources of information for employees to draw on for an employer to control their outlooks completely (to this extent, Orwell's 1984 scenario has become – for the moment – impossible). The best that we can hope to do is *influence*, not *control*, employee behaviour, in the same way that advertisers seek to influence consumers' behaviour. Second, it is virtually impossible to design a linguistic armour for a corporation which has no chinks in it. As many of the following chapters show, corporate-speak – in all its many guises – is fraught with internal inconsistencies and contradictions. Chapter 3, in particular, looks at how the language of privatisation – probably one of the most public and powerful examples of corporate-speak in recent history – ran into difficulties partly because of such internal contradictions.

Absolute control of corporate language is also not desirable. No sane business today would want a workforce of automatons: after all, anything an automaton can do we can automate. People are needed for dealing with customers, for communication, and for lateral thinking, none of which businesses will get if they attempt to regiment the way people talk too rigidly. Corporate-speak, therefore, is often a matter of balance between getting the benefits (a common culture) and avoiding the pitfalls (reducing personal autonomy).

Notes

1. *Computer Weekly*, 19 January 1995.
2. *The Observer*, 12 June 1994.
3. Mickelthwait and Wooldridge, 1996: 8.
4. Hampden-Turner and Trompenaars, 1993: 24.
5. Ibid.
6. Mintzberg, 1996: 78.
7. Baker, 1991: 3.
8. Ghent, 1902: 29.
9. Freedman, 1992: 26.
10. Senge, 1990: 267.
11. McMaster, 1996: 31–42.
12. Mickelthwait and Wooldridge, 1996: 12.
13. Pfeffer, 1995: 110.
14. Susan Corby, *The Observer*, 12 June 1994.

2 Case Study 1: Asda Stores

If you had visited the Asda head offices at the beginning of the 1990s, you would probably remember very little that distinguished it from the headquarters of any other supermarket chain across the world. True, its head office buildings were newer than most, but that might only have struck you in terms of the expenditure required, at a time when the company was struggling with a mountain of debt it had acquired when it purchased many of the largest stores of another supermarket chain, Gateway, in the late 1980s.

In fact, Asda was widely perceived to have 'lost its way'. Starting out as a dairy producer in the north of England (its name is an abbreviation for Associated Dairies), Asda expanded rapidly during the retail boom of the mid-1980s, spending on acquisitions in order to compete with the market leaders, J. Sainsbury, Tesco and Safeway. Although the traditional basis for that competition had been price, the store refurbishment and advertising campaigns of the time relentlessly pushed the chain up-market, into the traditional socio-economic catchment areas of its competitors. But by the start of the 1990s Asda had become stranded between its original price-conscious positioning and its more recent aspirations. Its competitors were expanding more quickly and into parts of the country where Asda had been dominant; at the same time, discount stores, many from continental Europe, were taking the lead in terms of price competition. Its share price plummeted.

Looking at the company then, it was clear that many of the operational staff did not know what to do: they sat there, helpless, waiting for what they felt would inevitably happen – a hostile takeover by one of the more successful chains.

Looking at it now, it is difficult to believe the change. In 1996, turnover increased by 15 per cent to £6.5bn and profits by more than 21 per cent. The company has returned to its traditional competitive edge – low prices – but has supplemented this with a series of high-profile campaigns to break up some of the few remaining areas of regulated pricing in the UK (books and over-the-counter medicines). More than it ever was in the past, the company is seen as a serious competitor to the top three supermarket chains.

At the heart of this transformation have been significant changes to the way in which the company is organised internally and to its corporate culture. The Asda Way of Working was introduced in 1993 as a means of bringing together a variety of initiatives, such as recruitment and personal career development, designed to increase the motivation and sense of involvement of the company's 75 000 staff. Effective communication was, and continues to be, at the heart of this initiative. This has taken many forms: establishing regular face-to-face meetings for staff in stores; designating a communication zone in all stores where all important communications are posted; senior management writing directly to all staff, on issues like benefits and the financial performance of the company. Nor is the communication all one-way. Early in 1992, Asda set up a telephone hotline inviting employees to put forward their own suggestions for improvements; now, the 'We're Listening' surveys are designed to elicit feedback from an increasing number of staff. The head office has been reorganised to reflect this emphasis: gone are the offices of middle and senior management, replaced by open-plan working arrangements.

What makes all these changes so important here is that effective communication is not confined to the channels of communication, it also extends to the language used: the new corporate cultural change has been accompanied by a new corporate language. Staff are 'colleagues'; they hold 'colleague circles' and 'shop-floor huddles' in stores in order to discuss issues which affect them collectively. In fact, it is significant that many of the 'new' words apply to communication-related areas. For example, all the meeting-rooms in the head office building have been given names, either of foreign capitals or pubs, allowing people to make jokes like 'I'll see you in Tokyo at 2 p.m.' or 'We could meet in the Hare and Hounds later'. Clearly, this move is designed to put discussions into an informal context, but it also demonstrates the extent to which the conventional business language had no words to accommodate the changes which were being initiated here.

Undoubtedly the most radical example of the extent to which the company's language has moved beyond typical business terminology is a wall in the head office foyer. Painted to look like an external brick wall, the objectives of individual people are scrawled across it as graffiti: 'I vow to reduce store paperwork by 10%' goes one; another is 'I promise to ensure that every customer to my store is a happy customer'. Both the style and the words used would be more commonly associated with evangelical Christianity than a business. Once again, the company has stepped outside conventional business language, in this case to borrow quasi-religious terminology.

Indeed, these changes were also viewed with suspicion by some of Asda's own people. The national officer of the GMB trade union at Asda, Donna Covey, asked Christine Maher, director of the Plain English Campaign, to look at the new language being introduced at Asda. In an interview at the time, Covey commented that:

> The staff complained to us that they felt the shop floor had become a sports field. Notice boards have become an art in double-speak words that say so much but mean nothing . . . This is typical management speak. The worst thing about these kind of 'improvements' is that they don't change anything. It's not much good calling Asda staff colleagues, if managers don't count as 'colleagues'.[1]

The approach adopted by Asda is an excellent illustration of corporate-speak as it has been defined in this book. Corporate-speak does not involve 'walking the talk': such ideas are simply irrelevant to it because it is not predicated on the notion that words have to link directly to actions and that actions make the words meaningful – this is management jargon. By contrast, corporate-speak is based on the idea that the words themselves are important and can have a direct impact without being evidenced in reality. Fundamentally, it is not about anything as straightforward as getting people to do things, it is about the effect these words have on the environment in which they occur.

To understand how this works at Asda, we have to look a little further into the grocery retailing market in the UK. Unlike their continental European and US counterparts, UK retailers have historically enjoyed high margins on their sales. These were the result of a larger proportion of grocery sales being concentrated in a smaller number of companies than is the case elsewhere. In the UK, supermarket own-label goods are rapidly approaching the status of branded goods – this has meant that prices for these goods are often not as low as they would be in comparable supermarkets in continental Europe (even allowing for regional differences in the cost of living). The status of the supermarket has also been reinforced by two decades of high-profile, high-quality advertising and the comparatively liberal shopping hours in the UK which has meant that, as in the USA, shopping has become a major social pastime. But competition in the 1990s has radically intensified: with increased government restrictions on opening new stores, the traditional method of organic growth is no longer an option for most supermarket chains. The market being saturated, the search is on to find different ways to compete and – more precisely – steal customers from competitors. Yet, with customer service, product quality and value at the top of all the major supermarkets' agendas, it has become increasingly difficult to find anything different to do. Introduce mother-and-baby parking bays today, and your competitors will do it tomorrow.

To succeed in this climate, Asda has had to stand out – especially since it was manifestly coming from behind. This is clear from the way in which the company has adopted high-profile campaigns against pricing codes and has been the first major retailer in the UK to adopt (although on a very limited basis) twenty-four-hour opening. At the same time, saddled with a high level of debt from earlier acquisitions, its options were limited – it could not initiate a massive store refurbishment programme. While it could afford to offer what it advertises to be 'everyday low prices', the company could not sustain a very intense price war or keep prices at very low levels for a substantial period of time.

Changing the language was the perfect solution. It is cheap to do. Done imaginatively, it can – as Asda has shown – be high-profile externally as well as internally. For the moment, it is also new.

Note

1. *Supermarketing*, 22 September 1995.

Part II

The Privatisation of Language

'That is the language of Church-management-speak, marm,' replied the slippery Slope, with a sanctified smirk. 'If we of the Church are going to network with and be a partner-in-charge with other parts of society then we must learn to speak their language of management and share our own theological jargon. Jargon after all is merely a way of e-mailing grid references for concepts . . . We need to maximise the potential of our human resources to empower the lesser clergy by assigning them areas of decision-making. This may necessitate an element of team-performance bonuses for the Cathedral Close Centre. And that must entail stipendiary equalisation.'

'I am not sure I quite follow that,' interposed Dr Proudie, scratching his head.

(*The Times* (with apologies to Anthony Trollope), 16 February 1996)

3 Learning a New Language – Nationalisation to Privatisation

There is no clearer illustration of the impact of corporate-speak than privatisation.

Since the late 1970s, more than 7000 enterprises have been privatised around the world and factors such as the collapse of Communism, attempts to reduce the scope and scale of government and a desire to promote the principles of the free market all mean that interest in privatisation looks set to continue. Privatisation, described as 'the full or partial transfer of government responsibility to the private sector',[1] was originally predicated on the belief that opening up public sector enterprises to the free market forces of the private sector would release the latent talent of the former, leading to significant improvements in operational and customer service. Linguistic change was the concomitant of this cultural change: passengers, patients, welfare claimants, even prisoners all became customers in this brave new world. The trend continues across the world: when Gennady Zyuganov published the second communist manifesto, in time for the Russian elections in June 1996, it was 'Marxism turned into McKinseyism . . . Not Das Kapital but Das Management'.[2]

> By now 'privatization' has become a household word, tripping lightly off the tongue of Sid and his mates, and is now ready to take its place in the OED between 'private' and 'privet'.[3]

In fact, such changes were just the tip of the iceberg: 'privatised' language was a complex affair which had wide-ranging implications for the organisations affected.

THE OFFICIAL LANGUAGE OF PRIVATISATION

Margaret Thatcher is commonly credited with coining the word 'privatisation' in the late 1970s. In fact, its first use seems to have been in Peter Drucker's *The Age of Discontinuity*, published in 1969, and it was subsequently adopted by right-wing thinkers and politicians, such as the MP David Howell who wrote in *A New Style of Government*:

> Peter Drucker uses the unusually ugly word 'privatization' for this process. This at least distinguishes it from denationalisation, which means something rather different, but it is still hideously clumsy.[4]

Clumsy or not, 'privatisation' became more than just a buzz-word, it became a way of speaking. The language of privatisation was – and still is – focused around words such as freedom, democracy and accountability. Take a book written by another British Conservative politician as an example: *The Myths of Privatisation* by Michael Forsyth appeared in 1983 and was an attempt to dispel much of the misinformation on the subject of privatisation which was – allegedly – being peddled by the trade union movement in the UK. Forsyth was writing at one of those cusps of time when theory (in this case, almost a decade of thinking on the subject of privatisation) was rapidly being converted into action:

> Privatisation is no longer a new and slightly odd-sounding world. It is now a major option for all local governments in Britain when they consider how to deliver the best and most cost-effective services to their constituents.[5]

For Forsyth, putting privatisation into practice was about breaking down the power of a small, unelected group of local government officials who were accustomed to exploiting public resources for their own ends. It was, he argued, the 'great paradox' of the so-called public sector that 'the public benefits from private services, the producers benefit from public services':[6]

> The real argument is about privilege and power. It is about whether a narrower elite shall continue to exercise a stranglehold on public services for its own gain or whether the wider public interest shall prevail.[7]

The shift in power which privatisation represented was to be accompanied by an equally dramatic shift in values: if the *ancien régime* of local government was associated with monopolistic control, rigid working-practices and quasi-totalitarian attitudes, then the privatisation 'revolution' was underpinned with notions of freedom, flexibility and democracy. It is this dualism – freedom versus constraint, democracy versus totalitarianism – which lies at the centre of Forsyth's book and of the language of privatisation as a whole. Although the values – and words – associated with the public and private sectors are polar opposites, they are in practice dependent on each other for their meaning; thus, *privatisation* does not just represent freedom and democracy but also *lack of constraint* and *non-totalitarianism.*

These are not the only sets of such opposites which occur repeatedly in Forsyth's book; take, for instance, the following extract:

> There is no doubt that contracting gives local authorities the chance to move up from the world of acquiescence to union demands, into the world of management level responsibility for the standards and quality of the services they provide . . . The administrators gain the opportunity to move up in status and become real managers. They replace the detail of labour relations and rostering with the more skilled and responsible task of monitoring standards and enforcing performance contracts. They gain the opportunity to shop around for the best services, instead of being prisoners of whatever their workforce feel ready to concede.[8]

There are several points worth noting here, all of which will become more significant as we start to look at the practical implications of the language of privatisation in practice. *Administrators* will become *managers*: it is a metamorphosis which includes becoming *skilled* and means abandoning passivity – the *acquiescence* to union demands – in favour of action and *responsibility*. It involves upward mobility, away from the humdrum routine of *labour relations and rostering*, and freedom to *shop* around after years of figurative imprisonment. Perhaps most tellingly, it is a metamorphosis to being *real* people, living in the real world.

In fact, it is possible to see Forsyth's book as an attempt to practise the values it preaches. Its purpose is to set the record straight – to dispel the *myths* of privatisation. By doing this it is giving individuals the real facts which make them *free* to choose; effectively, it empowers them. From this perspective, it is clear that there is a further pair of opposite values which lie at the heart of the book's philosophy:

privatisation is about truth – it is about setting out the facts and cutting a scythe through public sector rhetoric. Conversely, the public sector is associated with duplicity and deception – hence the lies being touted around by the trade unions *et al.*

Of course, Forsyth's book was just a beginning, but since its publication, the way in which we speak of or write about privatisation has continued to focus on these same sets of opposite values: freedom versus constraint; democracy versus totalitarianism; flexibility versus rigidity; active versus passive; management versus bureaucracy; skilled versus unskilled; real versus unreal; truth versus lies. To understand just how profound has been the impact of this – the language in privatisation – on the practice of privatisation, we need first to understand in more detail the nature of these sets of opposite values.

For Iain Vallance, the Chairman of British Telecom, privatisation allowed the company to:

> enter new home and overseas markets, to take full advantage of the many varying demands for what we could offer, now that we had the promise of greater freedom to do so.[9]

For BT and other public sector companies, privatisation meant freedom: 'privatisation released us from the Treasury shackles'.[10] In some cases – as Iain Vallance's comments indicate – this means freedom to do something (enter different markets, exploit new opportunities). But in many cases such aspirations are couched in terms of the end of the negative aspects of the public sector (primarily perceived to be bureaucratic control and commercial naivety), as these comments from *Management Today* illustrate:

> One clear advantage of privatization does seem to be the new freedom of interference from Whitehall, and the setting of objectives dictated purely by business criteria rather than political goals . . . At a recent gathering of the chairmen and chief executives of the Water Authorities, for example, a constant refrain above the tinkle of glasses was the desire to 'get Government off our backs'.[11]

This is the rule rather than the exception: a key point to the freedom versus constraint rhetoric is that the positive part (freedom) needs the negative part (constraint) in order to be meaningful and rarely carries any independent meaning of its own.

The same is largely true of the democracy versus totalitarianism opposition, which continues to be one of the most pervasive and potent images of the language of privatisation. According to this perspective, the relationship between government and nationalised industries is seen as too self-serving and symbiotic to be able to serve the public good: 'what should have been an independent authority becomes defender of a particular vested interest'.[12] By contrast, removing organisations from central control, via wider share ownership, makes them more accountable to the ordinary person. 'It's you we answer to', claimed a BT publicity campaign in the late 1980s.

In this respect, privatisation is feeding off the long-established rhetoric of free market philosophies. The democratisation of industry involved turning authoritarian bureaucrats into accountable managers ('outside revolution, there's been nothing like it'[13]), and consumers into shareholders ('there is no doubt that a new generation of private investors has been created'[14]). As one ex-minister pointed out this move met genuine resistance among the financial community more accustomed to dealing with a 'better' class of investor:

> [They were] not keen to expand that capacity by extending share ownership to the ordinary public. I remember one particularly acrimonious meeting . . . during which I had been extolling the virtues of wider share ownership . . . The head of a large brokerage house suddenly realised what I meant. *But John*, he said in a shocked voice, *we don't want all those kind of people owning shares, do we?*[15]

While such anecdotal evidence is entertaining it does not give much in the way of substantial definition (beyond the idea of wider share ownership) to the notion of democracy in this context. This is by no means unusual. Rather than defining *democracy* in practice, much of the talk surrounding privatisation substituted a democratic style, rather than anything more substantial. This meant using slang – *punters* for people and *tenners* for money invested:

> The beauty of [privatisation] has been that everybody could make money out of it – the brokers, the merchant banks, the public relations advisers and, of course, the ordinary punters. This last, providing virgin investors with what seemed like a golden chance

> to convert fivers into tenners, was all the more alluring for the City. It provided a populist dimension to the traditional City game of making money.[16]

But democratising language is not the same as being democratic: it is a substitute for giving a precise description of what this particular brand of democracy meant in practice.

Alongside democratisation, privatisation was perceived to involve 'freeing managers to manage', releasing them from the bureaucratic rigidity of 'an administrative culture'.[17] It is an attitude which is particularly visible around the time of BT's privatisation. The *Financial Times* drew this conclusion from a strike by telephone engineers in 1987:

> The dispute currently raging throughout the UK is part of BT's painful transition from a public company with a Civil Service structure of employment to a private enterprise looking for efficiency and growth, and with an employment structure it believes is needed to achieve the goals.[18]

The Sunday Telegraph concurred:

> How well BT performs in the increasingly competitive environment depends to a large extent on how far it has moved from – or intends to move from – the old nationalised industry public service 'culture' of the old days as a state-run institution.[19]

In this context, the notions of management became inextricably linked with ideas of freedom and democracy: management theory was the key to unlocking the benefits of privatisation in practice. Yet there is, if one stands back for a moment, no logical – or even historical – link between these concepts (quite the reverse, if one thinks of Marx). This is not to deny that considerable management thinking was and is focused on ideas of decentralisation and empowerment, but do these really add up to the broader dreams of privatisation? Is an empowered organisation more democratic, or does it just distribute power in a different way? Can the people in any organisation ever be 'free'? Surely it is inherent in the nature of any institution that individual wishes and actions have to be incorporated into the collective body. These are genuine points for debate but ones which were not part of the popular rhetoric of privatisation.

SPREADING THE WORD: PRIVATISATION AND PUBLIC RELATIONS

One of the factors which sets apart the language of privatisation from many of the other 'languages' covered in this book is the fact that it was a very public language. It was not a language which had evolved organically to meld a small number of individuals into an efficient group (in the way in which some of the more successful IS project teams work, for example); it did not act as a boundary between different groups (as happens in some multinational companies). The language of privatisation was a deliberate and integral part of a wider campaign to change public attitudes and behaviour: 'privatization has become an educational process by which the people of a country can grasp the fundamental beliefs and values of free enterprise'.[20] It is therefore hardly surprising that privatisation programmes across the world have been accompanied by massively expensive publicity campaigns.

The UK government spent more than £100m on publicity during its core privatisation programme in the 1980s. It spent over £20m alone on the first major privatisation – that of British Telecom; a further £36m was spent on the British Gas share offering.[21] In terms of effectiveness, it was money well-spent: between 1983 and 1987, the proportion of the UK owning shares rose from 5 per cent to 20 per cent.[22]

Such massive expenditure was necessary because of the size of the share issues involved. These were too large for conventional institutional purchasers, and the government was therefore dependent on mass sales to the general public. This posed peculiar difficulties for the advertising agencies involved, not least because there was no obvious model which could be adopted for this sort of campaign. The usual audience for share issues were the 200-odd financial institutions in the City: while bankers and their PR agents knew how to communicate with this market, no one understood how to talk to the general public. When the government first approached Dewe Rogerson, the agency commissioned to handle the PR campaign for the BT privatisation, very little research had been done on the target market – the private shareholder: 'Everyone had ideas, but no one had any confidence in them', recalled Kerry Martin, a director of the agency in a subsequent interview. Dewe Robertson and the other agencies involved compensated by carrying out extensive research on the target consumers in order to understand what their motivation would be in purchasing shares, and to identify the critical factors in appealing to them. 'Every decision seemed to be a trail-blazer', was how Iain Vallance summed up the BT campaign in retrospect: the meetings between BT and the PR specialists 'merged the cultures and requirements of occasionally almost incompatible interests into a force which was to achieve one of the greatest marketing conditioning achievements on record'.[23]

However, the resulting campaigns were also a continuation of the government's own publicity war by other means. This was unavoidable: after all, the privatisation and the language with which it was discussed were inseparable and it would not, therefore, be possible to promote the former without making use – consciously or otherwise – of the latter. As such, the PR campaigns became the single most effective way of disseminating the language of privatisation.

Examples of this are legion, but especially notable is the British Gas campaign which referred to (but never showed) an ordinary person – Sid. Hoarding advertisements reminded people to 'tell Sid' about the share offer, or reminded him to put in his share application before the closing date. Their language was a clear attempt to shift away from the conventional language of such campaigns (primarily directed at the professional classes) in order to speak directly to the blue-collar worker: popularist slang was thus used to indicate the democratic appeal of the share issue – but it was also a substitute for it. A similar approach has been adopted in other European privatisations, most recently that of the Spanish telecommunications company, Telefonica, and Deutsche Telekom.

Campaigns like this reinforced not only the central images and words of privatisation – freedom and democracy – but mirrored its comparative lack of meaning. But as such, these campaigns were highly effective weapons in the privatisation arsenal. Precisely because they provided a coherent but essential cosmetic patina of meaning – equivalent to that of the language of privatisation overall – they were difficult to argue with. When the dominant public images associated with, say, the privatisation of the water companies are clear running water and a clean, verdant environment, it was not easy to begin a debate on whether the underlying economic policy was flawed – the common ground between the two views of privatisation was too scant (and the publicity campaigns effectively kept it that way).

Thus, by disseminating the language of privatisation, these campaigns took the latter a stage further. The words used not only promoted a specific way of talking – and therefore thinking – about privatisation, they also provided what was in effect a barrier to entry for other ways of talking or thinking. Those who tried to argue against the policy found themselves not so much on a level playing field as on the same playing field. In the mid-1980s, for example, the London Borough of Wandsworth pursued one of the earliest and most aggressive campaigns to introduce compulsory competitive tendering, whereby long-established council departments were required to compete against outside suppliers for contracts. The aim was not, according to the council, ideological but was to increase efficiency.[24] While the trade unions were openly sceptical of the emerging management terminology, it was difficult to refute phrases such as 'value for money': after all, what can be wrong with the idea of ensuring that public money is well-spent? While such terms were the most visible evidence of a wider ideological shift by the council, they were not in themselves proof that the council was acting contrary to the public interest. The unions could only respond in kind – by launching their own PR campaign – in an attempt to reclaim both the ideological and linguistic initiative.[25]

But even where they organised counter campaigns, the opponents of privatisation found themselves increasingly forced to adopt the language of privatisation, even while they criticised it. A series of pamphlets produced during the 1980s by the Trades Union Congress (TUC) shows the change.

Public or Private (1982) makes the mistake of repeating the allegations made about the inefficiency of public services, thus giving them even wider circulation. It retaliates by turning the arguments in favour of privatisation against themselves – privatisation is seen to involve the cession of control to a small group of undemocratically appointed people – shareholders. Some signs of pre-privatisation thinking are still there: its stress on the need for central control of organisations, for instance. *Who Loses? Who Profits?* appeared the following year. While retaining the 'them and us' language of economic confrontation, the pamphlet relied more than its predecessor on the other side's language:

> Privatisation has certainly not resulted in a wider distribution of wealth. Nationalised industries have not, in the words of Conservative phraseology, been 'given back to the people'. Instead what used, in some way, to belong to the public as a whole now belongs like the rest of British industry to the rich.[26]

Two years later, the mode of opposition has shifted. According to *The Great Sell-Out* (1985): 'all of these claims [e.g. about a share-holding democracy] are lies'.[27] The booklet is intended to be an exposé of such lies and it centres on demonstrating that the government is not meeting its core objectives (share-holding democracy, value for money, efficiency). What it is not doing is arguing that the ideas themselves are wrong, and symptomatic of this is the increased use of the terminology associated with privatisation. Wait another two years, and the linguistic u-turn has been completed. *Paying the Price* (1987) talks about the 'reality' of privatisation in terms now almost wholly drawn from the private sector: it discusses merger and acquisition activity amongst ex-public companies; it analyses the return achieved for shareholders; and it praises the efficiency and profitability of companies when publicly owned. In the course of just five years, the language of privatisation had taken over.

Public relations did not stop at an organisation's front door: the majority of institutions affected by privatisation commissioned substantial internal communications programmes. And here we can see a further aspect of the language of privatisation.

These programmes were necessitated by the level of cultural change required in many of the organisations being privatised. Lord Sharp of Grimsdyke, chairman and chief executive of Cable & Wireless, recalled:

> On my arrival at the Cable & Wireless head office in London, I found a very comfortable board. None of the board papers seemed to have any bottom-line implications. The company was a highly centralised organisation; no one in the overseas regions had any true concept of profit and loss. The regional picture emerged only at the centre, which meant that decision-making was highly centralised, too. It was equivalent to the way the Admiralty worked in the seventeenth and eighteenth centuries when they used to send barrels of rum from the quarter master's stores to Jamaica.[28]

In fact, one of the prime changes which these programmes were attempting to initiate – and this is where they went further than the external publicity campaigns – was to improve the overall level and effectiveness of communication within the organisations concerned. Essentially, the programmes were aimed not just at teaching people the right words (freedom, democracy, management, and so on), but at getting them to talk in the first place.

This was an aspect highlighted in a recent study of British Airways before and after privatisation. The publicly owned BA was characterised by poor communication: 'each department was a fortress, and spent a lot of time battling against the other departments. Managers were not very visible to the staff. They never went out and talked to them'.[29] By contrast, privatisation was seen as having brought down internal barriers:

> We are more open to developing ourselves. For example, we are having a series of seminars on information technology which helps us not only to talk with managers from other areas but also to discover what other companies and industries are doing regarding specific issues in information technology.

As the employee of another privatised company, British Nuclear Fuels Ltd, saw it, people needed to talk because the environment around them was changing rapidly:

> Great emphasis is given to communication skills because, in a changing situation, the need to communicate is greater than in a static situation when things do not change over years and years (if you stay always doing the same job, you do not need to explain anything to anybody).

For staff at the British Airports Authority (BAA after privatisation), it was also a reflection of the need to learn a new language:

> The use of the word 'profits' was not very common. It was not in the front of people's minds. After privatization, the word 'profits' became a more common feature for people, and people's pay became more linked to profits.

The language of privatisation was not simply the right language, it *was* language: it made those who subscribed to the idea articulate and those who opposed it mute. This becomes clearer the more we think about it. It is interesting to note, for example, that BT's advertising strapline is 'It's good to talk': language and privatisation are inextricably linked.

In fact, it was not until 1993–4 that this started to change. This change has partly been the result of considerable criticism in the UK over the way in which some of the privatised companies have been managed. A notable example is British Gas which evoked a public furore by announcing – almost simultaneously – redundancies among its branch network and substantial pay rises for its most senior executives. The regional electricity companies (who have seen a substantial reduction in headcount since privatisation) have been criticised for reducing corporate strategy to lay-offs for their own self-interest:

> With generous share options giving senior managers a chance to build some personal capital, the need to support a strong share price has become a matter of personal interest to managers. The corporate strategy is effectively to keep the share price up.[30]

With incidents like this, chinks of light have appeared between private sector management techniques and the public good, most recently with Henry Mintzberg in the *Harvard Business Review*:

> 'We have customers,' Vice President Al Gore announced early in his term in office. 'The American people'. But do you have to call people customers to treat them decently? We would do well to take a look at what *customers*, this now fashionable word, used to mean before the Japanese taught us a thing or two . . . I am not a mere customer of my government, thank you. I expect something more than arm's-length trading and something less than the encouragement to consume.[31]

In Britain too, the tide is turning. Rising public concern with the profits being reaped by some privatised companies (while they continue to shrink their workforces) has led to calls for government intervention. There is, too, a growing sense of dismay at the amount of public money which is perceived as being spent on hospital 'managers' rather than front-line clinical staff. As the public mood shifts, politicians have been repositioning themselves:

> We politicians . . . need to call a halt to all this jargon-making. The politician has to break out and break through. We should say that we don't want our managers to keep drafting and redrafting strategy documents. We don't want to be out to consultation each week on some new change and restructuring or reviewing every year to make sure that the organisation is always being turned upside down . . . If you regularly use words like additionality,

> strategy, resources, commitment, you have been in the public sector too long. Take a break, knock on a few doors, talk to the people in the bus queue.[32]

Although perhaps no longer in its heyday, the language of privatisation remains a powerful example of corporate-speak. Its common terms were rarely defined: at least in ordinary usage, it was a series of conflicting values (freedom versus constraint, democracy versus totalitarianism and management versus bureaucracy), each of which was defined more in terms of its opposite (*freedom* meant not being constrained, for instance) than by concrete or practical evidence. The direct link – which, traditionally, we might have expected – between language and action was, in privatisation, always a remote and questionable one. It was also an irrelevant one. The language of privatisation was about getting people – the public and the employees of privatised industries – to talk differently, as this would ultimately result in cultural change. Corporate-speak is not a precursor to action: it is an action itself.

Notes

1. Salama, 1995: 3.
2. *The Australian Financial Review*, 4 June 1996.
3. *Management Today*, March 1987.
4. Quoted in Chapman, 1990: 15.
5. Forsyth, 1983: 5.
6. Ibid. 7.
7. Ibid. 10.
8. Ibid. 9.
9. Iain Vallance, quoted in Clutterbuck *et al.*, 1991: 100–1.
10. Comment of a BT official in the aftermath of privatisation (*PR Week*, 27 November 1987).
11. *Management Today*, March 1987.
12. *The Sunday Telegraph*, 16 August 1987.
13. *Management Today*, March 1987: 60.
14. *The Daily Telegraph*, 14 October 1987.
15. Moore, 1992b: 27.
16. *Post Magazine*, 3 September 1987.
17. Wiltshire, 1987: 11.
18. *Financial Times*, 22 January 1987.
19. *The Sunday Telegraph*, 1 February 1987.

20. Moore, 1992a: 115–16.
21. *The Times*, 28 October 1987.
22. *Financial Times*, 12 November 1987.
23. Iain Vallance, quoted in Clutterbuck, *et al.*, 1991: 103.
24. Benlow and Scott, 1983: 33.
25. Ibid. 14.
26. Labour Research Unit, 1983: 47–8.
27. Labour Research Unit, 1985: 1.
28. Quoted in Clutterbuck *et al.*, 1991: 193.
29. For this and subsequent comments, see Salama, 1995: 53–73.
30. *The Guardian*, 8 September 1994.
31. Mintzberg, 1996: 76–7.
32. Redwood, 1994: 10–11.

4 Case Study 2: The National Health Service

In 1983, the UK government commissioned Roy Griffiths, a managing director of the supermarket giant J. Sainsbury, to carry out a review of the management and organisation of the National Health Service. The Griffiths report, published the following year, concluded that:

> many of the problems of managing the NHS were similar in nature to those faced in big private-sector organisations: the fact that the NHS was seeking simply to deliver a service, not make a profit, made much less difference to daily management task than was popularly supposed.[1]

This was the basis on which the most radical shake-up of the NHS since its inception in 1945 was launched. An internal market was to be introduced whereby local health authorities purchased services from hospitals and in which many of the hospitals opted to become self-governing trusts. Introducing this element of competition would create the market forces necessary to improve efficiency and reduce costs: this, in turn, would cut waiting lists significantly.

More than a decade later, the Chancellor Kenneth Clarke was to sum up the results thus:

> We have achieved efficiency gains and delivered a better quality of service. We have put money into the hands of those directly responsible for purchasing the service as distinct from those who provide it. We have allowed the local providers in the NHS Trusts more freedom to manage their affairs and made them more responsive to patients and GPs. We have built on the strengths of the family doctor system by giving GP Fundholders more choice and influence over NHS care for patients.[2]

These words incorporate many aspects of the language of privatisation (hence the stress on accountability and freedom); they also included that familiar palliative for all ills – the idea of management. The way in which the NHS was run became, in much of the press coverage of the early 1980s, the only feature which distinguished it from a private company: the NHS had to manage suppliers (such as the pharmaceutical companies) just as a private company would; increasingly, it was having to accommodate competitors[3] (in the form of private health schemes established by companies for their employees): what it did not do was manage – the NHS 'administered'. It was a 'dismal combination of over-administration and under-management'.[4] The fact that, in 1986, 715 000 patients were reported to be waiting for treatment (33 000 of which were acute cases), in spite of the fact that around £11bn was being spent on the NHS, was blamed on lack of management.

Since 1990, the number of managers has grown to 23 000 from 4600, while the number of nurses has fallen by 50 000. The administrative costs of the NHS have increased from 5 per cent of the total budget to 10 per cent.[5] Cultural change – for example, the introduction of what were perceived to be private sector management techniques (such as new performance measurement and reward systems) – inevitably had to be accompanied by linguistic change.

> But if a business plan tells you where you want to go, and also the means of getting there, it develops other qualities when used as the vehicle for broader changes like those now going ahead in the health service. To begin with, it can do the strangest things to the English language, brewing up prodigious clouds of unknowing which often extend beyond the predictable boosterism of 'excellence' and 'efficiency' to achieve a positively Orwellian pathology. The prize so far goes to the London hospital doctor who asked a manager about intended reductions in clinical services, only to be told, 'we are not talking about cuts here. We are creating underspend.' This obfuscation goes along with a tendency to redefine confidentiality. There have been some disgraceful cases of persecution of health workers who have spoken out against aspects of the new order, and some trusts are now attempting to reduce professional loyalty to the individual contract of employment.[6]

There was no public sector equivalent to many of the terms being used. But hospitals were not places to which the language of management, or indeed any kind of non-technical language, came easily: administration was usually done by doctors or nursing staff rather than trained managers and the dominant vocabulary was a medical one. Not surprisingly, this had meant that many of these institutions had been poor at communicating with their patients.

In the new NHS environment, language was actively used to manipulate culture: for example, the management budgeting process was renamed 'resource management' as it was felt that the former gave out the 'wrong signals' and implied that the process was carried out by 'management' in isolation from the practical realities of the NHS. By contrast, the term 'resource management' was thought to imply the active involvement of medical staff.[7]

However, one of the problems in making this transition, from public sector to private sector language, was that the term *management* meant different things to different people.

In 1990, two sociologists, P. Anthony and M. Reed, carried out a study into managerial roles and relationships in a district health authority in Wales. What their work revealed was an organisation which was run along an extended network of collaborative relationships and where the formal organisational structure was sometimes regarded as irrelevant. Bound by a common goal (the care of patients), medical staff did not see what they did as management, but 'plain doctoring', although most of them were to some degree engaged in the management of resources:

> A nurse manager confessed that she did not know much about 'managing in the modern sense', but insisted that she 'managed all right'.[8]

'Management' was seen to be something imposed on the medical professions from the outside, involving a bureaucracy which was inimical to patient care: in effect, it was a strategy which forced medical staff to formally recognise the new structure but, simultaneously, to see it as irrelevant to their real work and a waste of their time: the concept of management had 'advanced to the point at which it has assumed institutional proportions in its own right'.[9] Indeed, management was not just seen as an alien concept, but as something faintly ridiculous:

> Three men sit in a room, joking, teasing each other, gesticulating wildly. They could be extras from a Monty Python film set but are in fact a team of people committed to making financial management in the health service work . . . These people are part of the

latest stage in the process of trying to turn the NHS into an efficient, well-managed organisation – a painful process so far.[10]

Looking at some of the material produced during the 1980s, it is not difficult to see how such perceptions arose. As with privatisation in general, using private sector language was often used as a sign that an organisation or an individual had embraced the ideology of the free market. Even simple matters like job descriptions could be recast in a politically correct mode, as these examples, taken from one for a ward orderly, illustrate:

> [The orderly should]:
> – demonstrate sound interpersonal relationships and an awareness of the individual clients' psychological and emotional needs;
> – understand the need for effective verbal and non-verbal communication; and
> – support clients and relatives in the care environment by demonstrating empathy and understanding.[11]

However the impact of corporate-speak did more than raise a few hackles, it also changed dramatically the way in which medical staff communicated with patients. The new style of language was more formal and structured: like any second language, it did not come naturally to the medical profession and many were unhappy using it. Suddenly, language had rules: like managing, talking has always been something which medical staff always did but now it seemed that they had to do something different. In this environment, informal chats to patients became less important, not just because increases in operational efficiency meant that staff's time was more precious, but more because it was a style of speaking which was outmoded. It is a trend which continues today: 'nurses do not have the time they used to', one health professional was recently reported as saying:

> Nursing is more intensive with shorter lengths of stay for patients. Only very ill people are in hospital and nurses cannot sit talking to them. 'This is a more efficient use of resources, and the taxpayer cannot afford the extra service'.[12]

This trend is seen to be part of a general decline in the amount of discussion and debate within the NHS. New arrangements for trust hospitals means that they no longer have to have local councillors and other lay representatives on the boards and they have to meet in public only once a year. Such changes also appear to have had an impact on external communications: NHS managers have been accused of becoming increasingly reluctant to make public any shortcomings or criticisms. They have, in a sense, been deprived of language – or at least this is the popular perception of the situation. Instead of increasing communication, the NHS reforms are now seen by many to have engendered an atmosphere of mistrust and intimidation.

As with privatisation in general, the wheel has now turned full circle, with many of the reforms, welcomed under the terms of improved management, being seen as inimical to the original intention:

> Yet the upshot of a decade and a half of neo-liberal policy has been the construction in Britain of a novel form of the corporate state – a species of market corporatism, in which a growing proportion of the nation's economic resources is pre-empted by an expanding managerial class charged with the task of overseeing internal markets. This managerial new class disposes of vast resources and exercises immense powers over individual lives, without being subject to the disciplines of democracy or of real markets, and – even when made up, as often it is, of decent people struggling to do an impossible job – without the guidance of any established professional ethos.[13]

Although, ironically, the old subservience to management theory persists: it is not so much that the use of private sector thinking in the public sector is ill-conceived, but that it was 'a primitive and anachronistic conception of business management'.[14]

Notes

1. Peet, 1987: 28.
2. 16 September 1996.
3. Chandra and Kakabadse, 1985: 9–20
4. Peet, 1987: 28.
5. *Accountancy Age*, 1 February 1996.
6. *The Guardian*, 1 August 1994.

7. *Accountancy Age*, 19 March 1987.
8. Anthony and Reed, 1995: 51.
9. Ibid.: 51–2.
10. *Accountancy Age*, 19 March 1987.
11. Reported in the *Medical Monitor*, 1994.
12. *Accountancy Age*, 1 February 1996.
13. *The Guardian*, 3 January 1995.
14. Ibid.

Part III

Language and Change: Failing to Talk about Technology

I saw the pale student of unhallowed arts kneeling beside the thing he had put together. I saw the hideous phantasm of a man stretched out, and then, on the working of some powerful engine, show signs of life, and stir with an uneasy, half-vital motion. Frightful it must be: for supremely frightful would be the effect of any human endeavour to mock the stupendous mechanism of the Creator of the World. His success would terrify the artist; he would rush away from his odious handy-work, horror-stricken. He would hope that, left to itself, the slight spark of life which he had communicated would fade; that this thing, which had received such imperfect animation, would subside into dead matter. . . He sleeps; but he is awakened; he opens his eyes; behold the horrid thing stands at his bedside, opening his curtains, and looking at him with yellow, watery, but speculative eyes.

(Mary Shelley, *Frankenstein*)

5 A Short History of Computer-Speak

By the time Mary Shelley wrote the opening lines of *Frankenstein* in 1816, technology was no longer the toy of the rich and eccentric likes of Dr Frankenstein, but had, like his monster, taken on a life of its own outside. Her nightmare – of a force created by man but outside his physical and moral control – was one that haunted the nineteenth century; if the evidence of films such as *Terminator* are anything to go by, it continues to haunt us in the twentieth.[1]

The following section of this book looks at how our unease with technology is shown in the language we use to discuss it, and at how this has an impact on the way in which we implement and use it in our businesses. We are all familiar with the picture of the cyber-nerd babbling over the Internet in a language which is all but incomprehensible to an outsider, but we have hardly begun to consider the impact that that babble, and all its derivatives, may be having on our businesses and lives. Given that more than $1m per second is being spent every minute on information systems (IS) in the world today, if that babble has only a microscopic impact on our ability to implement and use IS effectively, then its costs are enormous.

The evidence is not encouraging. As we shall see, the language in which we talk about IS first appeared at a time when only a few people knew not just what they were talking about but how to talk about it. They were experts in their field and, not having to worry about a wider audience, they inevitably communicated in expert-to-expert jargon. For the non-technical writers, who were responding to the growing popular interest in computing in the 1960s, there were no words which would make their then esoteric subject accessible to a broader readership. To put across their arguments and to expedite the acceptance of technological progress in their readers, they developed a language which drew heavily on non-technical images and analogies. While this language – which I term 'computer-speak' – quickly gained currency, it contained much that mythologised its subject matter and little of any precise meaning.

Yet it is this language which we use today to talk about IS. The whole means by which we select a new system, then develop, implement and use it is predicated on the belief that we know what we are talking about. Why else would we spend quite so much management time and effort in the production of mammoth cost/benefit analyses, specification documents and user training manuals, if it was not for the fact that all these words had some *meaning*, that they were *useful*. I shall argue that our faith is misplaced. 'Computer-speak' is a hindrance, not a help: if we cannot find a more effective means of talking about IS, we would do better to develop an approach to it which is not so heavily reliant on language.

CULTURE AND TECHNOLOGY

For much of this century, technological progress – in its broadest sense – has been viewed as an unstoppable force, changing profoundly and irrevocably a society which is passive to resist it: 'A powerful tide', wrote Alvin Toffler in his hugely influential *The Third Wave* (1980),

> is surging across much of the world today, creating a new, often bizarre environment in which to work, play, marry, raise children or retire. In this bewildering context, business men swim against highly erratic economic currents; politicians see their ratings bob wildly up and down; universities, hospitals and other institutions battle desperately against inflation; value systems splinter and crash, while the lifeboats of family, church and state are madly hurled about.[2]

The impact of such changes, Toffler argued, has gone far beyond anything anticipated by its progenitors:

> In altering the info-sphere so profoundly, we are destined to transform our own minds as well – the way we think about our problems, the way we synthesize information, the way we anticipate the consequences of our actions . . . We may even alter our own brain chemistry.[3]

To writers such as Toffler, the advances of the present day are part of a continuous line of positive technological development which stretches back to the birth of our civilisation. Step changes in technology – the invention of printing, for example – have brought immeasurable benefits to society: with books came rational thought, freedom of speech and the dissemination of scientific knowledge. Progress, in other words, begot progress. But others have drawn darker conclusions. Because computers are driving the trend towards global standardisation, they have become instruments of control, repressing society's energy and diversity: 'the computer has thus begun to be an instrument for the destruction of history. For when society legitimates only those "data" that are "in one standard format", then history, memory itself, is annihilated'.[4]

Whatever their perspective, most writers have until recently agreed on one point: society cannot and should not stand in the way of progress. Indeed, it is this attitude which has informed much government and social policy since the Second World War: the public, faced with an overarching wave of change, needs to be helped to adapt; failing to adapt will mean that individuals and nations will be left behind while the rest of the world marches forward.

But the past twenty years have seen an increasing recognition that society is not always the passive victim (or beneficiary) of progress, but rather that the nature of society – its organisation, economics and culture – moulds technological progress. This argument has been taken up by social anthropologists who, from carrying out comparative studies on the assimilation of technology in developed and developing societies, have argued that the rate and extent of technological progress is determined by culture and that it therefore varies widely between societies and between organisations.

> What is being queried is not just this or that 'result' of various information technologies in the past or present, but the whole idea that such technologies can be taken as self-standing or regarded of themselves as having 'consequences'. 'Technologies', after all, do not discover themselves, do not get developed apart from society, nor themselves make decisions – they are brought about by people, acting within particular institutional frameworks.[5]

This 'interpretative' approach to technological progress centres on the notion that culture is both the facilitator of change (it is the primary medium by which we communicate change) but also its constraint (we construct future technology according to our own – historical – image of what that technology should be like). 'Progress' therefore is firmly rooted in our collective pasts. To understand the nature and form that progress takes, we need to interpret its cultural environment.

In the 1980s, interpretative research was dominated by structuralists who were primarily interested in culture as a complex system of signs which, when decoded, revealed society's underlying value systems. For the most part, this was a debate which was carried on in isolation from other areas of social theory, and it was not until the late 1980s and early 1990s that researchers began to make explicit links between culture – by which was meant the dominant mode by which a group of individuals interpreted reality in theory – and organisational change – that is the impact that such interpretation had in practice.

Understanding how one component of culture – language – simultaneously affects technological change (in this case, IS) and is affected by it is the focus of the following sections.

THE ORIGINS OF COMPUTER-SPEAK

Any survey of the role language plays in the introduction of IS needs to begin with the very early history of computers. Much of the way in which we talk about computers had its origins in this period, and the manner in which 'computer-speak' was conceived continues to have an impact on our perceptions of and interactions with IT. Understanding the derivation of its terminology and how it is used is, therefore, the first stage in analysing the relationship between language and technology.

The concept of a 'cultural lag' was first proposed by the American social anthropologist William Fielding Ogburn; it occurs when 'one of two parts of culture which are correlated change before or in a greater degree than the other part does'.[6] The evolution of the car was a case in point: car design developed more quickly than road design, meaning that in the 1920s, the speed and manoeuvrability of the car was constrained, not by its own design but by that of the roads along which it was driven.

The cultural lag holds true for language – when something 'new' is invented, we do not necessarily have the words to describe it but have to construct a term which is based on our existing vocabulary: it was for this reason that the telephone was initially described as an 'electronic ear trumpet'. For the inventor and promoter of a new product, this poses a real problem – 'naming' the product becomes important, otherwise there is a risk that its 'newness' will be irretrievably dissipated as potential purchasers associate the new product with old ideas. It is unlikely that today's global telecommunications industry would have grown up if we had persisted in treating the telephone as an ear trumpet.

Although equipment for capturing information on punched cards was used as early as the 1880s, the first computer in its modern sense did not appear until the 1940s. From then on progress was rapid: there was less than ten years between the demonstration of the first electronic calculator at Harvard in 1944 and the installation of the first commercial computer – a payroll system for General Electric in the US. By 1970, it was estimated that there were more than 100 000 computers in use in USA and European businesses. In the public's mind, however, the computer did not come of age until the Apollo space programme; for the first time people became aware that computers – previously the butt of jokes – represented a quantum leap in technological progress. The resulting surge of interest was enormous and the demand for information about computers far outstripped the resources of experts in the field, leaving a gap which was filled by non-technical commentators and populist writers.

What strikes one in reading books and articles which were written on computing in the 1960s and 1970s, and which were aimed at the general business reader rather than technologists, is just how aware their authors were of this gap, and the implications it had for the language in which they wrote about computers.

The earliest books on computers, written by technical experts, employed the scientific terminology of computing with precision and attempted to introduce neologisms which were the linguistic counterparts of their 'new' technology. To their non-technical successors these words were both a source of excitement and a challenge. They were exciting in that their appearance was the first tangible evidence of a genuine revolution already under way:

> A specter is haunting modern society – the specter of computer revolution. Countless books, magazine articles, and news-media specials declare that this upheaval is underway, that nothing will escape unchanged. Such announcements are strongly reminiscent of a recurring ceremonial gesture in popular uprisings of nineteenth-century Europe. When it seemed that the forces of disruption in the streets had power sufficient to overthrow monarchical authority, a prominent rebel leader would go to the parliament or city hall to 'proclaim the republic'. This was an indication to friend

> and foe alike that a revolution was prepared to take its work seriously, to seize power . . . Like political revolutionists, advocates of computerization believe that a glorious transformation is sweeping the world and that they are its vanguard.[7]

But the use of technical terms was also an obstacle to making the subject accessible to the general reading public: 'even the qualified engineer may have difficulty in grasping its concepts and modes of employment'.[8] Yet, at the same time, it was recognised that the 'newness' of computers would be lost if the language used to describe it was adapted too far for the needs of the lay reader. Many writers therefore defended the use of these specific and essentially technical terms on the grounds that the computer was:

> unique, original and rapidly evolving . . . An unfortunate consequence of this is that simplistic concepts like 'glorified adding machine' or the 'electronic clerk', which tend to direct attention away from the more valuable sorts of job a computer will do, have gained too wide a currency . . . Computing is undeniably jargon-ridden. Some computer specialists seem to take almost as much pleasure in the development of a neologism or acronym as they do in the invention of the component or operation it describes. But much of computing terminology is legitimate and necessary. To try to reject it makes as much sense as insisting on saying 'device for transmitting sound between two speakers placed at a distance' rather than telephone.[9]

In theory, there were two main options to resolving these problems: writers could either attempt to develop and pass on a quasi-technical vocabulary, or they could talk about computers in non-technical terms. But practice was not quite as clear-cut as this suggests and, as we shall see, there was considerable confusion between the two methods. How this confusion originated and the form it took determined fundamentally the way in which we talk about computers today.

BUILDING A TECHNICAL LANGUAGE

It may be that the attempts to develop a technically precise language for talking about computers in everyday life were doomed from the outset.

The 1960s and early 1970s saw the publication of a stream of books which were intended to educate their business readers in the scientific language – as well as the scientific use – of computers. Typically, these books included extensive glossaries of terms such as central processors, storage devices, magnetic tapes, magnetic disks, input and output devices, and on-line terminal processing equipment. While not making for gripping reading, the real problem with these books was that their authors were having to make some fairly broad assumptions about how business people would use computers. They did not, for example, anticipate the rise of the IT department which in the early 1970s became the keepers of computer knowledge within an organisation and which minimised the need for the rest of the organisation to understand computers. The average business person, therefore, never had any need for the technical vocabulary which these books were attempting to disseminate.

Technical language did not, however, disappear. Rather like the English pilgrims who first settled America and who took with them a wealth of seventeenth-century regional accents which are still audible in American English today, IS staff took over the technical language of the 1960s and 1970s. It became one of the ways in which they marked themselves out from the rest of the organisation. Perhaps the most fascinating study of this trend was carried out by Tracey Kidder: *The Soul of a New Machine* (1981) charts Data General's development of a computer which could compete with ICL's newly launched VAX mainframe. Amongst the excitement, the setbacks, the personalities, Kidder notes how the product development team evolved their own language:

> A phrase book, such as *The Penguin Dictionary of Computers*, could be useful. *ECO* . . . meant 'engineering change order'. Hence this remark: 'A friend of mine told his girlfriend they had to ECO their relationship'. *Give me a core dump* meant 'Tell me your thoughts', for in the past, when computers had used 'core memories', engineers sometimes 'dumped' the contents of malfunctioning machines' storage compartments to see what was wrong. A *stack* is a special small compartment of memory, a sort of in-box inside a computer; it holds information in the order which the information was deposited and when its gets overfull, it is said to 'overflow'. Hence the occasional complaint, 'I've got a stack overflow'. 'His mind is only one stack deep', says an engineer, describing the failings of a colleague.[10]

It is in moments such as these, rather than in any statement of organisational theory, that we witness the birth of the IS department as an entity which was culturally, as well as logistically, distinct from other functions.

Faced with the problem of having to describe something which was outside the experience and language of their readership, and therefore beyond their comprehension, other writers turned to metaphors, and in particular to the image of the computer as a 'being'. Even in some of the earliest articles on automation, man is the benchmark against which the performance of a machine can be measured:

> The human machine tender is at best a makeshift . . . This development is only in its infancy, yet already we have machines that see better than eyes, calculate more reliably than brains, communicate faster and farther than the voice, record more accurately than memory, and act faster and better than hands. These devices are not subject to any human limitations. They do not mind working round the clock. They never feel hunger or fatigue. They are always satisfied with working conditions and never demand higher wages based on a company's ability to pay.[11]

These comments need to be seen in their historical context: 1946 had seen massive labour unrest across the whole of the USA as the economy attempted to adapt to peace time production – hence the reference to demands for unrealistically high wages. To the employers of the day, factory automation and the very early types of computer under development represented the trouble-free labour market of the future: machines were essentially 'good' workers.

Over the next thirty years, as the use of computers in business became widespread, it is remarkable how constant this analogy is, as, for example, in this guide to computing, written in 1976:

> In this chapter we are going to start developing the theme of how a computer can be made into one of the workhorses of the management team. Lesson one is recruitment. You may recruit a high-flyer on the basis that he is obviously a good man, straight from business school, 'come in and learn the business' and so on, knowing that a niche will be found for him later. You don't recruit a workhorse like this at all. You define the job that has to be done, then you find someone with the right experience and teach him,

> within his capabilities, how to do the job you have defined . . . The most useful, which means cost-effective, computers are invariably those where the management team have worked out a complete objective well in advance . . . The least successful installations are those where the objective keeps shifting.[12]

The notion that the computer is 'a rapid and obedient servant'[13] – that computers could do the work of humans, but without the latter's tendency towards independent political and economic activity – had two profound implications. In the first place, it engendered fears amongst economists and workers alike that the introduction of computers would result in mass unemployment.[14] This in turn led to the fear of extensive strike action in the 1970s in the USA and Europe – something which was much less dramatic in practice – and contributed to the chronic deterioration in employer/employee relations which marked this period.

Second, it conditioned many organisations to view computers as effectively blue-collar workers, able to do only menial and highly routine tasks. To this extent, we were transferring our contemporary prejudices about the rigidity of labour to the computer itself. We might have replaced the unionised worker with a willing 'workhorse', but we had retained many of our preconceptions about the nature of work itself. For this reason, computer automation was not universally deemed to be a quantum leap in technology; indeed, some social theorists during the 1970s questioned the value of computerisation where the end result produced no material improvement in performance.[15] It is also interesting to note that, as computerisation moved from the factory and to the office, clerical work began to be defined in the same terms of blue-collar mundaneity. This was a self-fulfilling prophecy. If computers were like men, then it followed that men were like computers, and it was typical of the literature produced in this period that any distinction between man and machine became blurred. Take for example:

> A simple model of the human as an information processor consists of sensory receptors (eyes, ears, nose, etc.) that pick up signals and transmit them to the processing unit (brain with storage). The results of the processing are output responses (physical, spoken, written, etc.). . . The capacity of the human to accept inputs and produce outputs (responses) is limited. When the human processing system is overloaded, the response rate can decrease.[16]

There is, however, a further twist to the use of this metaphor. The machine as an autonomous being was not an image original to computing, and it carried with it some dark associations – as *Frankenstein* demonstrates. Indeed, it is ironic that a metaphor which was intended to make computers appear more accessible (and thereby aid the process of technological assimilation) was one which was rooted in our historical fears of forces beyond the control of man. Its choice suggests that at least some of the early writers on computers were more ambivalent about the technology than they may have admitted, although the occasional equivocation still surfaces.

The other image most commonly deployed by early writers on computers was that of a revolution, but, in an article which first appeared in *Database* in 1990, Kling and Iacono argued that the term 'computer revolution' is not a description of historical fact, but is a rhetorical device used by writers who want to engage their readers' attention and commitment to the technological advance which computers seemed to represent. This is effectively propaganda: 'The future hasn't yet happened; yet computer revolutionaries are quite confident in describing an emerging revolution. They develop legitimacy and authority for their claims through a variety of rhetorical devices and simplifying conceptualizations that merit our attention'.[17]

Kling and Iacono identified two particular traits consistently used by the 'computer revolutionaries'. The first of these was *isolation*: computing was almost always analysed without reference to the environment – social, political and economic – in which it was used. Thus, it became possible to talk about computers from a wholly technical perspective. Second, the overwhelming majority of writers gloss over any detailed discussion of the issues and problems which surround the actual implementation of computers. The world of these writers was a pure and idealised one, untroubled by practical realities. It was also an inherently optimistic one. They didn't want to know what could go wrong'. Like the image of the computer as a proto-human, the persistence with which the image of a computer revolution appears has had a fundamental impact on the language we used to talk about IT. The very 'revolutionariness' of computers became a fixation and it forestalled any in-depth discussion of the real problems associated with their implementation.

> Every argument and analysis uses some kind of rhetorical style and associated devices to enlighten or convince readers. The rhetorical

> devices used by computer revolutionaries undermine a serious enquiry into the nature of the very social relationships that they claim are being formed.[18]

In these circumstances, it is not surprising that the attempts to educate the lay public in the scientific language of computers failed. A language studded with words like 'inputs' and 'outputs' could hardly compete with the richly resonant language of the non-technicians; moreover, the scientific vocabulary had to be learned with precision – something English-speakers have traditionally been bad at; it could not be simply picked up or inferred from everyday speech. The metaphoric language may have been less precise, it may even have distorted our perceptions of the 'newness' of IT, but it was simpler to construct and easier to communicate.

No one typifies the dilemma this posed more than Alvin Toffler. Toffler is firmly one of the technology-as-an-irresistible-force school of thinking who sees IT as the 'third wave' of progress (the first two being the agrarian and industrial revolutions). In trying to find in language the counterparts to the 'newness' he saw in the technology, he coined new words – infosphere, prosumer, telecommuting – and bolted old words together to create new phrases – electronic cottage, intelligent environment. Toffler is clearly aware of the impact that choice of words may have, and the way in which their associations may determine his readers' reactions; yet at the same time he himself finds many of these associations beguiling. Take the following extract:

> There is nothing magical about [computers], and they are assuredly not 'spirits' or 'souls' in our environment. Yet with all these qualifications, they remain among the most amazing and unsettling of human achievements, for they enhance our mind-power as Second Wave technology enhanced our muscle power, and we do not know where our minds will ultimately lead us.[19]

It is a passage which goes full circle. We start with a straightforward rejection of the metaphor of the computer as a sentient being, but Toffler immediately qualifies this: while the analogy is misleading, he seems to say, there is some truth in the mythic qualities which it implies (the power of computers to change our lives). Indeed, through the introduction of phrases like 'enhance our mind-power' he has, by the end of the paragraph, reinstated the connection with human life and computers.

Toffler's new words are a measure of his enthusiasm. Like other 'computer revolutionaries', he is creating the new world, not reporting its existence. It is a world untrammelled with worries about practical realities, one without history.

The type of writing adopted by Toffler was not unique to him. Other researchers found this style similarly beguiling; some exploited its isolation from the issues of the 'real' world in order to construct a new image for the products or ideologies they were promoting. An advertisement for ITT in the USA, which first appeared in 1974, is a good illustration of this; it showed a young girl looking through what appears to be a pair of binoculars:

> Without them, she couldn't see in the dark. She has good reason to fear the dark. She has retinitis pigmentosa. This eye disease usually begins with night-blindness. But little by little, many of its more than 100,000 victims will go totally blind. The electronic binoculars you see here can help during the night-blindness stage of the illness. They detect light even in near-total darkness – then electronically amplify it so even failing eyes can see. We developed these binoculars with the help of the Government's Night Vision laboratory. Now we're working with the National Retinitis Pigmentosa Foundation to make a less expensive, pocket-sized model. So that more of the children and adults who become afflicted each day and need them, can have them. To us, there's a particular satisfaction in putting science to work for the benefit of people. Letting some light into the darkness, where we can.[20]

The advertisement is remarkable if only because it neglects to mention that this 'science' had first been put to work in night bombing raids in the Vietnam War.

In many respects the hyperbole which preceded the widespread introduction of computers into business was no different to that which accompanies the launch of any new product. However, where products are concerned, the constant exposure to such hype has immunised us against accepting the message uncritically. The problem with the early computer – which was due partly to a lack of technical knowledge and perhaps also to a less sophisticated approach to media promotions – was that people started not so much believing it, as acting as though they believed it.

> The moment the word 'computer' is mentioned we step into a mythological world as powerful as surrounded Homer and his ancestors. There is meaning and power and even a sense of 'being' attributed to the technology . . . Programmers unhesitatingly attribute a 'mind' to the computer. 'I tried it with the library keyword, but it threw it out', they will say, adding things like 'There's something in that code that it doesn't like'. They know well that all they are talking about is an electronic control program . . . They do not really think it is a mind, but, and here is the rub, they find it the most convenient way to think about it, and to discuss it, as if it were a being with a mind.[21]

It is these last comments which are the most significant – the fact that even technologists were speaking and acting as though the computer was human. We noted above that commentators on technology had two main strategies for dealing with the combined problem of a non-technical audience and a phenomenon whose newness could only be understood in technical terms. While these two strategies frequently reappear, the division between them became blurred in practice. What Rothery was witnessing was the introduction into technical language of non-technical metaphors. This is the reverse of what the commentators themselves were seeking to achieve – either, in the interests of greater discursive precision, to educate a lay audience in technical concepts and terms; or to translate those technical terms into images which their audience could understand. In this instance, it was the non-technical images which were feeding back into technical language.

It is interesting to note that the technologists used the human analogy because it was 'convenient': they recognised that it was misleading but, we assume, it was quicker and more easily understood. What they ignored is the effect that using such analogies was having on the way in which they used and thought about the technology. The phrase 'artificial intelligence' is a case in point. The use of the word 'intelligence' clearly relates to the computer-as-man analogy, yet the term does have a precise meaning. In the 1950s, Alan Turing devised a means of rating the 'intelligence' of a computer by testing the extent to which a person could distinguish between the same activity as performed by another human and by a computer: a computer was judged to be 'intelligent' when its performance matched that of its human counterpart. Of course, the phrase 'artificial intelligence' also has a popular, non-technical meaning as well, conjuring up images of brighter-than-normal robots. Thus, the same phrase, which is a product of the machine-as-man way of thinking, has different meanings to a technical and non-technical audience: such is the nature of computer-speak.

CONCLUSIONS

The lessons we can learn from the evolution of 'computer-speak' are directly relevant to business today. Many of the problems we continue to encounter in attempting to design and implement computer systems have their roots, I would argue, in the language we use.

Educating a non-technical public to use technical language was difficult. Despite the heroic attempts of some writers, it was not possible to change the way people spoke by engineering what was effectively a new and artificial language. Computer-speak evolved instead via popular preconceptions (the computer as man) and through usage.

Overall, people were far better at adopting non-technical words and giving them a technical meaning than at learning technical words. This had two primary repercussions. In the first place, the words used inevitably carried with them their prior associations, and these associations in turn affected the way in which we thought about and used the technology. Second, these words had no precise technical meaning: they may have been substituted for technical terms in discourse, but they did not express the same meaning. Thus, from a very early stage in its evolution, computer-speak was loaded with words whose meaning was imprecise: the umbilical cord between the technical context and the way in which we spoke and wrote about the technology had already been severed. Technical language, meanwhile, did not disappear, but migrated to the IS department where it was first revered as evidence of the IS professional's skill and then marginalised as IS departments failed to meet the demands of the wider organisation.

The spread of non-technical jargon led to the mythologisation of the computer, often intentionally by companies and governments which were keen to promote their use. Computers may have been built in the 1940s, but it was not until the 1960s that the concept of the computer was invented. With the mythologisation of the computer, it became almost impossible to discuss the practical realities of computer implementations – and indeed failed implementations – with any degree of meaningfulness. The dominant tone, at least up to the mid-1970s, was one of relentless optimism.

It is my hypothesis that we did not, when computers first appeared, 'learn' a reliable language with which to communicate about them, and that this problem continues to be a significant obstacle to the successful use of IS in businesses today, as we shall see in the following chapter.

Notes

1. See, for example, Stanley, 1978.
2. Toffler, 1980: 17–18.
3. Ibid.: 188.
4. Wisenbaum, 1976: 238.
5. Finnegan, 1988: 12.
6. Ogden, 1964: 86.
7. Winner, 1984: 90.
8. Rose, 1969: 104.
9. Ibid.: 104–5.
10. Kidder, 1981: 52.
11. *Fortune*, 1946; quoted by Noble, 1984: 70.
12. Birkle and Yearsley, 1976: 20–1.
13. Bagdikian, 1975: 249.
14. See, for example, Jenkins and Sherman, 1979.
15. Whisler, 1970, for instance.
16. Davis, 1974: 60.
17. Kling and Iacono, 1991: 68.
18. Kling and Iacono, 1991: 68.
19. Toffler, 1980: 189.
20. Quoted in Mattelart, 1979: 46.
21. Rothery, 1971: 2–3.

6 The Impact of Computer-Speak in the 1990s

We can hear the impact that computer-speak continues to have all around us. How many times have we heard someone exclaim, when presented with a new computer system: 'But it doesn't do what I asked for! You haven't listened to what I told you.' Of course, there are many reasons why IS fails to meet its expectations – needs change, technology arrives late, systems have bugs, projects go over budget. But it is my belief that the language that we use to talk about IS still has a significant impact on its results.

To demonstrate this, we first need to understand the cultural (and, indeed, linguistic) context in which a new computer system is introduced and the kind of changes which its introduction will bring. Next, we have to look at the process itself, from the moment at which someone in the organisation hears about a new IS product and starts to promote it to the point at which it becomes operationally 'live'.[1] We will find that computer-speak is poorly suited to the challenges of this process in most organisations, yet with technical language the sole preserve of the IS department, business users have no alternative means by which to talk about computers. And we talk about computers a lot: try and calculate just how much time is spent talking about IS in your organisation – steering committees, project teams, training, help desks. How much of what is being said and written down in these activities is actually of any value? – by which I mean that it can be translated into an action which yields precisely the results expected. And what do we do when we perceive there is a problem? We convene a meeting to discuss it, we write a memo to highlight it. Until we can accept that the way in which we communicate about IS within organisations is fundamentally flawed, we continue to be trapped in a vicious circle in which talk begets talk. What we need, I shall argue, is to develop a way of implementing and using computer systems which bypasses computer-speak.

THE CHARACTERISTICS OF IS CHANGE

Information systems are all about change. Research has shown that IS remains the single most important internal driver for change within organisations: indeed, there is evidence that organisations find change easier to accept if it is initiated by IS (because it represents progress, and because investment indicates confidence in the future) than by corporate restructuring. But the organisational changes which result from implementing a new computer system in the 1990s clearly differ from those associated with the initial introduction of computers into the workplace: although most people are now accustomed to computers at work, implementing the latest generation of computer systems offers a new set of challenges.

Many of the systems now being implemented by businesses do not represent a quantum leap which is visible to their users; often they are re-automating already computerised procedures, perhaps introducing greater flexibility or storing more data. Customer service systems are a good example of this. Most UK companies who serve wide customer bases, such as utility companies, installed their first systems in the 1960s. These systems were designed to carry out the mechanical procedures of the time (primarily billing) and are poorly suited to the priorities of a modern service company – being able to look at all the information held on a specific customer or being able to customise bills. Installing systems which meet these new priorities may have a noticeable impact on its customers and may enhance a company's competitive position, but it is improbable that it represents a step change to those accustomed to operating the old system; if anything there may be a tendency for these people to operate the new system just as they used to operate the old one. In lieu of visible differences, what these operators are more likely to notice is the new system's greater complexity and, perhaps as a consequence, its lower resilience to human error; they may also find that they have to become more technically proficient to compensate.

Moreover, because many of the activities now being automated cut across the traditional organisational boundaries of a firm, the introduction of a new computer system is much more likely to involve changing the way in which people work together and communicate with each other. Communication is becoming more impersonal (e-mail is replacing face-to-face conversations), faster (people require immediate responses), and briefer (long documents will become a rarity). One effect of this is that the distinction between written and spoken language will become blurred; if we accept that text and speech are different languages, in the sense that they have their own distinct grammar and vocabulary – we do not write as we talk, nor do we talk as we write – then future communication will be a third language, a hybrid which combines elements of the written and spoken word: 'a sort of universal Pidgin may emerge, similar to the special patois that airline pilots use as they take off and land in a multinational range of cultures'.[2]

THE SOCIAL SYSTEM OF IS

While the nature of the changes which a new computer system brings differs markedly from that which accompanied their mass introduction in the 1970s, the social system which provides the context for such changes has – in most organisations – ossified. The earliest computer systems were implemented by those who intended to use them: thus payroll and ledger systems were introduced by finance departments, stock control systems by warehouses. But as computer applications became more complex and fulfilled functions which increasingly crossed traditional organisational boundaries, it made little sense to keep the management of them in the hands of discrete business units. A business-wide perspective was called for, and a centralised IS department promised economies of scale and trans-functional systems. Since then the pendulum of opinion about the role and structure of the IS department has again swung away from centralisation, but it is a rare organisation which has found a practical balance between the needs of the centre and those of individual business units. Instead, there appears to be a state of constant friction between the IS department and its internal customers in most organisations.

Because it is almost always carried out by one set of people on a different set of people, the implementation of computer systems continues to be invasive, rather than organic. Even where some of the final users of a system are included in its implementation team they tend to be seconded from their departments for the duration of the project and returned at its end: the project team always remains a distinct entity. All but the smallest IS implementations therefore contain some degree of us-and-themness.

As a consequence, implementing IS is partly about control and power. It is the reassertion of the authority of the IS department; it is the establishment of the authority of the project team; executive sponsors use it to strengthen their position within the organisation; managers use it to control the way in which their subordinates work.[3] Thinking about computer technology as hardware and software obscures the fact that, while IS may be a driver for change at some levels within an organisation (via the introduction of new working practices) it is not an inherently revolutionary force. What it does have is a legitimising influence. New working practices which might, in isolation, have provoked some resistance from employees can be disguised with the simultaneous introduction of a new system because people accept that technology changes how they work.

It is worth stressing at this point that IS decisions are also inherently undemocratic: the decision to introduce a new system is taken by the few (the board, an IS steering committee) on behalf of the many (the end users of the final system). It is hardly surprising, therefore, that it continues to be common for those affected by a new system to see it as an impersonal technological force which is 'without conscious human control'.[4]

In this context, the 'management of meaning' – the official reasons for the implementation and the formal means by which it is communicated to those affected – becomes vitally important. The reasons for a new system may be clear or they may be opaque. Given that most areas where there would be a transparent justification for using computers (such as highly labour-intensive manual procedures) have already been automated, the rationale behind IS decisions in the 1990s is often much less clear. Why, for example, do organisations replace one word-processing package with another, especially since the majority of its users will only be using a fraction of its facilities? And because its meaning is unclear, those affected by the introduction of a new system are much more reliant on those who took the decision to interpret and communicate its value to the organisation.

Central to controlling the way in which staff interpret events like an IS implementation is controlling the language they use. Take, for instance, the names given to computer systems. When the Scandinavian manufacturers of electronic cash registers wanted to diversify into point-of-sale systems and wanted to promote them to a suspicious market, they gave their new products homely and non-threatening names like 'Laura' and 'Sarah'. Of course, it is a strategy which can easily misfire: one UK retailer inaugurated a programme of updating existing systems called COMA and was nonplussed to discover that delays in the programme were interpreted as 'COMA has gone into intensive care'.

Controlling interpretation clearly goes way beyond naming a system. Where the purpose of a new system is not obvious to the people affected, those who have taken the decision to implement it also have to define it; by defining it, they also start to establish how the system should be talked about. The lexicon of a new system, like the system itself, starts off by being imposed on those who will use it; part of the communication process, indeed part of the training they receive, is designed to teach them new words as well as new ways of working.

Because introducing a new system in the 1990s tends to have less of a visible impact than introducing those implemented in the 1960s and 1970s, meaning, interpretation and language all play far bigger roles than they have done in the past. But, although it bridges the gap in knowledge between the IS department or the project team and the final users of the system, computer-speak inevitably reinforces the fact that that gap exists. Because it contains so much non-technical language applied loosely to a technical subject it creates and propagates misinterpretation, as we will see from examining the decision-making and implementation processes in detail.

COMPUTER-SPEAK AND THE DECISION-MAKING PROCESS

To understand the impact of computer-speak in business today we need to analyse how its role and the process of communication in general changes during the different stages which make up a typical IS project:

- the point at which knowledge is acquired by an organisation;
- the means by which members of the organisation are persuaded to support the proposal;
- the basis on which a decision to go ahead with the proposal is taken;
- the way in which it is implemented in practice; and
- the acceptance of the completed project by those affected by it.

As we will see, the nature of the communication process varies at each stage: different people and different channels of communication are involved.

In an IS context, the acquisition of knowledge would typically be learning about a new hardware or software product from a supplier, a competitor, or from the technical press. One of the key features of IS change is that it is almost always an IS professional who acquires the first knowledge; in some instances, non-IS staff may acquire an awareness of an new product, but they only very rarely acquire a detailed knowledge of it and usually pass it over to the IS professionals to evaluate.

This immediately presents an organisation with a serious problem if the knowledge about a new product is to move outside the confines of the IS department. In the first place, there will be a tendency for the knowledge to be articulated in technical terms and this leads to 'knowledge' and 'technical knowledge' becoming synonymous; thus any information about a product which is deemed not technical is not considered to be knowledge. As a result, there is a fairly common tendency for IS professionals to rubbish ideas put forward by business colleagues: because these ideas are not expressed in technical terminology, they cannot be regarded as reliable knowledge. For this reason, the speed with which knowledge is picked up and disseminated within an organisation will initially be determined by the ease with which its IS and non-IS parts can communicate.

The gap in understanding between the technologists and the non-technologists at this stage is no different to that which occurred with the sudden surge of interest in computing in the 1960s. It is therefore not surprising that the strategies available for resolving the problem are the same: either to improve the technical skills of the business audience, or to express the technical 'knowledge' in a way in which the business audience can understand it.

These two options – educating their audience or pandering to it – run through the bulk of research into IS implementations and are readily observable within businesses. For obvious reasons, academia has almost invariably sided with the first option – to educate business people about technology:

> Top management has to develop a language and a facility for talking about and directing technology. We don't hear about technology in the boardroom, except for some progress reports

> that we pretend to understand or criticize, because we don't have a language or conceptual framework for managing technology.[5]

But in practice, as the introduction of computers in the 1960s demonstrates, communication is much easier when the technologists abandon technical arguments and opt for 'mythologising' the new product, something which (at least, historically) their position outside the mainstream business tended to reinforce:

> To user management, to whom [IT staff] are a power that may dramatically change their lives, they emanate intelligence. They can talk not only about the new hardware and software, but also about the company's information in new terms . . . When we add to this ability to talk about another man's job, the computer technology jargon and the brilliant concepts of M[anagment] I[nformation] S[ystems], the computer man attains awesome proportions.[6]

If these comments seem a little dated – after all, the statements of IS departments are treated cynically by most organisations in the 1990s – then we should only consider the extent to which we – the non-technologists – have learnt to gull ourselves without any help from the IS department. The computer-speak is the only language which is available to the majority of us: we simply know no other way of talking about IS. Just as our predecessors in the 1960s and 1970s spoke of the 'computer revolution' before it had begun to happen, so do we end up constructing an image of the changes a product will bring about before we have begun to implement it. Like them, we use a language of optimism – after all, no one can promote a bad idea.

All of this is hardly an encouraging foundation on which to build a business decision, but what else do we have to go on? Our only facts are presented in a technical jargon we do not fully understand, so it is hardly surprising that we find computer-speak much more attractive. Unfortunately, computer-speak creates more problems than it solves when we come to implement our decision.

COMPUTER-SPEAK AND THE IMPLEMENTATION PROCESS

The acquisition of knowledge, the promotion of the idea and the decision-making process are all activities which are primarily language-driven: actions and hard facts have only walk-on parts. Implementation is where all this changes. Suddenly, we are expected to turn words into reality; as one project manager commented:

> The really difficult job is to move from the 'never-never land', the unbounded optimism of the early phase, as yet imprecisely defined and protected by corporate muscle, to a phase in which you must narrow down, become tough-minded, become clearly aware of what you need . . . Sometimes you have these dreams: it is like at a party after a couple of drinks, when you start seeing all these great ideas and everything looks possible. But then the next morning it always seems a little more difficult.[7]

Implementation is the stage at which people (IS staff and users) realise that the words which they have been using up to this point have had no precise meaning and are not understood in the same way by both sides. Yet implementation is also the moment when discussions suddenly need to become much more detailed and precise if the project is to be completed with any chance of success. It is therefore not surprising that research has shown that a substantial proportion of errors in completed computer systems can be traced back to communication problems during the specification phase.

Faced with this situation, IS project teams are going to increasing lengths to familiarise themselves with the users' environment; typically, they either go and observe the users at work in order to understand how they do their jobs or they second users into their teams to provide the 'expert' business knowledge. But understanding their users' business is not enough; in order to design and develop a computer system (or even in order just to order the correct off-the-shelf package from a supplier), the project team need to articulate their knowledge: at the simplest level, they need to write it down so that other parts of the team (programmers, for instance) can work from it. And however well the project teams learn what people do, it does not resolve the problem of how this knowledge can be converted into a specification for a system which has the same meaning to both sides. It does not, in effect, deal with the inherent difficulties of translating actions and working practices into words. To resolve this particular problem, the project team will still have to fall back on the IS methodologies developed to aid the specification process: in other words, developing a closer relationship with their users only defers the moment when language becomes a problem once more.

System specification methodologies are the modern descendants of the technical jargon which IS departments annexed in the 1960s; as such they have some serious constraints. They are stories. By their very nature they have to assume that there is a natural flow to work which can be captured in a narrative: inputs and outputs become characters; procedures become plots. But the limitations of the specification story-line have become apparent as the way in which we work (and the way in which we expect our computers to work) has become increasingly unstructured. Like a good story, a specification has to have a beginning, a middle and an end, but work itself can be open-ended, its plot can change half-way through, characters disappear: 'one problem with the life cycle concept is that as a narrative tool it does not fit the "natural" flow of work for a given application' comments one IS expert.[8] Moreover, specifications documents are linear in conception: they divide work up into activities which can be analysed sequentially; in practice, work is usually iterative, often circular. 'Specifications', an IS professional recently concluded, 'do not improve communication because user requirements are hard to verbalize and they are likely to change between the requirements specification phase and the operationalization phase of the system life cycle'.[9] Despite this, IS professionals are usually unwilling to accept that their approach is flawed: to do so would be tantamount to questioning the value of their skills.

But even if we were to deflate the need of the IS department to stamp its authority on every project and to eradicate their conceptual weaknesses, we would still be unable to resolve the fundamental problem of these methodologies – which is the attempt to replicate the real world in an objective language which holds good across different organisational units and over a period of time. In fact, when we start to analyse the way in which the language used to describe an IS system evolves during the course of its implementation, we can see that both the words used and their meaning change over time and have to be constantly renegotiated:

> [The] use of information systems is not just the physical transfer of material objects and their efficient manipulation. It is based on users' ability to see these transfers as having a common significance . . . that goes beyond their peculiar physical properties . . . IS change is about coming to an agreement on the conventions that governs language use: its form, signification, use-intention and so on . . . During systems development languages evolve: new

> meanings and words are defined, new uses established and so on: syntax of language is restricted to preselected forms, and its use-patterns and contexts are fixed.[10]

Almost all of this negotiation is carried out by those involved in the detailed specification process; it is not something which makes the agenda of the project steering committee. Because of this, the language used by those at the top of a project hierarchy is inevitably out of step with that being used 'on the ground'. Moreover, as soon as any part of the process becomes formalised – a requirements specification document is finished and circulated – it is immediately obsolete; the meanings attached by the different sides to the words used will have moved on. Where computer-speak is most culpable is that it encourages us to believe that it is possible to talk about computers: this is its fundamental myth.

Yet the absence of a language in which we can consistently communicate meaningfully has a high cost, not just in terms of the errors in the delivered system, but also in the reaction of those affected by its implementation. Uncertainty makes them afraid, and the fear makes them resistant to change.[11] Few studies have highlighted the importance of *meaningful* communication more than Enid Mumford's comparative analysis of several IT implementations in the UK towards the end of the 1960s. One of the case studies was of the Royal Exchange Bank, where a computer system had just been implemented in the local branches. Among the branch staff's comments are:

> We should have had someone who understood the computer to tell us about it. We just had a pile of notes to read.
>
> People didn't know what the system meant, and they still don't.
>
> We were not given any practical experience, only a pile of notes to read. The whole office could have gone in turn to a computerised branch if we'd started the change-over six months earlier.[12]

These remarks are borne out by a survey which Mumford carried out into the sources of information among branch staff which demonstrated the extent to which the staff relied on informal means of communication and their own experience, rather than formal, corporately sponsored approaches. Mumford concluded that:

> Communication is a most complex subject which, because it is to a large extent a reflection of existing social relationships, firms have great difficulty in handling successfully. A period of technical change places extra demands for speed and accuracy on communication lines yet, because it also arouses a great deal of emotion, easily causes these lines to become blocked and ineffective.[13]

Mumford's research brings together many of the issues noted above which are central to any understanding of the effect of the communication gap on IS implementations: those affected did not understand the 'meaning' of the new system; there were too many wordy documents and too few hard facts; there were no opportunities to learn about the new system other than through words; and the formal channels of communication could not compete with the informal routes. It cannot come as a surprise that the Royal Exchange systems were implemented later than planned, that they cost more than anticipated and that they were received less enthusiastically than expected. Nor should we be surprised that most IS projects have a similar ending.

AN ALTERNATIVE APPROACH

How can we get round these seemingly intractable problems? I would suggest several possible actions we could take.

- We should recognise that the language in which we talk about technology is more of a hindrance than a help: it is inherently inaccurate; it contains no consistent or precise meaning; it can be interpreted differently by different groups and over time; it mythologises rather than represents its subject.
- We need to be acutely aware of, and therefore cautious of, the language used when we evaluate new IS products and projects. Overselling in the early stages of a project, both to ourselves as well as those immediately affected, creates difficulties in the implementation stage. Rather than waking up with a hangover, we should drink less during the evening. We need to read cost/benefit analyses in the same way that we read advertisements because, often quite unintentionally, this is what they are.

- Nothing keeps the hyperbole of computer-speak at bay more than facts and actions; the more we can introduce these into our decision-making processes, the better will be the decision that we take. We need to make sure that useful facts are not embedded in technical jargon, and we need to ensure that we consider the non-technical facts which IS professionals are prone to dismiss. Rather than talk about a product, we should go and look at it being used.
- We should work to minimise the extent to which we rely on language in IS implementations; this means ditching the bulky specifications documents which are so often assumed to be a prerequisite of a successful project. Instead, we may find non-verbal means of systems development – by building a prototype, for example – considerably more effective.
- We need to manage 'meaning' more proactively and more imaginatively. As we have seen above, meaning has become an increasingly important part of an IS implementation simply because it is not immediately obvious to those involved. Language abhors a vacuum as much as nature does, and it is inevitable that people will start to fill this gap in their understanding with their own interpretations of events. Controlling this process more effectively than most organisations do at the moment is fundamental. Formal corporate statements do not address this issue because they fail to keep up with the pace of linguistic change over the course of a large project and because, all too often, they are not regarded as the main source of information. To overcome these problems we have to identify ways of getting much more up-to-date information about progress to key members of staff (and this does not necessarily mean the most senior) who can then disseminate it.
- We also need to reconsider the value of the kind of documentation and training which usually accompanies a new system. People cannot learn how to use a new system from reading about it, or from hearing someone else talk about it: they need to do it. Clearly we have already gone part of the way towards this if we organise hands-on training for groups of new users, but we might do even better if either we train a small number of 'expert' users who can then pass on the skills which are actually required to do their job (and these will not always be those taught on a formal training programme) to their colleagues or we second people into a part of the business where the new system is already in use so they can observe how people work with it in practice.

The following case study – of Storehouse – is intended to illustrate the points raised here. For each, I have taken a single, large IS project and looked at the evidence of how computer-speak affected their progress and the means by which those involved sought to resolve the problems which arose as a result.

Notes

1. This framework is based loosely on that proposed by Rogers (1983) who saw the change process within an organisation as comprising four distinct components: the nature of the change; its social context; the time frame over which the change took place (a process which was itself broken down into five distinct phases: acquisition of knowledge, dissemination, decision, implementation and confirmation); and the type of communication.
2. Quoted by Dizard, 1985: 14.
3. Scarbrough and Corbett, 1992: 29; for examples of the fears engendered by technology see Boguslaw, 1965, and Galbraith, 1967.
4. Friedman and Cornford, 1989: 193.
5. Foster, 1986: 42.
6. Rothery, 1971: 16–17.
7. Foster, 1986: 53.
8. Friedman and Cornford, 1989: 205.
9. Ibid.: 205–6.
10. Lyytinen, 1987: 14.
11. Davis, 1974: 426.
12. Mumford and Banks, 1967: 123-4.
13. Ibid.: 218–19.

7 Case Study 3: Storehouse

RETAILING AND TECHNOLOGY

Retailing is one of the most competitive environments, but since the early 1990s a combination of several factors has meant that many of the traditional strategies for expansion (and, indeed, survival) in this market have become redundant. The boundaries between shops and other service providers have become blurred – so much so that grocery chains see fast-food restaurants as legitimate competitors. Increasingly mobile and discerning consumers are demanding personalised products at mass-production prices: Levi's now offers a service where your measurements are entered into a computer and a pair of perfectly fitting jeans are dispatched within days. Ever more stringent planning controls mean that the most common method of increasing sales is not an option. Overall, retailers are having to find new ways to compete.

In this environment, technology is playing an increasingly important role. It is not just the case that a new logistics system, complete with satellite tracking, will significantly reduce distribution costs and relieve (even if only momentarily) the mounting pressure on retailers' margins: technology also provides retailers with the opportunity to focus promotions ever more precisely on their target market segments (through using data on consumer behaviour from the point-of-sale scanning systems); to reduce shop-lifting (which accounts for more than £0.5bn of sales in the UK alone each year); and to entertain their customers (in-store holograms and video-bearing shopping trolleys are just two of the ideas being trialled).

In the 1960s, if technology came into retailers' thinking at all it was in the form of automatic vending machines or 'electronic systems' which would allow customers to go round a store collecting stamps on a card, rather than picking up the actual items; once they had finished, this card would be machine-read, leaving the customer to pick up the goods from a collection point. What is most remarkable about the evolution of retailing technology since then is not so much the increasing complexity of individual systems as the way in which retailers have gone from seeing technology as a support tool to exploiting it as a form of retailing in its own right. For the bigger stores, retailing and technology are indistinguishable: touch-screen menus help you decide what to cook, videos at the point of sale can show you (and order) a product which is out of stock. The advent of electronic home shopping, via the Internet, will be the ultimate expression of this trend.

In recent years, the pace of change for the retailers themselves has been phenomenal. Back in the 1960s, the use of computers in retailing was confined to generic activities such as sales accounting, purchasing and stock control; only in the 1970s did applications more specifically designed for the retailing market first appear – merchandising aids and marketing information systems. The dramatic change of the 1980s was to take computers beyond the back office and into the customer front line, with electronic point-of-sale and fund transfer systems, and scanners.[1] As in other walks of commercial life, the introduction of computers into stores met with resistance both from retailers' own staff and from their customers. Particularly high on their list of suspicions in the 1970s was that computers meant that individual goods would no longer have price labels; and it is interesting to note that it is this kind of concern – not the technological difficulties – which is still inhibiting many retailers experimenting with electronic shelf-edged labelling (where the price indicated can be changed by a computer system).

Information technology also brought significant changes to the way in which retailers organised themselves and this had implications for their corporate culture. The supermarket has become a factory shop-floor, with individual staff playing their part on what is effectively an assembly line:

> The development of the supermarket form of work organization has enabled shopwork to be broken down into specialized elements of stock control, pricing and so on, while the customer queue provides a useful pacing effect on the work of the check-out operators. Now the advent of IT in the form of EPOS technology enables even greater management control.[2]

But reading trade journals such as *Retail Automation*, you would be forgiven for thinking that all these changes have happened relatively smoothly, that the implementations of major new computer systems on a continuous basis have been without problems. The public language of retailing technology is an almost remorselessly successful one: unlike computer fiascos in the public sector or in heavily regulated industries, those of the retail world happen in relative privacy. There may be the occasional visible blip – food may not be delivered quite as fresh as it should have been because of problems with the distribution system or certain items may be missing from the shelves because the parameters of the automatic reordering system have been set incorrectly – but most difficulties are invisible to the shopper. Unlike banks, retailers do not offer bank statements; unlike telecommunications companies, they do not offer complex tariff structures and payment arrangements. (Although all of these things may change.) Having such an optimistic public face may be helpful to the retailers' reputations, but it does not necessarily provide a constructive basis on which to talk about technology in this market. The rules of competition mean that retailers cannot exchange notes or learn from each other's experience. How, then, do they manage to talk about IT?

STOREHOUSE PLC

Storehouse is one of the largest fashion retailers in the UK. From a rather chequered past (the Storehouse Group was originally formed by Sir Terence Conran, based around his highly successful Habitat furniture chain which was subsequently divested), the company has succeeded in carving out for itself a substantial niche, offering good designs at low prices, In 1996, the company had a turnover of more than £1bn and comprised two main chains: Bhs, offering exclusively own-label fashion, accessories and home furnishings, and Mothercare which focuses (almost uniquely among UK retailers) on the mother and baby market. While it remains largely UK-based, the company now operates a small number of overseas stores, principally in the Far East.

Despite the problems caused by the evolution of the group (such as the incompatibility of some of the merged companies' technology bases), Storehouse companies have often been early adopters of some of the newest technologies. Given its relative newness, acceptance by staff has always posed a challenge, and one which the organisation historically solved by allowing its staff to evolve its own language to accommodate the changes. In 1975, Mothercare installed an early type of electronic tagging system. To integrate the new system with existing working practices (and the logistics of fashion retailing), the implementation programme developed its own vocabulary which had a precise, specialist meaning in the Mothercare context. As the then director of IS commented:

> If a sales capture system of our kind is installed it is vitally important that the staff are trained to operate it and are motivated to observe the operating rules. To this end we have written self-administered learning booklets which explain all our in-store systems in a very simple manner . . . At present we operate a kinball tag system on a two level basis. We have firstly a single tag which is attached to such items as maternity dresses and prams and are detached at the point of sale . . . The other tag we call a 'bulk' tag and this is attached to the outer packaging of high volume merchandise. IBM, I believe, term this kind of system 'seeding'.[3]

Talking to Nigel Pilkington, the current Director of IS at Storehouse, confirms this. Language, according to Pilkington, is the biggest problem his department faces. Every year Storehouse, like other companies, invests in writing lengthy specifications for complex new systems, yet however detailed these are, they seem to offer no guarantee that the final system will be implemented according to plan. While preparing these specifications seems to be the 'right thing to do' – after all they are what every textbook on technology recommends – it is not easy to see that there is any link between these documents and the final system, between words and actions.

In fact, Pilkington sees the words as potentially contributing to the problem. It is easy in his view to 'get sucked in' to a project by the image which is constructed by a specification for a system, to become preoccupied – mesmerised even – by the words used rather than using them as a tool to communicate a particular issue. It is a problem which affects IS staff and users alike, and one which is almost impossible to prevent, especially working in an environment – like IS at present – in which language is valued. Despite the lessons of practice, the working assumption remains that the more words associated with a project the more likely it is to succeed.

Language, from Pilkington's perspective, poses several specific problems. In the first place, a single – even apparently innocuous – word can mean different things to different people: when an IS person talks of 'sales' he or she is probably referring to a precise definition, taken from a data dictionary, used in just one area of a complex management information system; for a buyer or store manager 'sales' may have a slightly different meaning, one which relates to their operational experience and one which they may use more flexibly than the IS person's term.

This points to a further difficulty with the relationship between computers and language: computers need precision, but human beings prefer flexibility and are not naturally very accurate creatures. Language is effectively the bridge between the precision of computers on the one hand, and the imprecision of humans on the other: it fails because it can never satisfy both demands at once. There is also a working assumption that using technical language will resolve this problem, as it provides greater precision than lay English (this assumption tends to go hand in hand with the idea that the more words the better). In fact, what this does in practice is drive a wedge between the IS department and the rest of the business: retailing may becoming increasingly dependent on technology but the gulf of understanding between the two remains great. Technical language may be interpreted by the IS department as a sign of success – its appearance in a specification for a system could indicate, for instance, that the user who wrote it has become comfortable with and knowledgeable in the system's technical aspects. But it remains a barrier to the majority of people in an organisation: the inclusion of technical terms in a document may not be welcomed by this community, who may interpret it as a sign that the author has 'gone native'.

Pilkington sees these attitudes becoming polarised. Technology is becoming ever more sophisticated: its successful implementation into an organisation requires more decisions by more people with a greater understanding of the technical issues involved. At the same time, the language of IS staff is seen as increasingly specialist, detached from operational – 'real' – issues. The gulf between the two grows daily: preventing a discussion about technology becoming completely subsumed into a technical vocabulary is a 'desperate struggle'. The problem is exacerbated by the emergence of other subcultures within the organisation – effective merchandising who build up a strong *esprit de corps*, or store managers who develop their own operational jargon for the practical issues they deal with. As each team starts to evolve a distinct language of its own, it becomes increasingly difficult for members of the IS department to communicate precisely with all those involved: the areas of commonality recede and the chances of misinterpretation increase exponentially. The reaction of the IS department is to write even more – ever more complex systems have to be tied down to an ever increasing degree of detail. As a result there is too much information, and no one person can absorb all of it.

One of the interesting things which emerges from these practical examples is the extent to which IS practitioners think very differently about language to most non-technical people: for an IS person, language is as important as doing – indeed for much of IS-related work it *is* doing; by contrast – as we see from many of the other examples in this book – mainstream business managers prefer doing to talking. Given that the latters' attitude is reinforced by a long-standing cultural bias against language, it raises the question: why should IS people be so different? The answer is probably two-fold. First, more of the work done by a typical IS department – whether it is writing a systems specification or a computer program – is language-based. For the IS department, therefore, words and actions are indistinguishable. Second, this difference is something which is promulgated by IS people themselves, simply because they want to be different – if they worked in an environment in which words were perceived to be less valuable than actions, then much of the work they did would be similarly denigrated. To be able to gain any sense of job satisfaction, IS people have to invert the conventional framework of talking/acting values. Seen from this perspective, it is hardly surprising that there can be such tensions between IS and non-IS people – the former value words, the latter actions.

For Nigel Pilkington, there are two possible solutions. One is to use non-IS analogies where possible; for example, when describing the potential of a large-scale system, he remembers likening it – to his non-technical audience – as 'a cathedral not a bicycle-shed'. What he loses in precision, he gains in terms of immediate understanding and impact. The second and more important approach is to attempt to move the business away from relying on substantial tomes of specification and analysis, and more towards prototyping. As we noted in the previous chapter, prototyping has the advantage of being 'beyond' language. There is no need to describe a system in detail in order to get its final consumers to sign off its specification: with prototyping, no words are required, a user can simply sit in front of a computer screen and experiment with the dummy system, discussing possible improvements with its developers along the way. In some ways, as Pilkington recognises, it is not the perfect solution: it certainly constrains the kind of systems you develop and the software that you use to those areas which can be prototyped: large-scale systems whose programs still require extensive customisation are not easy to accommodate on this basis. This in turn implies that the skills required from IS staff will change in the future: detailed technical expertise may be less valuable than the ability to develop small-scale applications rapidly and in close collaboration with their ultimate users. But in a world where it is becoming, if anything, more difficult to talk about computers, this is beginning to look like the only feasible solution.

Notes

1. Newman, 1975: 6–10.
2. Scarbrough and Corbett, 1992: 35.
3. Sanderson, 1976: 35.

Part IV

Communicating with Customers

8 Changing the Way We Talk to Customers

> The premise . . . is that you cannot manage a quality customer-service operation unless you understand the nature of what it is you are providing, not unless you fully realise what your customers want from you and how they perceive you from the start.[1]

'Understand your customers', we are frequently exhorted. If we understand them, we will serve them better – and earn ourselves more sales and profits in the process: 'your customers will tell you how to be successful, if you will only listen to them'.[2]

But what is rarely pointed out is that, in order to understand our customers, we have to talk as well as listen to them: our entire relationship is mediated through language. In fact, talking to customers is part of the service we deliver, whether it takes the form of the end product (information on train times, for example) or as part of the service 'package' (the friendly greeting of a hotel receptionist).

LANGUAGE AND THE CUSTOMER

What makes language so important in dealing with customers is that the traditional dichotomy between language and action – we habitually use language as a means of getting to an action and are suspicious about using it for its own sake – does not apply:

> Corporate takeovers and mergers can fly or fail depending on the properly timed release and management of information. Product introductions are carefully planned to get the most publicity in the media. Organizational crises are worsened or minimized in part by how skilfully information about the problem is handled . . . What you *say* to customers has become just as important as – if not *more* important than – what you *do*.[3]

Language is crucial at every stage in the process of delivering, consuming and evaluating a service.

Customer expectations are no longer necessarily accepted as *de facto* quality standards (since it was recognised that these were unmanageably complex and changeable), but they still provide some essential benchmarks of what consumers are looking for when they purchase a given service. Such expectations are almost invariably expressed in linguistic terms. When we go to the hairdresser, we might expect the environment to be 'stylish', 'relaxing', 'colourful', whereas a hospital would be 'clean', 'efficient', 'white'. We do not tend to use such expressions when we are buying manufactured goods – or at least they represent what is available rather than what we aspire to. We might, for instance, want to buy a washing machine which is 'clean', 'efficient' and 'white', but this is only to distinguish our choice from other possible models; the adjectives are given to us, we do not supply the adjectives. There is, of course, a broad grey area between the two, between the subjective service and the objective good. When we buy a car, we may be looking for something which is 'red' and 'fast' – to distinguish it from those that are 'green' and 'slow' – but we are probably also looking for something which is 'stylish'. Goods which fall into this grey area are those which are accompanied by a service 'package' and which are marketed by appealing to our subjective taste as much as our practical requirements (and it would be fair to say that – as marketing techniques become more significant and competition more intense – an increasing number of manufactured goods are falling into this grey area).

The difference between goods and services is therefore not simply – as it is often conceived to be – that of tangibility versus intangibility: it also involves the relative importance of language in the transaction. The more language, the more the 'good' is in fact a service.

Of course the problem this raises – and this is why customer expectations are no longer taken to be the sole benchmarks of service quality – is that with qualitative words, such as 'stylish', the exact meaning is unclear and will certainly vary from customer to customer. It would therefore be true to say that, as the proportion of language associated (i.e. the service component) with a service increases, so does the extent to which the 'meaning' of that service is outside the control of the service provider (Figure 8.1).

The picture is one of increasing vulnerability: as what were manufacturing companies shift gradually towards providing a service 'package' around their core products, they are relinquishing more

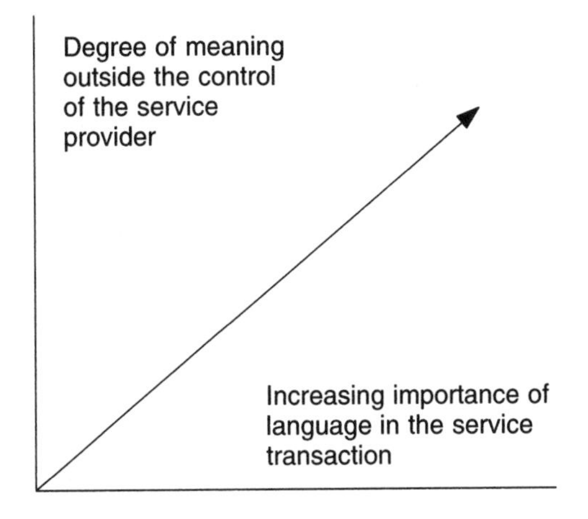

Fig. 8.1

and more control over their performance – customers are a force for democratisation.

Ownership of meaning empowers the customer – language is therefore the prime means by which customers exert control over their service purchases. The more language a customer uses – or is allowed to use – during a service transaction, the more powerful the customer becomes: articulate customers are more likely to exact the service they require – and be vociferous in complaining should the service not meet their expectations.

Compare, for example, the experience of having a washing machine repaired with going to the hairdresser. When the repair-man arrives, we may engage in a short, desultory dialogue (weather, traffic) but we want to move fairly rapidly on to to the core topic: the fault with the machine and how to fix it. This conversation tends to be short too, as it develops from our lay view of the situation ('there's water pouring out of a hole in the back') to the repair-man's technical analysis ('sounds as though it's the . . .'). Shifting to technical jargon puts the repair-man back in charge: unless we are technically proficient, we have to accept his diagnosis. At the hairdresser, by contrast, we remain in control. Clearly, we don't hold the scissors, but we can say: 'No, that's not enough – I want you to cut more off.' The absence of technical jargon means that we remain in control.

Of course, it could be argued that this contrast is less a function of language than the inevitable result of one profession (repairing washing machines) being more complicated than another (hairdressing). This would be a simplification: there is nothing in the technology which stops the repair-man giving a clear explanation in lay terms ('the water is pouring out of the back because . . .') which we, the customer, could understand and, where appropriate, challenge. What stops the repair-man doing this is much simpler: time. It could take some minutes to go through the problem and the repair company will probably have scheduled the engineer's appointments on the basis that his time – which costs money – is better occupied mending as many washing machines as possible per day than in providing explanations to customers.

Bigger assumptions lie behind this. First, efficiency is important, both in terms of costs and in keeping to a planned timetable (so as not to irritate customers whose appointments come later in the day). To be efficient, the repair company has to remain in control: letting the customer take charge would disrupt the engineer's work pattern. The control of the individual customer has therefore to be sacrificed to the collective good of all customers (and – implicitly – that of the company itself). Second, the repair company has taken a decision on our behalf: that efficiency is more important to us than control; that we are not interested in understanding the problem, we just want it fixed. While this assumption may be true where washing machines are concerned, there are plenty of occasions where we want a better explanation but the 'system' is based on the assumption either that we should not want an explanation or that it is more important to invest time in dealing with the issue (acting) than in telling us about it (talking); see Figure 8.2.

Visiting a doctor is an obvious example: most of us want an explanation for whatever our complaint is, but the length of our appointment rarely allows enough time. As a means of processing their patients efficiently, doctors use a kind of shorthand – medical terminology. This has two benefits: it allows the doctor to refer the patient to another doctor with minimum preamble and maximum accuracy ('this patient has an . . . .' provides an immediately comprehensible guide to a colleague); it also allows the doctor to curtail the conversation with the patient (the 'you have an . . .' statement which few patients would contest). The system (such as the number of appointments a doctor has in a single morning) is designed to promote action not discussion. In practice, doctors therefore often have to weigh up the benefits of providing an explanation to an individual customer against seeing a large number of patients, and late-running appointments are the inevitable consequence.

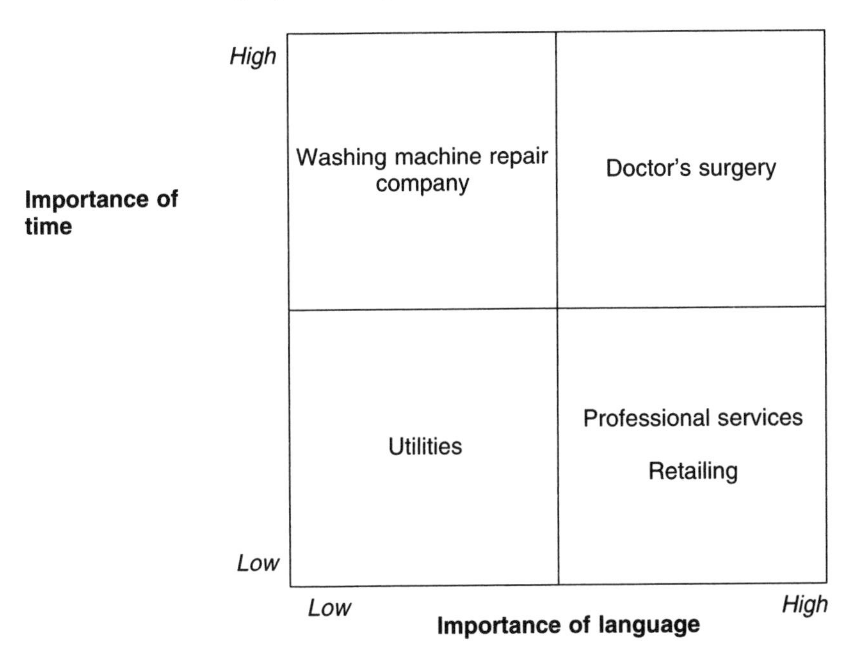

Fig. 8.2

Going to the doctor is an interesting example in another way. There appears to be an increasing body of evidence that shows that talking to patients, involving them in their treatment, even giving them control over aspects of it (such as pain relief) all aid recovery. If we extrapolated this to the 'service' which a doctor provides, we might conclude that giving patients more of an explanation – thereby increasing their sense of control – might actually increase the overall efficiency of the medical service. We might also argue that the assumption that patients are willing to trade explanation for cure is an old-fashioned one: better education, an increased unwillingness to accept unquestioningly the authority of the medical profession and perhaps even the growing complexity of modern medicine all mean that explanation is as important as treatment.

That the scheduling of medical appointments has yet to recognise this fact should not surprise us: it is a paradigm shift which few service businesses have made. Many organisations still assume that we want action rather than explanation.

In some cases they may be right. As long as a company provides a unique or rare service, the explanation component of its service will be comparatively unimportant: as customers, our priority will be to obtain the service, not to understand it. However, as competition increases, the explanation component grows in importance: the basic service functions simply as starting point – an 'order qualifier' in the jargon of operations management – and not as a source of differentiation. We are accustomed to the idea that as goods manufacturers face greater competitive pressures, they are forced to add service components to their core products in order to differentiate them. Language may be the next stage in this evolutionary ladder: as service providers fail to find any conventional points of differentiation within their offering, they will start to rely more on language. Language – we might conclude – grows in proportion to competition (Figure 8.3).

Language is therefore becoming a competitive weapon. This is not as simple as getting your front-line staff to say 'have a nice day' with greater conviction, it means – literally and figuratively – speaking your customers' language. We have already looked at the importance of being able to use the native language(s) of your customers, as a means of ensuring both that you match their meanings as closely as possible, and that you have a common basis of understanding (the idea that a shared language is a form of social contract between individuals), but the idea of speaking your customers' language extends beyond this.

For example, we are familiar with the idea that customer contact is all-important: for this reason, we all spend vast amounts of money and time in staying in contact on a regular and systematic basis. More

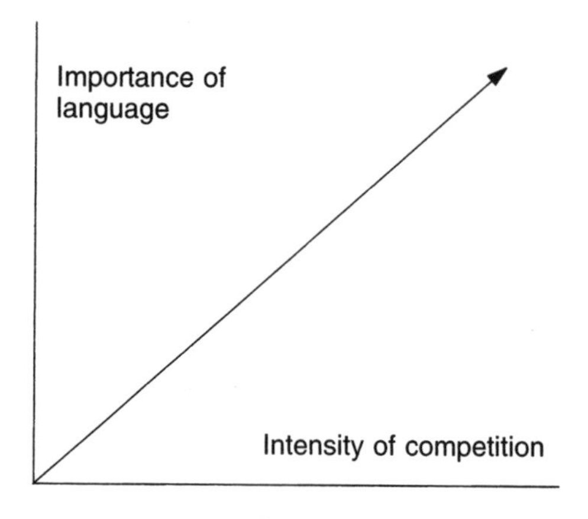

Fig. 8.3

often than not, this communication is one-way: it rarely provides an opportunity to gauge a customer's expectations and needs. As organisations, our words usually fall on deaf ears. How precious (and rare) are the times we manage to open up a dialogue. Getting customers to talk back is all-important – not just, as we usually tend to think, because this provides useful feedback on our quality of service – but because even the act of having a dialogue helps to cement our relationship with our customers. It means that we are worth talking to and that we have something to say which the customer is interested in hearing. Moreover, when customers talk to us, they cannot be talking to our competitors: dialogue can be exclusive and self-perpetuating.

This is where language comes into play. We have already seen how language can reinforce group dynamics by creating common words and links between members of a team, especially where the collective focus has a technical or similarly esoteric bent, as is the case with IS project teams. The same 'jargon' which makes the team an effective unit is also a barrier to those outside the team. This pattern can be deployed to our advantage with customers: if we can create a set of common words, we not only tie our customers to us more effectively (because we at least sound as though we share a common set of values), but we also exclude our competitors. Clearly, being first is an important part of this equation: if one of our competitors has got there first, we may find ourselves excluded because our potential (former?) customer now speaks our competitor's language – which we may not understand but which we are forced to mimic (something which is far more difficult than speaking our own language).

Establishing the primacy of our organisation's language is the nearest we can get to directing our customers' wishes, aspirations and – ultimately – purchases. Earlier, we looked at the important role played by words such as 'stylish' in certain types of service; while we will never be in a position to completely control the meaning which customers attach to such subjective words, we can set the agenda by creating the link between the word and our service in the first place.

Imagine that your company decides to launch a new insurance product. Insurance is not renowned for excitement: indeed, it is popularly associated with niggling conditions, incomprehensible jargon and illegible small print. It is a reputation which is much less deserved in the 1990s than it might have been ten years ago. Growing competition and increased regulation have improved both the essential product and the service package associated with it (many insurance companies, for example, now offer helplines for their customers). However fast the gap is closing between what people want from insurance (a new roof when a tree has fallen through the old one) and what they think they will get (quibbling over whose tree it was), it still exists. So when you look around for a means to differentiate your new insurance product, you might decide that this gap – between wish and expected reality – is one that you can exploit to your advantage. Rather than promote a particular aspect of the cover you are offering, you might try to associate your product with honesty and plain-talking: 'direct' insurance in a new sense. And to reinforce this message, your advertising might show that your company is staffed not with buttoned-down actuaries primed to obfuscate any issue with legalese, but with 'ordinary' people. You may find that this approach touches a nerve: suddenly, the words that you are employing (and 'ordinary' is a good example) acquire a common currency: they become the benchmarks against which your competitors are judged.

Setting the linguistic agenda allows us to exclude our competitors because people – in this case, our customers – tend to be lazy about the words they use. We are all guilty of using words we have recently heard, as it requires considerably less effort than thinking for ourselves (this is the basis of clichés, after all; indeed, it is also how we learn language in the first place). Although language empowers us, we are often willing to abdicate responsibility. So when we associate a particular word with one of the services we offer, the chances are – as long as our delivery matches expectations – our customers will start to use these words too.

Before you decide that this is far-fetched, look at the world of management consultancy. Consultancies face an especially difficult task in making their ideas both tangible (and therefore worth potentially considerable expense) and different. A key way of doing this is to use specialist – usually resonant or exciting – words. Words, as we have seen, imply there is an associated action, something which is particularly important where consultancy firms are trying to convince potential purchasers that the service they offer is a concrete and substantial one. Methodologies are a traditional but frequently time-consuming route to doing this, but new words – 'buzz-words' – are the short-cut: they are the advance party which allows a firm to take the intellectual high ground while the main army is still some way behind. As the consultancy world becomes more competitive, and as issues like time to market become increasingly important, we can expect to see the use of buzz-words growing and the length of time for which they are current shrinking. While they are used, however, these words represent a competitive advantage. They are not simply – as we traditionally assume words to be – the precursors of action: they are actions in their own right.

All these different functions of language provide opportunities for organisations to exploit. But to do so, they need to discard some of their preconceptions.

Most companies – like most training manuals and most textbooks on improving customer service – see language as a matter of getting their employees to say a few key phrases; employees should not gossip in front of customers; they need to listen to customers; they should look as though they mean what they say.

Perhaps the most sophisticated way of looking at the role of language has been to draw parallels between service provision and drama: both are 'live' performances; both consist of an actor (or actors) and an audience; both rely on behaviour, gesture and language. In some services, customers themselves may play an active role and one of the key aims of the service provider is to ensure that this role is managed and that the message being transmitted is not distorted, by educational or cultural differences for instance.[4] But it is a testimony to our suspicion of language that the linguistic element in service delivery and consumption is rarely considered – indeed, it is often explicitly excluded from any analysis, as we can see here:

> In a drama, the script is the vehicle through which all key details of the drama are conveyed (dialogue, staging, lighting, scene changes, etc.). In short, a script is a very detailed plan of action. For service, a scene might consist of a detailed description of appropriate behavior(s) for a given situation, yet might not include the exact spoken words. Service scripts should contain all of the behaviors necessary to fashion a credible performance and should always be mindful of audience expectations.[5]

Even where research has been carried out specifically on customer communication, there has been a tendency to analyse this within a conventional customer service (and primarily process) framework, rather than focus on the content of the communication. Thus, while the findings may provide useful information on the critical points at which the communication process breaks down – where a customer's expectations are unrealistic or the performance of the firm or employee does not match the capacity to deliver a service (a product is unavailable, for instance – which apparently account for 75 per cent of incidents[6]) – they provide little insight into the origin of these lapses. How, for example, have customers articulated their expectations?

It is in having answers to this sort of question that the real potential for making use of language in serving customers can be exploited.

MAKING THE MOST OF LANGUAGE

The benefits which can be realised from using language more effectively come from recognising the role it plays in communicating with customers and consciously making the most of the opportunities this provides. Most companies fail to exploit this resource simply because they do not see it as one: language is invisible to them and you cannot get a return on an asset which you do not know you have. There are four key steps to changing this:

- You need to understand the role that language either currently plays or could potentially play in the context of the services you provide – something which will vary with the type of service. Doing this is partly a matter of simple communication (who talks to whom and how), but it is also about understanding the type of language used and the way in which language and actions are linked.
- Where the potential benefits justify (and they will not always) changing the way your organisation uses language, you need to develop a plan for encouraging your customers to communicate with you as frequently and widely as possible.
- You have to take a proactive stance, setting out to influence the words used by your customers in relation to your services, because this will help you control more effectively not only the direct interaction you have with your customers, but also the indirect interaction with all the people your customers go on to talk to.
- Finally, having established – and, to some degree, helped to form – the vocabulary with which your customers associate your services, you need to ensure that your organisation speaks the same language: that communication inside the organisation

mirrors that outside so that the boundary between internal and external communication disappears.

As we saw earlier, every organisation – hairdressers, washing machine repair companies, doctors' surgeries – makes choices about the part played by language in the services they provide. Usually, this choice is an implicit one, and it differs from service to service. Few companies think through the implications and trade-offs.

For instance, the mid-1990s in the UK have seen a growth in the prevalence of loyalty schemes amongst retailers: what started in the early 1990s with stores offering their own credit cards rapidly escalated into much broader schemes offering customers loyalty points every time they shopped. Today, in 1997, the majority of the UK's largest retailers run loyalty schemes of one form or another. The perceived value of these schemes (which are immensely expensive to operate) is that it gives the retailer direct access to their customers (their home addresses), information about the likes and dislikes of individual shoppers (from analysing till receipts) and a whole host of tangential, but potentially highly useful, information about demographic profiles, family sizes, hobbies and even incomes. All this data can be used to focus promotional campaigns much more effectively at those who are most likely to react positively. Leaving aside the practical issues involved (much of this is as yet untried and its ultimate financial return still questionable), what is worth noting is that loyalty schemes of this sort do not in fact significantly change the relationship between the retailer and its customers. The essential shopping experience remains unchanged (having a loyalty card does not give you better treatment or access to, for example, the supermarket equivalent of the club-class store): communication from the retailer to the customer may increase but the (more radical) attempt to encourage customers to talk back is rare.

It is an approach which obviously differs from the smart boutique, where the clientele is small enough to be known individually. For supermarket chains, the implicit assumption is not simply that customer loyalty is driven by greed (loyalty points), rather than by the nature of the supermarket shopping experience. Also assumed is that the financial return from this type of scheme is greater in total (by getting a large number of people to spend a small amount more) than it would be if the chain tried to get to know its customers on an individual basis (where the costs in staff time would be huge and not matched – because the average price of supermarket goods is low – by increased expenditure). This economic decision has an impact on the way the supermarket communicates with its customers and the language it uses. The theory is that investing in some degree of direct communication with retailers will increase sales (via focused promotions); further investment in communication – encouraging customers to enter into a dialogue – cannot be justified because the cost will outweigh the benefit. Given the scale of their operations, supermarket chains cannot afford to engage in protracted, two-way communication with their customers. For this reason, their market research will tend to be based around closed and multiple-choice questions, and the approach to customer queries and complaints will be to resolve the issue, where possible, with a single letter or call. It is probably one of the reasons why these companies often give immediate money-off vouchers to dissatisfied customers: they want to curtail the conversation. This is not to suggest that these companies do not want to ensure customer satisfaction or that they do not take seriously any short-falls in their services, but that they do apply some commercial criteria to resolving these issues.

Because their average sale per customer is low – at least in comparison to a department store – large supermarket chains can afford to take this attitude as long as the proportion of dissatisfied customers remains very low and geographically dispersed. The views of a single customer are immaterial when compared to the customer base in total. Thus, when a small number of customers complain about a particular product, the supermarket can ascribe this reaction to individual preferences because it can take comfort in the fact that the vast majority of purchasers have not complained. Even where the entire stock of a faulty product has to be withdrawn (perhaps because of multiple complaints), the supermarket can minimise the impact by substituting alternative goods, an action which protects the supermarket's name but damages that of the original manufacturer (as happened when it was discovered that a batch of Perrier water had become contaminated with benzine in the early 1990s). The basis of supermarkets' communication with customers is therefore quantitative, rather than qualitative (Figure 8.4).

Clearly the same equation produces a different result for the chic boutique. Interestingly, it can also vary depending on the relationship between the company and its end customers. Supermarket chains have the advantage of a large customer base with which they can communicate directly. For the companies which manufacture the goods sold in supermarkets, their relationship with their consumers is

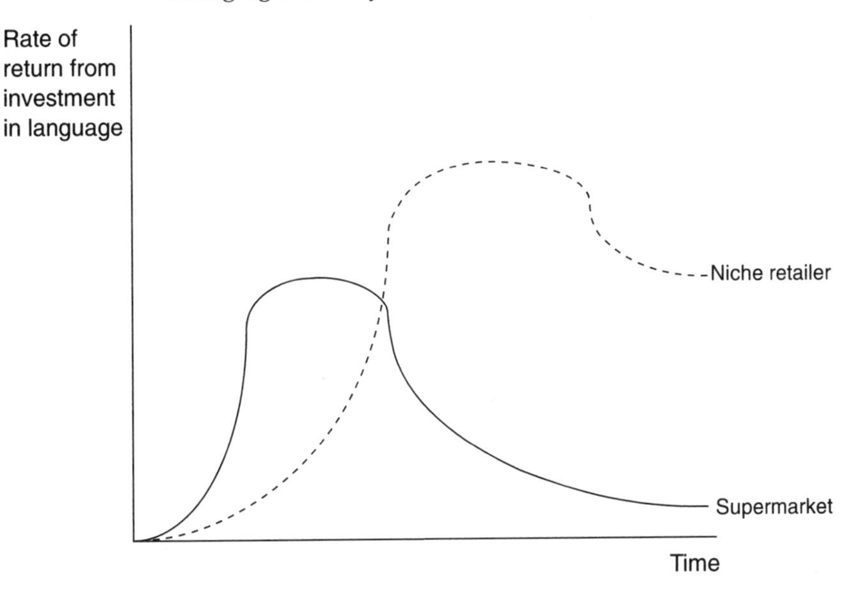

Fig. 8.4

less direct and more problematic. Without the detailed information on purchasing trends which the supermarkets have, these companies are cut off from their customers and making direct contact with them is therefore considerably more valuable. These companies tend to be more willing to engage in longer correspondence with customers, and rely more on them for qualitative information. These companies also have to invest in different types of market research, asking more open-ended questions, encouraging customers to respond.

Knowing where your own organisation fits on this particular spectrum is fundamental to understanding the economic value of *communication* to you, but it is only one side of the equation: you also need to understand the importance of *language* to your customers. This is where the examples of the washing machine engineer, the doctor and the hairdresser all come in. When our washing machine floods the kitchen we want it fixed more than we want an explanation; when we go the doctor's, we want an explanation as much as a cure; when we get our hair cut, we want to be able to tell the hairdresser what style we want. One of the factors which influence the value we attach to language is the speed with which that language turns into action: the quicker this is (for example, hairdressing), the more important language is.

Conflict occurs – and we become dissatisfied customers – when there is a mismatch between the importance we attach to language and that attached by the organisation with which we are dealing. Of course, this works both way: companies may want to talk to us, as customers, more than we want to talk to them – something which grows in proportion to the tenuousness of the link between the organisation and its customer base (good examples of this are many financial services companies and all political parties – see Figure 8.5).

Understanding where you fit on these two scales – the importance of language to you and to your customers – is, therefore, the first step in being able to make strategic choices about the ways in which you can exploit the opportunities language brings with it. You may find that overall the economic return on increasing communication with customers will not justify the expenditure involved. However, plotting your services on to these two scales should allow you to segment your portfolio of services, in order to distinguish between those services where increased communication would have positive or

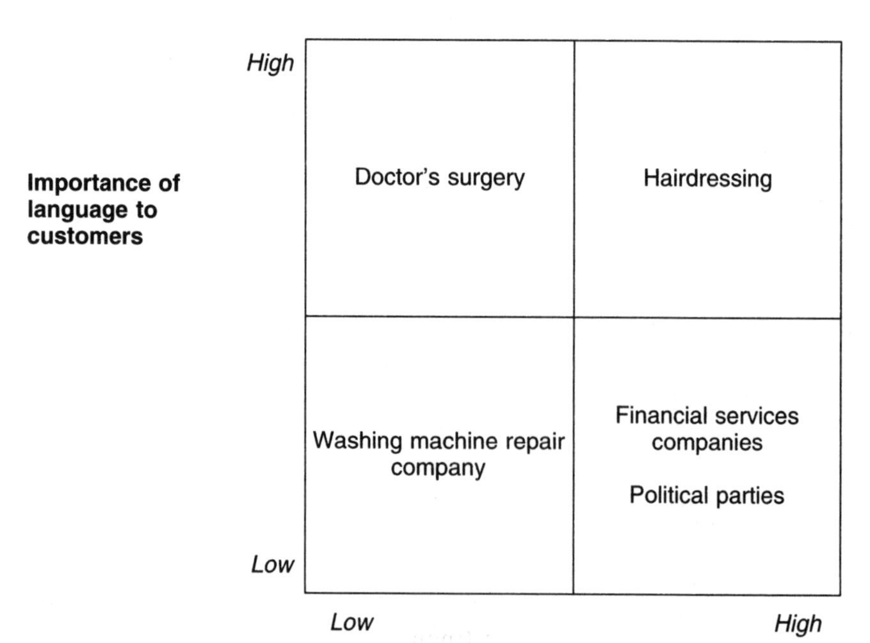

Fig. 8.5

negative returns. This, in turn, will allow you to focus your investment most effectively. On this basis, you can target a specific – and profitable – subset of your main customer base and invest time in encouraging those people to respond. It is a technique being increasingly adopted by financial services companies. Banks are identifying high net-worth customers and promoting their local branches to contact them directly in order to establish a more personalised service for this most valuable segment. Card issuers are discriminating between ordinary and high-value users, where the latter enjoy an extended range of services. It is also a technique heavily used by British Airways, as the case study in the following chapter illustrates.

Once you have highlighted those services where language plays a particularly crucial role, you need to start to identify the kind of language being used: this involves developing a plan to encourage your customers to communicate on a wide and regular basis. It is an approach used by the high-quality UK retailer, Jaeger, who in 1996 was the overall winner of a customer service competition organised jointly by BT and *The Daily Telegraph*. In order to widen the gap between themselves and the high-street fashion retailers, the company introduced 'listening posts' to find out what their customers really want. Every year, it invites 4000 of them to participate in shopping 'exercises' to test the quality of service being provided and additional needs; as a result, many stores now offer extended opening hours, provide toys and videos for children and make home deliveries.[7]

There are two aspects to getting your customers to talk to you: organising an effective communications channel and providing the stimulus to use it. Historically, the depth of communication (in terms of quality) has decreased in inverse proportion to its breadth: the more people whom you try and contact, the less you are able to say to them (hence the fact that our opinions are not solicited along with our votes in elections). This is a straightforward result of the logistics involved, and the only way round it has been to limit in-depth research to samples, an approach which is useless where an organisation wants to open up a dialogue with its customers rather than just get feedback.

Segmenting the services you offer in order to identify those where language could play a more important role is one solution, as this allows you to prioritise investment in those services where it is particularly important (and profitable) to encourage customers to talk to your corporation. But new technology and communications networks offer an alternative solution. The Internet is perceived as a powerful form of corporate advertising because it allows – or at least appears to allow – companies and their customers to communicate more directly. But perhaps its real importance lies not so much in the extent to which it allows companies to make much more information available, but in the way in which it enables potential customers to access this information in a non-threatening environment, one in which they – and not the company – seem to be in control. When, for example, the Chrysler Corporation set up their home page, this was precisely the intention:

> We are branching out from traditional media and investigating alternative ways to reach current and prospective consumers, and the Web fits that description . . . With a growing number of consumers tapping into the Web, our home page will allow more people to be exposed to detailed information on Chrysler and its products in a way that is most familiar and comfortable.[8]

By putting customers in control, the Internet both encourages its users to interact with companies' web sites and provides an easy-to-use means of doing so. As such it potentially offers companies the most powerful and effective way of talking with – rather than to – their customers.

By getting your customers to talk, you are effectively empowering them, giving them some degree of control over the services they receive and the way in which those services are delivered. Customers can articulate what they want the service to be, setting the agenda for the service provider to follow.

But, by empowering your customers, you are also increasing your own dependence on them and therefore your vulnerability. This was a lesson which the computer chip manufacturer, Intel, learnt the hard way. Intel is a classic example of a company with remote and indirect relations with its final consumers: its products are literally invisible to them. To counteract this, the company promotes its 'Intel Inside' message (see the case study on this in Chapter 14). As a high-tech company, Intel has been in the forefront of using the Internet to promulgate this message and to help establish a community of Intel users. But in 1994, news that the company's Pentium chip had a fault surfaced. It was a fault of which Intel was already aware but, having calculated that the probability of it affecting an average spreadsheet was once in every 27 000 years, it did not think that prevented it from launching the chip. Its 'community' of users thought otherwise and the Internet provided them with a channel for rapidly disseminating this information until it became headline news.

This anecdote illustrates just how fundamentally important it is that companies do not become passive bystanders in the debates they initiate: 'virtual' groups of customers are just as prone to mass hysteria as any other crowd. Moreover, beyond every immediate customer is a network of informal connections through which information and opinion travel quickly:

> In many cases a service is an experience which cannot be shared, passed around or given away to someone else once it has been delivered. It can, however, be described to other people. If the customer believes that the service was a good experience, that is what he will tell other people. If he thinks it was a bad experience, he will tell even more people.[9]

Directing how people talk is essential. I use the term 'directing' quite deliberately. Even if companies wanted to control how people talk, it would not be an option. The mass brain-washing envisaged in *Nineteen Eighty-Four* is only made possible because all information is controlled: the customer of the 1990s has access to a wide range of possible data sources – informal or formal, often mutually contradictory. In this world, the most we can achieve is to attempt to direct how people talk about us.

There are several ways of doing this. The simplest is to say something first. Unless provoked by a particularly good or bad experience, our reactions to most services are neutral: if asked to describe the service, we are often unwilling to invest much energy (even unconsciously) in giving our opinion, by default we are likely to use the first words which come to mind. Effectively, we are likely to use the words that someone else has given us rather than our own. This phenomenon applies equally whether the words are acquired from an individual or from an organisation. Thus, if someone tells us that a particular dentist offers a good service, we will visit that dentist with the preconception that the service will be good and – unless it is unexpectedly bad – we will tend to describe the dentist's service in the same way to others. Descriptive language is an inert force: contradicting it requires a degree of deliberate energy. Organisations can make use of this by establishing in advance the kind of vocabulary they want their customers to apply to its services. It is critical to recognise that this does not necessarily mean trumpeting their good qualities: in fact, this course can clearly be counterproductive, where it encourages incredulity and cynicism. Much more important than unilaterally trying to place its services on a scale of quality is to establish what the nature of the scale is in the first place. A company which is trying to promote personalised service will not automatically want to be judged according to its response time; an organisation which is marketing highly specialised services may not also want to be measured by price. Linking its services to a handful of key words allows an organisation to direct its customers to the most appropriate way of evaluating them. Advertising is important for this reason: in addition to all its conventional functions (building customer awareness, increasing sales), advertising helps to orientate customers' expectations: a company which advertises its flexibility is likely to be measured by it.

The second step in directing how people talk about you is to say something distinctive. Words which fail to differentiate you from your competitors or which are obvious are unlikely to be adopted by your customers. Saying that a parcels delivery service is fast is not saying much, but saying, as Federal Express does, that it allows you to stay in touch with your parcel (via the Internet) as it travels across the world says a lot more. It is – quite simply – more memorable: it invites us to judge it against a standard it has set itself (giving the customer a sense of control), not the standard set by the industry in general.

The third step is perhaps the most obvious – you have to keep saying it. The only way your customers will use the words you want them to is to make them learn them: consistency and repetition must be the order of the day.

A good example of this strategy in its entirety is given by Andersen Consulting which, in the early 1990s, launched an advertising campaign in the UK to promote its services. The move was a brave one: historically, the big accountancy and professional services firms had steered clear of this kind of promotional activity, partly because they regarded programmes of individualised client contact as more effective than public campaigns. The Andersen campaign – on television and in the press – centred on the phrase 'metamorphosis in a world of change'. Analysed at length, this is an unexceptional message, although it helped promote the firm's business-orientated brand of consultancy. What made it powerful was: first, that the firm simply said it first – it must have taken considerable courage to break rank with the other professional services firms; second, that it was different ('metamorphosis' is not a common term in advertising copy); and, third, that they carried on saying it.

Changing the way your customers talk about you is something, but it is not enough. This chapter began with one of the many exhortations we hear to understand our customers better, but one of the criticisms levelled at organisations which explicitly espouse this approach is that they rarely convert words into action: 'seldom', complained *The Sunday Times* in 1995, 'have so many words been spoken about the importance of meeting and exceeding customers' expectations, yet how often is the talk translated into reality?'[10]

Our usual assumption is that translating talk into reality means translating it into action. Yet – as we have seen in relation to customer service – talk often constitutes action in its own right. Action is only part of the equation. If language is the medium through which customers perceive and evaluate their experiences of a particular service, part of ensuring that the service organisation matches those customers' expectations is for the organisation to deliver its services in the same context – effectively, to speak the same language as its customers. This is partly a matter of ensuring that communication with customers does not stop there, but runs through the whole organisation:

> Excellent communications systems, both internal and external, are also vital if a customer care management scheme is to work. If people within the company don't talk to each other, how will they ever be able to talk to the customers[11]

However, the idea of speaking the same language has more profound implications than this. Using the same linguistic style as its customers implies that a company shares their values – that it is one of them. Exactly the same approach means that the style of a daytime television chat show host differs from that of the presenter of a late-night documentary. It is a principle which we take for granted in many areas of life, but often ignore in business. Even more fundamentally, using the same vocabulary implies that a company and its customers are a team. Words here are acting in exactly the way they do in any group of people. Shared words or phrases evolve which both make the team efficient (the time spent spent explaining is minimised) and cohesive (only the team players know the 'pass words'). If you evolve a specialist vocabulary – however limited its scope (it might just be a single word) – for your products or services *and* get your customers to adopt it, you have scored a major success in directing how your customers think about you. But think how much more powerful it would be if you could pick up the key words that your customers use and play those words back to them. What you would do is project the image of an organisation which is so strongly committed to putting its customers at the heart of its operation that it is prepared to change its corporate culture (as evidenced by its collective vocabulary) to match that of its customers.

It is not as if it is difficult to do. We are accustomed to internal communications campaigns which promote certain company values or goals: what we need to do is replace the words of the organisation with those of our customers.

Notes

1. Martin, 1991: 11.
2. Goldzimer, 1990: 9–10.
3. Ibid.: 3–4.
4. Katz, 1987: 105–52.
5. Fisk and Grove, 1995: 112–13.
6. Nyquist, Bitner and Booms, 1985: 195–212.
7. *The Daily Telegraph*, 16 February 1996.
8. *Corporate Advertising*, 12 June 1995.
9. Brown, 1989: 26.
10. 11 June 1995.
11. Brown, 1989: 14.

9 Case Study 4: British Airways

'Without customer satisfaction, we do not have a business', comments Robert Ayling, the chief executive of British Airways in the 1996 annual report.

In the 1970s, the airline barely had a business. Years of operating inefficiencies and a declining reputation amongst air passengers meant that the company was the butt of popular jokes. In 1996 the BA group of companies made £585m on a turnover of £7.7bn, making it not only one of the largest and most popular airlines, but also one of the most profitable. In 1995, for the eighth year running, BA was voted the best overall airline in the *Business Traveller* magazine.

It would, of course, be simplistic to attribute a change of this magnitude to the stress the company places on customer service, but the latter clearly has played a very important role in bringing customers back and keeping them.

For BA, like most companies, customer service was originally defined in terms of the actions taken by staff – grandiose statements were not enough:

> The most important ingredient of success, however, would be the attitude of staff towards their customers. Unless they were perceived as friendly, understanding and genuinely helpful, then the glossy new corporate image would only emphasise the gulf between the implied promise and the actual performance. For enduring success, the airline must be run at every level by people who really wanted to do a good job for their customers, and who believed that their management was trying to help them do it.[1]

This approach resulted in the 'Putting People First' programme, an extensive training initiative, aimed primarily at staff in the front line of dealing with customers, to instil the values of excellent service. Even while some airlines, particularly in the USA, have pursued a policy of competing on price, BA has stuck to its approach of offering premium service to those passengers who are willing to pay for it.

Language has played a crucial role in sustaining this positioning. Like other previously publicly-owned companies, there is a link at BA between privatisation and better communications, both internally and externally. Privatisation effectively created an environment in which words were valued. What distinguishes BA from many other privatised companies and from other airlines is the extent to which this shift towards language has involved incorporating customers' language. Thus, privatisation was not just about the company, but also its customers, acquiring a voice:

> Before 1983, we were quite 'arrogant', we tended to know what was the best for our customers. It was one of our beliefs that the customers didn't know what was best for themselves.[2]

BA recognised that customers who complained could be seen as 'willing communicators' who genuinely wanted the airline to solve a particular problem: only 13 per cent of them defected to other airlines

How easy is it for customers to contact British Airways?	*Don't complain*	*Complain*
Easy	Walking wounded – could complain but do not; not happy but repurchase	Champions – active in providing British Airways with information on quality of its services, loyal
Not easy	Missing in action – defected, not complaining	Detractors – defectors – vocally critical

Propensity to contact British Airways

Source: *Harvard Business Review*, 1995.

Fig. 9.1

as the result of a problem. The company found that, by contrast, 13 per cent of its customers who were completely satisfied – and who did not actively communicate with the company – defected in any case. Using this research, the airline was able to categorise customers by the relative ease or difficulty they encountered in communicating with BA against their propensity to communicate (Figure 9.1). What the company found was that there was a correlation between a customer's loyalty and his or her propensity to communicate.

'The key, therefore, was to lower the 'waterline', that is, to get more customers to communicate either directly or indirectly with customer relations', commented Charles Weiser, the head of BA's Customer Relations department from 1991 to 1994.[3] The establishing of a dedicated Customer Relations group was a direct result. The group's remit extended beyond providing the conventional – feedback forms and focus groups – and encompassed the proactive identification of problem areas in specific business units and helping to resolve them. Where possible, customers were encouraged to describe what they want in their own language, not in the airline's language: 'we continually ask customers in focus groups to tell us what such an experience should look and feel like', stresses Chairman Sir Colin Marshal. In essence, the strategy was to encourage customers to talk to the airline as much as possible and to convert these comments – not the directives of senior management – into action. The company thus created an atmosphere in which the language of its customers, and not its internal people, drove its actions. Asked in the *Harvard Business Review* how the company manages to maintain its standards of service in the face of increased competition and problems (such as air traffic congestion) which are beyond its control, Sir Colin Marshal replied, 'by creating an organization which excels in listening to its most valuable customers'.[4]

However, with competition in the airline industry increasing at what appears to be an exponential rate, such advances in customer service give only a brief respite. The challenge now for the industry is to cease to treat customers as one amorphous mass, with similar needs, but as individuals. As Robert Ayling sums it up:

> Last year, over 32 million people chose to fly on British Airways' mainline services, nearly six per cent more than the previous year. Each of them expects to be treated as an individual. Each customer has a different reason for travelling, different reasons for choosing to fly with us, and different expectations of us.[5]

Of course, airlines have distinguished between different classes of customer in the past and, indeed, continue to do so. But technology, database marketing techniques and loyalty systems (such as the BA Executive Club) all mean that it has become possible to cater even to individual needs.

The challenge BA therefore faces is how to translate its extensive use of customers' language into this new environment. Listening to an amorphous, massed voice of the crowd will not be enough: the company will need to be able to distinguish individual voices within this. The repercussions are enormous:

- How do you distinguish between the words of different customers? Can you categorise some of them into distinct groups – languages, in effect? If so, where do you draw the boundaries between different groups?
- To what extent are these distinct languages mutually exclusive? Is one language dominated by proactive words (verbs, for instance), while another is more passive (more descriptive)? Do you have to prioritise these languages, so that you react to the words of some (presumably the most profitable) groups of customers?
- Once you have distinguished between your customers' languages and identified their relative importance to your business, how do you act? Do you need to select just one language and stick with it, that is, use the same words on all your promotional material and advertising? Or can your internal organisation and external brand or reputation accommodate more than one language? Can you be all things to all people? If not, where do you draw the line?

We are already starting to see some of these issues addressed on the Internet. At the moment, BA, like most other companies, faces a logistical problem in trying to move from a mass customer voice to individual voices in that it has no obvious communication channels or conceptual frameworks to assemble what is potentially a very large volume of data: the output from focus groups is usually summarised; statistics on complaints are collected, but the individual vocabulary used is not analysed. The Internet offers a partial solution to this problem: via it, individuals can communicate with companies – they can express preferences, give feedback, even e-mail specific executives. It is no coincidence that some airlines have started to auction unsold tickets across the Internet, allowing individual consumers to bid a price. All this information can be collated, allowing a company to build up a picture of who (a subset of) its customers are.

BA operates an extensive web site, offering a variety of information services and a facility to check seat prices and availability. In line with its emphasis on making its customers talk to it as much as it talks to them, the web site offers users the chance to supply feedback – either by e-mailing the Customer Relations group or filling in a structured questionnaire. Although still embryonic, Internet sites offer companies like BA the opportunity to gain much more detailed information about individual customers. And, as the whole operation is carried out via computers, many of the other factors which can have an impact on customers in the conventional service experience (body language, whether the person serving you is gossiping to his or her colleagues, the physical environment, and so on) are irrelevant. Only two factors remain: the virtual environment on the web site and, of course, language. From this perspective, gathering information on the language of individual customers, not all customers on average, will not just be fundamental to sustaining competitive advantage in the future; it will be essential to survival.

Notes

1. Quoted in Clutterbuck *et al.*, 1991: 133.
2. Quoted in Salama, 1995: 57.
3. Weiser, 1995: 115.
4. Prokesch, 1995: 106.
5. 1995–96 annual report.

Part V

The Native Language of Transnationals

10 Globalisation and the Evolution of Business Pidgin

In 1996 the car manufacturer Honda operated 89 production facilities based in 33 countries: it is a global network which allows the company to export cars from Canada and the USA to the Middle East, power products from Thailand to Columbia, and motorcycles from Brazil to Italy. Thirty, or even twenty, years ago, the picture for firms like Honda would have been very different. Multinationals typically addressed each national market individually – co-locating production and marketing resources, and stressing the financial independence of the local subsidiary. Management was mostly by numbers.

The set of market-driven, economic and technical changes which, in the 1980s, challenged this way of doing things is a now quite familiar one: better-informed consumers demanded the best and cheapest products available worldwide; producing these goods required the integration of both resources and knowledge on a global scale; at the same time, it became possible to transport information around the world at vastly reduced costs. While multinational organisations had tended to pursue one of the three basic strategies – achieving economies of scale through the centralised management of resources, having a strong (decentralised) national presence, and sharing worldwide a central pool of skills and experience – the problem for the new 'transnational' corporations was to combine these three, often contradictory, approaches into a single strategy:

> To compete effectively, a company had to develop global competitiveness, multinational flexibility, and worldwide learning capability *simultaneously*.[1]

All these changes require an unparalleled degree of organisational interdependence and individual interaction – something which the conventional structure of a multinational (the head office hub surrounded by satellite subsidiaries) is not designed to accommodate. Control has to give way to coordination, and corporate culture becomes an issue of central importance.

Any sizeable organisation is likely to have a multiplicity of cultures within it – the traditional rivalry between production and sales departments, for instance – but the situation is clearly more complicated for transnational companies who face national, as well as functional, demarcation lines. For the multinational, culture has a necessarily homogenising function; like saline solution before an injection, its role is to ensure that the corporate message passes into the bloodstream of an organisation as swiftly as possible. With the transnational it is different: here, culture has to be embracing rather than exclusive, capable of balancing national differences with collective action; common goals values have to replace managerial dictates. 'Planting for a global harvest', writes Kenichi Ohmae, 'is a painstaking, iterative process of balancing local needs with shared values and balancing particular growing conditions with the requirements of each crop'.[2]

A networked culture, like the strategic tenets of transnationalism which it underpins, is itself heavily dependent on effective communication. Up to the end of the nineteenth century, communication was virtually synonymous with transportation. Both goods and words moved around the world at the same rate: a communiqué from a company might well be accompanied by tangible evidence – news of a good crop would arrive simultaneously with the crop itself. But the arrival of the telegraph radically changed this situation: ideas and information could be transmitted more quickly, thus allowing organisations to decentralise their operations. Words were no longer accompanied by things.

This means that we have to be much more conscious of the words we use, their meaning and possible interpretation. When sixteenth-century explorers introduced potatoes and tobacco leaves from the New World, they had the advantage of being able to bring back examples: a modern equivalent would probably send an e-mail. While multimedia and virtual reality may help us to some extent, they will never be able to resolve the problem that in most of our business lives we are dealing with representations of things (people, products, problems) rather than the things themselves. For this reason, the way in which we choose to represent these things is crucial: putting in our e-mail that the potato is small and rounded obviously gives a different impression to saying that it can be grown for consumption. For the transnational corporation, such issues are particularly pertinent: not only must its employees communicate with colleagues spread across different continents and time zones, but they may have to do so in more than one language. Technology now allows national subsidiaries to communicate with one another directly, rather than through a centralised point: 'each point would become a center on its own, and the distinction between center and periphery would disappear'.[3]

Traditionally – as we shall see – the problems of multilingualism have received little serious consideration. Yet, when we start to look at it, we discover that the issue is a complex one, that there are different models for language use, just as there are different models of organisational design. Indeed, managing language is a very important part of managing a business.

ORGANISATIONAL COMMUNICATIONS AND MONOLINGUALISM

What does it mean for an organisation to communicate in a single, national language? A company may – and most do – have the equivalent of dialects (we have already looked at the use of management and technical jargon, for instance), but a common native language has important implications which override 'regional' differences such as these. To understand such implications, we need to look first at the role which communication, and language in particular, plays in an organisation.

At the most simple level, communication serves two functions – gathering and disseminating information. As we have discussed previously, the ultimate purpose of both functions is to precipitate action: a head office might react to feedback from customers channelled via its field sales force; workers on an assembly line may change their working practices in accordance with new guidelines from the operations management. Such actions are not restricted to those officially sanctioned by the organisation: information, and the actions which result from its transmission, can be official or unofficial. Indeed, every organisation consists of subgroups who have different information needs and channels, and whose reactions to the same set of stimuli differ.

Language is not just the means by which people communicate (that is, the medium in which items of information are expressed), it is also the purveyor of meaning. Data is only information when it has meaning, and data without meaning cannot precipitate action. Language therefore provides a means by which we interpret the relative significance of any information and decide how we will respond. Within an organisation, the role of language is therefore analogous to other – and more familiar – aspects of cultural behaviour such as myths, rituals and stories. They all provide a context from which we can infer meaning; they therefore largely determine how we interpret information, and this in turn determines how we act. Take for example the manager who comes in and – unusually – closes his or her office door. How people interpret this will depend on, among other factors, the symbolism of a closed door in that particular environment (problems? privacy?) and myths ('Smith did that just after being fired'). Just as with myths and stories, individuals in an organisation (or organisations as a whole) may seek to influence the way in which both translation processes take place by managing the meaning of the language used: the greater the ambiguity of the language, the less controllable or predictable the resulting action.

Starting with the same basis of meaning which sharing a common language gives is clearly fundamental to this process, although the success with which this can be achieved also depends on many other factors (and we will be examining some of the most significant of them later in this book). Anthropologists and philosophers have argued that a national language represents a 'contract' within society which underpins its common culture.

Having a monolingual corporate environment means that we share the same fundamental preconceptions about the world: whatever our individual differences, we have a common outlook. This engenders a sense of trust – we only need to think of how uncomfortable we can feel when two people in front of us converse in a language we do not understand to see how true this is. It also promotes a sense of equality. While we may not all have access to the same information, sharing a common language means that in theory we could access it. Working in a language other than our own, we feel disadvantaged. As a result of this, a single national language has a homogenising effect on the corporate culture of which it inevitably forms a part. This is perhaps most visible at the micro level of project groups:

> Evidence in meetings and groups teaches all of us how quickly culture forms in even a few meetings. The group forms a language of its own, attaches its own meanings to events, and develops assumptions about itself and its environment that can begin to operate as silent filters on perceptions.[4]

This may not always be a good thing: a group which develops a distinct culture and sense of identity may have problems communicating with outsiders. In the 1970s, Thomas Allen analysed the relative efficiency of different engineering laboratories: each one, he noted, tended to develop its own culture – the result of shared goals and experiences over time – and this, in turn, determined the way in which they interpreted and communicated their findings.

> The coding scheme is a common viewpoint manifested in a shared language and a common set of attitudes. It enhances the efficiency of communication among those who hold it in common but can detract from the efficiency of communicating with anyone who follows a different coding scheme. Engineers in an organization are able to communicate better with their organizational colleagues than with outsiders because there is a shared knowledge on both ends of the transaction and less chance of misinterpretation. It is amazing to see how misinterpretation can creep into the communication between organisations.[5]

Similarly, a monolingual company will have difficulties dealing with customers beyond its national markets.

At a fundamental level, therefore, sharing the same language reduces the level of potential distortion in translating action into language and language into action.

THE IMPACT OF MULTILINGUALISM

But, if it is true that a monolingual environment engenders a homogeneous corporate culture and facilitates cohesive action, is the converse also true – can multilingualism fragment an organisation? Multilingualism clearly changes the action-language-action process, simply by the introduction of more than one language:

	→	Language 1	→	
	→	Language 2	→	
Action	→	Language 3	→	Action
	→	Language 4	→	
	→	Language 5	→	

But this change only matters in the extent to which it precipitates multiple actions as well as multiple languages:

	→	Language 1	→	Action 1
	→	Language 2	→	Action 2
Action	→	Language 3	→	Action 3
	→	Language 4	→	Action 4
	→	Language 5	→	Action 5

If this proliferation of actions – effectively caused by mistranslation from language into language – occurs, can it be overcome simply by employing professional interpreters or by structuring language usage within an organization much as we might structure other aspects of management, or are we faced with more profound problems?

Does multilingualism matter? There is certainly evidence to suggest that multilingualism can fragment economies: 80 per cent of linguistically heterogeneous countries are also underdeveloped; linguistic uniformity – evolving either in the form of 'lingua francas' or as a hierarchy of official and unofficial languages – is frequently recognised as a necessary precondition of economic development.[6] There is plenty of anecdotal evidence to suggest that when a company reduces language difficulties it also increases its efficiency. Back in the 1970s, *Business Week* quoted the example of the General Foam Division of Tenneco whose Spanish-speaking employees worked under USA managers: 'The resulting shaky communications brought high [staff] turnover, high accident rates, unsatisfactory quality control, and constant tension'.[7] A programme of practical, work-related language training in company time was set up:

> The classes were considered a success. Worker motivation was high because classes were held in company time and the content was tailored to job requirements and advancement. The firm's reward was evident also. According to the manager: 'We saw results immediately. Everyone relaxed. We had fewer accidents. We even

> had fewer grievances. Production moved along better and we expect employee turnover to go down'.[8]

But without definitive proof on this issue, opinions inevitably vary. In one camp, there are the people – commentators and business people – who believe that cultural differences (including language) are unimportant when balanced against supra-national similarities.[9] Facing them are those who argue the opposite: 'language', argued Michael Argyle in *Social Skills and Work*, is 'one of the most important differences between many cultures, and one of the greatest barriers'.[10] Culture diversity is both so strong and so long-standing it overwhelms any cosmetic, short-term unifying factors: 'the multiplicity of languages and the parallel diversity of cultures in the world economy have a constraining influence on the operations of international business'.[11] This is an approach which has been reinforced by more recent research: in a 1985 study of the impact of different national management styles on the operations of an international business, Andre Laurant concluded:

> The findings summarized here provide an illustration of nationally bounded collective mental maps about organizations that seem to resist convergence effects from increased professionalization of management and intensity of international business.[12]

And somewhere between these two factions are the people who believe that cultures can be grouped into clusters where similar social and economic levels of development provide a degree of cohesion within, but not outside, the cluster.[13]

The majority of business people would probably subscribe to the last of these views, although there is comparatively little research to justify this. Our working assumption is that, however heterogeneous the constituent parts of our organisation, we are held together by common goals and by similar economic and cultural values. To see it from a different perspective, we assume that the language of business is stronger than any national language. To quote Ohmae again: 'commonalities in a business culture are so important to economic success that they easily outweigh traditional differences in language or secular culture'.[14]

It is, however, possible to see all three of these views as simply different points on the same continuum, rather than as mutually exclusive. What is at issue here is not the way in which national languages and cultures affect the corporate entity – almost everyone agrees that they can have a fragmenting and destabilising effect – but the severity with which this impact is felt. Everyone seems to agree on one fundamental point – multilingualism can have a negative impact; successful organisations have traditionally been those which can minimise this impact.

Today, however, the management of language – if one can use this term – is clearly subject to the same economic drivers as other management decisions within an organisation. Thus, organisations trying to grapple with the conflicting needs of transnationalism – finding a compromise between central coordination and local autonomy – also need to balance linguistic cohesion with retaining those national languages which, for example, give it direct access to its consumers in local markets.

But if squaring this particular circle is clearly a microcosm of the issues to be resolved across the organisation as a whole, the solutions have been more limited and have principally been a means of reintroducing monolingualism by the back door.

Official Languages

One such approach to multilingualism is to establish one official language for internal communication: the Swiss firm, ABB, has been pursuing a strategy of integrating people of different nationalities at all management levels but the company's official language is English.

There are, however, two problems with this approach. First, it necessarily draws a line between those people within or outside an organisation who can communicate effectively in the organisation's 'native' language, and those who cannot: the haves and the have-nots. For western companies, this was not – historically – a problem. Our colonial outlook meant that we tended to put expatriate managers into national subsidiaries who would be responsible for directing the local workforce: the language divide therefore mirrored and reinforced the management/worker divide and the wider social context. With the rise of transnationalism, this distinction is much less clear-cut, as organisations try to communicate more complex issues, more frequently, to more people. Internally, all the notions of cross-functional working and organisational learning depend on all employees being able to communicate equally. Externally, an organisation also needs to communicate with its suppliers and customers:

while it may have been acceptable in the past to deem some employees second-class, classifying customers in this way is going to cost business.

The second problem with establishing a single official language is that the use of the language chosen may in practice cut across a conventional organisational hierarchy in a way which is outside management's control; it may even subvert it, as more than one study has shown:

> The official international language of this company is English. However, whenever the home office people show up they tend to cluster together with their countrymen and speak Japanese. That's why I'm trying to learn Japanese. Let's face it. They say all you need to know is English, but if you really want to know what's going on you have to talk *their* language.[15]

Thus, junior employees who speak a company's native language may be better informed than more senior staff for whom the company's language is not their own. While language training can mitigate against this problem, it can never totally overcome it. Effectively, this means that different people get access to different interpretations outside an organisation's control – the more important the communication the more likely it is to travel fast down these important but unofficial communication lines – again ease of control is in inverse proportion to the importance. It is a problem which surfaces in the use of terminology:

> Who is 'foreign' in a worldwide company? Or, what is 'domestic'? As a company expands internationally, the 'home country' is not home for more and more executives. These handy, but inaccurate, labels lead to the blatant mismanagement of people. Further, the constant reference to 'home' versus 'abroad' reveals a deep-seated ambivalence about multinationalism in today's MNCs. Such ambivalence necessarily influences intraorganizational consensus on which version of multinationalization is best for the firm.[16]

Business Pidgin

An alternative solution is for an organisation to allow a lingua franca to evolve – the peculiar form of English used in air traffic control is one of the most familiar examples of this.

It was this approach which the Caterpillar Tractor Company adopted in the 1970s to overcome the problem of servicing and repairing machine parts in different parts of the world: the company developed a form of pidgin English – Caterpillar Fundamental English (CFE) – a condensed form of English in which engineers could be trained over just 30 lessons. The service manuals were rewritten using the 800 essential CFE words allowing any engineer to understand them: the language was a wholly written language – engineers were not taught how to speak CFE.[17]

While this approach is effective in a narrow and specialised field, it is more difficult to apply in a wider context or in a more fluid environment. Language is limited – in this example – to operational matters: communication in areas beyond this is not expected. In effect, this approach works because the action–language–action links are close and direct, because the ratio of action to language is high: the task of replacing a broken part is translated into CFE and then actioned by the engineer. It would work less well where action plays a proportionately small role in the whole process. Take a typical sales meeting: this begins with a desired action – perhaps the need to increase sales in the following month if targets are to be met. This is followed by a series of discussions (at the meeting itself, between the sales representatives after the meeting, with customers) which eventually translate into action (sales). In this situation, a form of pidgin English could not cope with the complexity of the discussion and the number of different people involved.[18] Thus, while the business pidgin approach may initially appear more 'democratic' than the idea of establishing an official language, the underlying process is identical – in both cases the organisation is imposing a structure of monolinguistic communications.

Translation

Translation has the apparent advantage of allowing more than one language to function side by side, with at least the semblance of parity.

It is, however, rarely a uniform process, even within a single organisation: a professional linguist translating a long document word for word clearly provides a different translation from someone who summarises the contents of the same document during a meeting with colleagues from a different country. The process by which a foreign subsidiary (in this example, a German company) typically reports to its (US) parent illustrates this:

- staff conference would be held in German, agreeing specific details of the report
- an initial draft in German would be prepared by a staff member
- agreement would be sought on the German draft
- the German draft would be translated into English
- a middle manager would read both the German and English drafts, and would attempt to improve the English version
- the vice-president of the subsidiary would review and attempt to improve the English draft
- the managing director of the subsidiary would further improve the English draft before sending it on to the USA.[19]

At each stage in the process and every level in the management hierarchy, the content changes, so that – finally – the subsidiary's managing director is the only person in the company who knows exactly what is being said to the parent company (and he cannot control the way in which it is interpreted): all the managers below the managing director have a slightly different view of 'reality'.

Style of translation is primarily determined by the extent to which translation is important to an organisation. This is not simply a function of whether a particular item of information needs to be transmitted to all parts of a multinational organisation (after all, it is quite likely that certain management layers will share a common language), but more the extent to which it is important that all stakeholders (inside and outside the organisation) have access to it and to the same version (i.e. (mis)translation) of it. This last point is the most fundamental: translating a document does not just mean that an organisation is minimising the risk that some of its stakeholders may misinterpret (i.e. mistranslate) what it says, but that it is actively seeking to influence the way in which people interpret what it says.

It is a process which tends to subvert itself, as those people who commission translations are rarely in a position to verify whether a given document has, in fact, been correctly translated:

> All German managers commanding oral English stated [in the survey] that their grammatical competence was not sufficiently honed to produce a written English report of top quality. Even

> when professional translators from outside the company rewrote the German into English, German middle managers were unable to verify whether the report captured the substantive intent or included editorial alterations.[20]

The downside to translation is that it is costly both in money and time: the most important communications are often the most urgent and translation can add a delay into the process – something which the requirement to be precise (as will be the case with critical communications) exacerbates. The ease of translation is therefore in inverse relation to its importance: the more important the translation, the more difficult, time-consuming and expensive it will be; the easier the translation, the less important the information.

PUTTING THESE APPROACHES IN CONTEXT

It would be unfair to say that it is lack of imaginative thinking which is responsible for the paucity of approaches to dealing with multilingualism. We would do better to point the finger of blame at the organisational context in which these solutions have been developed.

The structure of an organisation can help or hinder different types of communication. At the simplest level, the structure adopted by multinational organisations has tended to follow one of two models – centralised or decentralised – with the pendulum of preference and fashion swinging between the two. At any one time, every organisation will be subject to a variety of pressures for and against centralisation, which may manifest themselves in different ways within both the parent company and its subsidiaries.

A second factor, which combines with the pressures for and against centralisation, is the extent to which an organisation relies on vertical or horizontal communication. The need for vertical communication will occur in any organisation where one point acts as a hub for similar activities spread across different geographical locations (such as marketing for a worldwide brand or coordinating the shipping of goods made in more than one country). By contrast, horizontal communication will predominate where an organisation operates discrete functions in different locations which must then communicate directly (rather than through a central point) in order to function effectively.

The dominant mode of communication within an organisation will vary with the stage of evolution which the company has reached, as firms usually evolve in response to problems they encounter. Thus, an international company – one which may simply be engaged in exporting their goods on to sales and marketing agents overseas – will require little horizontal communication, but a multinational company, with suppliers and customers in many countries, may be much more reliant on it.[21]

Communication preferences will also be dictated not just by an organisation's particular culture, but by the wider external environment in which it is operating: a high degree of difference between cultures, for example, generates uncertainty and makes the need for information more pressing. They will also be affected by the bias of any country towards certain modes of communication. There have been studies, for instance, showing that American firms tend to rely more heavily on formal reporting than Japanese firms.[22]

Such tendencies are also reinforced by the degree to which an organisation relies on formal communications – how much its subsidiaries rely on policies and procedures from the parent company, the extent to which they make use of these in decision-making and the frequency with which they have to report to their parent company. Such dependency varies from company to company, but the greater the subsidiary–parent reliance, the more likely that monolingualism will develop.

Therefore, although vertical communication might be most commonly associated with a centralised structure, other permutations occur, and these dictate the method used to manage multilingualism (Figure 10.1).

For centralised structures where the need for vertical communication is paramount, the logical form of 'language management' is translation as it is linear and therefore facilitates communication up and down the hierarchical ladder. The more decentralised the management structure, the more appropriate the use of business pidgin. Like translation, this approach eases vertical communication: a parent company can focus the language around those components which it requires centrally, rather than those which might aid lateral contact. This applies equally, even where the pidgin language has evolved unofficially, as the result of necessity: the form of English used by pilots primarily came about as a result of their need to communicate with single hubs (air traffic controllers), rather than

	Centralised structure	Decentralised structure
Vertical communication	Translation	Business pidgin
Horizontal communication	Official language	Language tuition

Fig. 10.1

talk between themselves. For an organisation which, while being centralised, also needs good horizontal communication, establishing an official language will be the more appropriate method of managing multilingualism: here, a degree of equality is introduced by putting all subsidiary organisations on the same linguistic footing as the parent company.

Of course, identifying the logical communications method in each of these three environments does not ensure that the method is adopted in practice: indeed, the world is full of examples of unmatched communication systems. The European Union, for example, uses translation to ensure that communication between member states is as effective as possible: while this approach has the merit of being very precise, it tends to reinforce the centralising aspects of the EU's administration[23] and may inadvertently reinforce its remote and bureaucratic image.

Of the four possible structures in Figure 10.1, only one – the decentralised organisation where the need for horizontal communication is great – offers the potential for a genuinely multilingual environment. Here, the approach adopted – in so far as there is one, as such organisations are comparatively rare – has traditionally been to invest in teaching some people the languages they require to communicate directly to their peers in other countries. Yet the way in which this approach has functioned in practice – although theoretically the most liberal – illustrates the underlying principles of all four forms of language management.

Language Tuition

It is ironic that one of the ways in which our prejudice against multilingualism has manifested itself is in some of the thinking about language tuition in business. The first real impetus for this came in the USA in the 1950s and 1960s:

> If the businessman wishes effective communication with laborers, government officials, customers, and others, he must be able to communicate directly with them in their own language.[24]

And again:

> Only a handful of foreign managers speak fluent Japanese and even they sometimes find themselves at a disadvantage. The result is that most American managers rely heavily on interpreters, communicate little with most of their employees, and suffer from indifferent relations with many customers and government officials.[25]

But language tuition was in practice motivated less by the desire to communicate with overseas customers more effectively than by the perceived threat of Soviet infiltration into American business: 'it is now widely known in the USA that Russians are rigorously trained in languages before they are sent abroad to live and work'.[26] The learning of foreign languages by Americans was a primary means by which the USA hold on the western world at least – following the end of the Second World War – could be consolidated. It is not surprising that many of the intensive learning techniques which business adopted at this stage (such as language labs) were pioneered during the Second World War. Language tuition was effectively the war continued by other means, the aim being control rather than communication:

> It is essential that we be able to make ourselves understood in at least one language. Communication is so fundamental to good management that failure from this point alone could undermine an otherwise well-rounded performance . . . [People] want to know where they stand. The American owners to whom the foreign manager reports and those reporting to him want to know, have to know, what the foreign manager is trying to accomplish and whether or not he thinks he and they are succeeding. Unless he is willing or able to tell them, they are lost: and so is he.[27]

Monolingual Americans let their side – implicitly, their country – down:

> With [the foreign manager] language is vital. If he is unable to communicate his thoughts to a staff of nationals, to the authorities and to his business associates, he will be severely handicapped and can hardly claim to offer even the minimum of what can rightly be expected from him . . . How much better for America's worldwide interests when tourists, but more important, chief executives and travelling representatives of our largest businesses manifest their interest in other lands and peoples by speaking their languages instead of expecting and demanding that all the world speak American.[28]

MULTILINGUALISM AND CONTROL

Control underpins everything: all that the conventional forms of language management do is shift it around the organisation.

For instance, research into multinational companies indicates that those where the management structure is focused around products (so that, for example, product group managers have direct control over subsidiaries) exhibit a higher incidence of inter-group communications problems than those organised on a geographical basis. This primarily appears to be the result of conventional communication barriers (for example, between departments and functions) – which usually occur in the holding company of geographically-organised organisations – being pushed outwards and surfacing in difficulties in communicating between the holding company and its subsidiaries.[29]

Each approach to language management exhibits a different means of management control: with translation, little is left to chance – the possibility for varied interpretations is kept to the absolute minimum; with business pidgin, it is the scope of communication which is limited; with an official language, the number of people who have access to it can be restricted. In other words, however decentralised an organisational structure, however horizontal the communications, the management of language – effectively, the control of meaning – remains hierarchical: 'Even in medium-sized firms the number of channels needed to allow each unit of the firm to communicate directly with all the other units is prohibitively large. The hierarchy provides a system of channelling the flows of information among the units through a series of co-ordinators'.[30]

> It is not technology that creates inequality; rather, it is *organization* that imposes a ritual judicial asymmetry on the use of intrinsically symmetrical means of communication; it arbitrarily creates unequal capacities to initiate and terminate exchange, to store and retrieve information, and to determine the extent of the exchange and the terms of the discussion. Just as the colonial powers in the past linked each point in the hinterland to the metropolis and inhibited lateral communications, preventing the growth of independent centers of decision-making and creativity, multinational corporations (backed by state powers) centralize control by imposing a hierarchical system.[31]

Multilingualism, essentially, lies outside this type of control.

FINDING AN ALTERNATIVE APPROACH

From the majority of research carried out into all types of multinational organisations, two things seem clear. First, communication within tends to be bad, irrespective of the structure or the perceptions of the organization: however efficient the internal systems, tension and conflict exist which distort the dissemination of information.[32] Second, most organisations which recognise there is a problem try to re-engineer their structure rather than their means of communication:[33] 'the mistake, so often made, is to change the organization in order to solve communications problems. There is little evidence that this works'.[34]

What is needed instead is a very different way of thinking about – and managing – the issues of multilingualism in a transnational business.

To start with, we need to move away from our very deep-rooted view that multiple languages in a single organisation are a bad thing. As was pointed out earlier, in most of the thinking which has been done in this area – and this is borne out by the practice of a large number of organisations – we habitually work on the assumption that multilingualism is a divisive influence. The role of the organisation in this context is to minimise the impact of multilingualism, traditionally by either establishing an official language or by legitimising some form of business pidgin. But it is only divisive because our concept of organisational design is so heavily biased towards the monolingual model. What we need to do is throw away this model.

We could instead begin with the view that if we believe that future competition will focus on meeting our customers' varied needs with greater speed, precision and quality of service, speaking directly to those customers represents our single most important opportunity to strengthen our reputation in their eyes, to put space between ourselves and our competitors. There are two points to this. The first is that it involves switching our focus to what our customers mean, not what we think they mean, in other words exploiting the opportunity to demonstrate to our customers that we understand their needs. The second is that it means that we are establishing a contract of common understanding and trust with our customers – we appear to be on their side. Both of these aspects involve recognising that language can be a positive – not negative – influence.

However, the ability of organisations to exploit this opportunity is constrained by the organisational models conventionally available to them – centralised or decentralised. These favour the monolinguistic approach and start from the view that all organisations either are inherently, or aspire to be, monolingual. Companies have recently been experimenting with turning the traditional organisational chart upside down, to put their customers at the top in place of their chief executives. For transnational corporations, wanting to gain as much direct access to their customers as possible, we need to mirror this structure in terms of language. Managers should be encouraged to learn the language of their locality, not because it means that they can tell their employees what to do, but so that they can understand what customers want them to do.

The implication of this is that a single meaning to language can no longer be guaranteed – the customer has usurped the chief executive, and it is what the customer (not the organisation) says and means that is translated into action. This is an immensely threatening notion for organisations, as their accepted structures start to lose their authority. Like any other threat to their cohesion, organisations are frightened of inconsistency in the language/action process – which is why they spend so much time and money trying to minimise it via interpreters, a lingua franca, and so on. But the problem is really one of their own making. They have started from the premise that monolingualism is the optimum structure: they believe that the only workable model for a business is one that has a single, consistent set of meanings throughout its organisation, that the same words always result in the same action. They cannot accommodate the idea that it might be possible for different meanings to co-exist in different parts of the organisation without threatening the unity of the whole.

Yet it is worth noting that those transnationals where communication is generally good often tend to be those where authoritarian structures are less rigidly imposed: where the head office demands less control over the subsidiaries and is willing to stand by decisions made by the latter; where there is a greater sense of team work within the subsidiaries; and where there is less personal contact between the senior management of the parent and subsidiary companies. Informal communication, within subsidiaries or across groups of subsidiaries, may offer a better paradigm for the transnational:

> In an organization consisting of a close, permanent web of relationships, communication takes on a special meaning. There is less need for verbalization; things do not have to be spelled out . . . Communication thus often takes nonverbal forms: one is expected to read the minds of others without resorting to verbal articulation. In fact, in a closed system where everyone is intimately acquainted with one another, one may be accused of insensitivity and naiveté if he seeks a clear articulation of someone else's point of view.[35]

The two following case studies – of Schlumberger and Inchcape – examine how these issues are addressed in practice.

Notes

1. Bartlett and Ghoshal, 1989: 16.
2. Ohmae, 1994: 112.
3. Hymer, 1979: 163.
4. Schein, 1985: 41.
5. Allen, 1977: 139.
6. Terpstra, 1978: 6.
7. *Business Week*, 28 February 1970; quoted in Terpstra, 1978: 19.
8. Terpstra, 1978: 19.
9. See, for instance, Brooke and Remmers, 1977: 185.
10. Argyle, 1981: 175.
11. Terpstra, 1978: 14–15.
12. Laurant, 1985: 54.
13. Kerr, 1964: 77–94.
14. Ohmae, 1994: 112.
15. USA manager working for a Japanese multinational; quoted in Hodgetts and Luthans, 1994: 375.
16. Heenan and Perlmutter, 1979: 60–1.
17. Terpstra, 1978: 22.
18. Hofstede, 1991: 212–15.
19. Hildebrandt, 1973: 9.
20. Ibid.: 9.
21. Brooke: 1986: 172–91.
22. Negandhi, 1990: 564.
23. Michelmann, 1978: 205–17.
24. Fayerweather, 1960: 17.
25. *Business Week*, 18 November 1972; quoted by Terpstra, 1978: 17.
26. Cleveland, Mangone and Adams, 1960: 241.
27. Bryson, 1961: 4.
28. Ibid.: 22–6.
29. Brooke, 1984: 261–9.
30. Stopford and Wells, 1972: 12–13.
31. Hymer, 1979: 164.
32. Brooke and Remmers, 1977: 184–5.
33. Ibid.: 185–6.
34. Brooke, 1986: 183
35. Yoshino, 1976: 166–7.

11 Case Study 5: Schlumberger

BACKGROUND

Founded in the 1920s when the brothers Conrad and Marcel Schlumberger invented 'electrical coring' – a means of analysing remotely the geological strata through which a drill bit is moving – Schlumberger is now the world's largest oil services company, with a 1995 worldwide operating revenue of more than $7.6bn. The company attributes much of its success in recent years (it has grown by 25 per cent since 1991) to its transnational strategy:

> To be successful in the global marketplace of the 90s and beyond, futurists say, organisations must become truly transnational by recruiting worldwide for outstanding employees and by reaching across Europe, the US, Japan and beyond for the best research and engineering to develop cost-effective products. While other companies struggle with the meaning and complexity of 'globalisation', the Schlumberger companies are building on knowledge and experience gained in over 60 years of international operations . . . Operating in more than 100 countries, they comprise what is probably the world's most truly transnational large enterprise, numbering more than 50,000 employees of 100 nationalities from six continents.[1]

The single most influential factor in the performance of Schlumberger's oil services business is the price of crude oil. As well-head revenues fall, exploration activity (from which Schlumberger gains the overwhelming proportion of its oilfield services revenue) declines sharply. When, in 1986, the price per barrel fell to $10, rig utilisation (that is, the percentage of worldwide rig fleets being actively used in drilling and production) fell from its 1982 peak of 55 per cent to 24 per cent. At the same time, the number of active seismic survey crews fell by 80 per cent, from the 1981 peak of 744 to 150 by 1987. Since the oil crisis of the mid-1970s, the price of crude oil has been very volatile in response to world events (in the immediate aftermath of the Iraqi invasion of Kuwait in 1990, the price of oil soared to $40 per barrel). However, the overall pressure on the price has been downwards because of the substantial overproduction which has resulted from OPEC's consistent failure to balance the supply of oil to world demand. The fall in the price of oil has not been offset by an increase in the volume of sales. Historically, demand for oil has been inelastic as in the short-run industry and consumers could not move to alternative energy sources. However, the cumulative price shocks since the 1970s (notably the 1976 oil embargo) have been gradually increasing the longer-run elasticity of demand; a trend which is likely to become more marked as environmental pressures grow.

The increasing elasticity of demand has very significant implications for the oil services industry in the future. While the overall OECD outlook up to the end of the twentieth century is relatively optimistic – the 13 per cent fall in prices 1990-95 is expected to be replaced by a 35 per cent price rise in the period 1996–2000, with the price ending at $20–25 per barrel – it takes no account of short-term fluctuations in prices as consumers find it easier to switch between alternative fuel sources. This will have repercussions in the oil exploration sector where price swings are likely to deter investors and speculators and therefore dampen exploration activity disproportionately.

The impact of these changes on the oilfield services market has been to increase not only the number of potential purchasers, but also the variety of services demanded (the independents want a low-cost 'one-stop' service because they lack the resources to manage multiple subcontractors, while the multinationals are 'cherry-picking' contractors to suit very precise requirements); the Schlumberger of the future will need to sell more varied services to more customers.

While the oil-producing market has been fragmenting, the oil services industry has become more homogeneous, and is now dominated by three companies – Schlumberger, Halliburton and Western Atlas – all of whom offer a comparable range of services. In an effort to differentiate themselves (and therefore to continue to command the high margin which the industry has enjoyed historically), each company has developed high-tech flagship products, such as intelligent drill bits (Schlumberger) or satellite networks (Western Atlas).

SCHLUMBERGER'S STRATEGIC RESPONSE

Schlumberger's strategic response to its external environment can be summarised using Porter's coordination/configuration model (Figure 11.1). Its highly geographically dispersed clients need services which are both globally integrated (to achieve economies of scope and scale) and simultaneously responsive to local needs (for example, seismic surveys which have to be adapted to the requirements of a particular terrain). Much of Schlumberger's efforts are therefore concentrated on investing in its overseas operations and in ensuring that its subsidiaries coordinate their activity effectively.

There are two main strands to Schlumberger's international investment – its sustained programme of overseas acquisitions and joint ventures, and its R&D strategy.

Much of the company's historical growth has been through acquisition and joint ventures (for example, Dowell Schlumberger which was a joint venture with Dow Chemicals). In the 1970s and 1980s this activity was aimed at the diversification of the company, both in terms of its product mix and its geographical spread. Hence

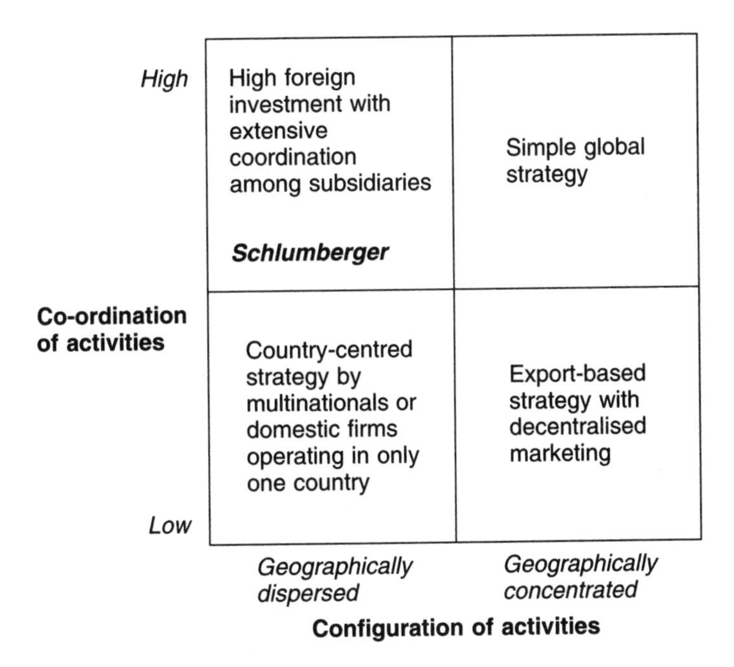

Fig. 11.1

the acquisition of companies as varied as a high-technology printing house in France and an environmental consultancy in the USA. The 1986 fall in the price of oil curtailed this aggressive expansion programme and forced Schlumberger to divest its least profitable subsidiaries (mainly on the Measurements & Systems side). Despite this, the diversification strategy continued, although on a smaller scale than previously, until 1991.

Since 1991, Schlumberger's acquisition activity has returned to its pre-1986 levels, but its objective is retrenchment rather than diversification. Almost all of the $1.1bn spent on acquisitions since 1991 has been directed at the oilfield services business, and at seismic survey companies in particular, as Schlumberger has sought to strengthen what it regards as its core competencies. Although focused more on a single product set, the acquisition strategy continues to be a transnational one, with seismic survey companies being acquired in Sweden, Germany, Canada and the UK. As well as boosting annual revenue, international acquisitions have brought Schlumberger considerable non-financial benefits:

- operating bases in more than 100 countries which have ensured that the company remains in touch with, and responsive to, the needs of its local markets;
- a pool of international skilled staff which is large enough to ensure that most well-head teams have national representatives to liaise with the client's on-site staff; and
- a continuous source of fresh blood and new ideas which has helped the company's culture remain flexible, entrepreneurial and innovative.

Schlumberger's R&D programme has been one of the main beneficiaries of the company's transnational strategy and is now a key source of competitive advantage; as the technical director commented in a recent article, 'technical innovation remains a key factor for improving the bottom line'. Investment in R&D has more than doubled since 1980, despite a drop in the aftermath of the 1986 fall in the price of crude oil. Overall, the trends in investment have largely mirrored those in Schlumberger's acquisition strategy. Between 1980 and 1988, more than half the R&D expenditure was directed at diversification – building up the Measurements & Systems side of the business; since then (and particularly since 1990), expenditure has been switched to the oilfield services business. Like its acquisition strategy, Schlumberger's R&D programme is a transnational one, which now boasts sixty research centres in ten countries. The company's heavy investment in technology has been the primary source of its organic growth (for example, directional drilling enabled the Schlumberger subsidiary Anadrill to grow by 31 per cent in 1995).

THE IMPLICATIONS FOR INTERNATIONAL COORDINATION

While these externally-facing strategies have contributed much of Schlumberger's recent growth, the company has had more difficulty in configuring its internal operations to address its increasingly distributed markets and clients. In the early 1990s, for example, it blamed a fall in revenue partly on the collapse of the market for 2-D seismic surveys; these have been superseded by the vastly more accurate 3-D surveys, but Schlumberger was not able to convert its 2-D resources to meet the demand of the 3-D market. Slow reactions have also meant that Schlumberger was not able to fully exploit the regional variations in demand for oil; its performance in the Gulf of Mexico, for instance, was outstripped by the independent specialist operators who did not have to move equipment and people into the area.

As this trend towards geographical distribution and new product development continues, and as the number of opportunities for external expansion decline, the future of Schlumberger rests increasingly on its ability to make its transnational vision a reality. Effective communication is fundamental to this, not just because the company is operating in some of the most inaccessible terrains in the world but also because of the technical complexity of its products.

Despite being originally a French company, Schlumberger has long adopted English as its official language and it is English, therefore, which acts as one of its most fundamental means to coordinate its worldwide activity. All Schlumberger employees must speak fluent English; meetings and documents are all in English, as it is rare – because of the company's policy of actively moving its staff around the world – that a meeting or a distribution list will contain only people of one nationality or language.

To some degree, this linguistic integration is formally promoted by the company. In addition to its overall policy on the use of English, it has invested heavily in internal communications, such as e-mail, which enables staff to coordinate their work across different time zones and it has a standard training programme for all employees. However, these official initiatives are backed by others which promote integration on a more informal basis: project teams, for example, are multicultural and drawn from different areas of the business to cut across functional and national boundaries; networking between subsidiaries is encouraged. The organisational culture is also helpful, as it minimises the kind of bureaucracy (such as circulating papers and minuting meetings) which would exacerbate language difficulties. Instead, rather than communicate on paper, Schlumberger employees are actively encouraged to travel to discuss issues face to face. It is also part of the company culture that people – even the most senior ones – are available to talk to: this is not an organisation in which people's diaries are full for months in advance – a practice which ensures that only formal communication is guaranteed to get through.

Unquestionably, some of this informality stems from the markets in which Schlumberger operates, for three reasons. In the first place, the sheer logistical difficulties and dangers posed by its type of work has meant that action, rather than words, has always been at a premium: when something goes wrong at a well-head site, writing a memo is not going to fix it. Indeed, often the speed of response required to solve problems precludes anything but the most succinct communication. Second, even as the company diversifies, its product range remains heavily technologically dependent and this brings linguistic advantages because the accompanying (international) technical vocabulary means that there is no need for translations or interpreters: the scientific language of engineering ensures that actions and words can be precisely matched. The scientific terminology is almost exclusively English-based and is egalitarian in the sense that all technical staff share the same language so that it is more difficult for hierarchies of languages to develop. If anything, the importance of technical vocabulary is likely to increase, as the services Schlumberger offers grow in complexity and demand specialist skills, rather than labour from the local country of operation. Finally, Schlumberger currently sells to a relatively limited number of companies (the likes of Exxon or Royal Dutch Shell), and most of its selling is done to the head office, not to a local country operation. Thus the multi-billion dollar contract for drilling in a particular field is likely to be negotiated with a small number of English-speaking executives, and it is their needs which Schlumberger needs to understand and service, not those of the local representatives.

These external factors all help to make Schlumberger's approach to language straightforward, and one which has worked very effectively to date. However, it is important to note that it inevitably involves some degree of compromise, the most obvious trade-offs relating to innovation and to addressing the non-technical needs of customers. Most of the company's sources for new products are external and come as part of newly acquired subsidiaries: Schlumberger's own R&D expenditure goes on developing the market potential of these typically nascent products, rather than 'blue sky' thinking. The same is true of Schlumberger's wider relations with its customers: while it provides an excellent technical service, it has been less good at putting forward anything more than a technical service.

Historically, this has been a comparatively unimportant weakness as the big oil companies have seen companies such as Schlumberger as the providers of specific – and indeed technical – solutions. But as these companies outsource more of what a decade ago would have been considered to be core services (and BP is an example of a company in the forefront of this trend) their relationship to all their suppliers is changing, with the latter taking on more and more of the operational management of the business, leaving the oil company to focus wholly on its role as the owner of the oil assets.

At the same time, computer technology is having a dramatic effect on those parts of the business which are being outsourced. Even in the 1980s, the major risk for oil companies lay in deciding whether to carry out exploratory drilling in a potential new oilfield: drilling is an expensive process and the continuing search for new reservoirs has meant that it is taking place in increasingly hazardous conditions. This changed with the advent of 3-D seismic surveys: while these are themselves very costly, they are also much more accurate than 2-D surveys. This means that the nature of the risk for the oil companies has changed: rather than applying to the actual drilling it now applies to the decision to carry out a 3-D seismic survey. In effect, the point at which the risk to the oil companies is greatest is continually moving forward: it is only a matter of time before an oil services company like Schlumberger develops a method for carrying out pre-seismic survey studies, in order to reduce the risk in carrying out the seismic survey itself. As a result of these trends, the oil companies are becoming increasingly distanced from the physical oil-well: ever more of the operations which are critical to them are being carried out by computers rather than human beings; more and more of their core processes are becoming 'virtual'. Schlumberger has been responding to this by investigating how it can make its own services more virtual – to match the needs and expectations of its customers.

All of these developments pose a direct challenge to the way in which Schlumberger manages its linguistic environment. The traditional vocabulary of oilfield engineering around which the company has been centred is beginning to be superseded by the terminology of computing: it is true that this is still English-based and retains many of the advantages of engineering language (notably precision and equality among users), however, it is still a new language being introduced into a resolutely monolinguistic environment. It will take time to assimilate and there will – inevitably – be points of conflict and division.

But potentially the greater threat comes from Schlumberger's own attitude to language. What Schlumberger has done so successfully is make language invisible. Because the company uses an engineering vocabulary and because it primarily relies on informal, face-to-face contact, language as such has been irrelevant. But as the services which it provides become more virtual, so will they involve more language. As its customers outsource more of their operations to companies like Schlumberger, the linguistic ground for the relationship between the oil companies and their suppliers is changing. The traditional technical vocabulary is giving way to a more broadly-based business vocabulary. Thus, Schlumberger's current solution to managing language may cost them long-term differentiation and competitive edge.

Note

1. Euan Baird, CEO, 1992 annual report.

12 Case Study 6: Inchcape plc

If one wanted to find a different approach to managing language in a multinational environment, it would be difficult to find one more different than that of Inchcape plc.

With its head office in London, Inchcape companies operate across the world in three primary sectors: cars (distributing Japanese cars such as Toyota mainly in Europe, the Far East and Australasia); marketing consumer products (an area of business which ranges from Coca-Cola bottling plants in Russia to a joint venture with the Italian shoemaker, Salvatore Ferragamo, in the Far East); and services (shipping, insurance and mineral-testing laboratories). While the strategy of the new chairman, Sir Colin Marshall (who joined the company from British Airways at the beginning of 1996), has been to focus the group increasingly on its core services and markets, disposing of or distancing those which are not central to its portfolio, these three sectors still betray the group's past as a highly diversified organisation, grown during the 1970s and 1980s through acquisition and joint ventures rather than organically. The group remains very dispersed in geographic terms: although a third of its income comes from the UK, 14 per cent comes from continental Europe, 24 per cent from the Far East, 23 per cent from South East Asia, 6 per cent from the Americas and 10 per cent from other parts of the world.

Although highly successful up to the end of the 1980s, that strategy has more recently had a high price associated with it. The 1995 results saw the second consecutive year in which profits declined. The motors division saw a 4 per cent rise in turnover (mainly from its UK operations), but a 34 per cent drop in profits in the face of economic uncertainty in many of its markets and a strong yen which significantly reduced the competitiveness of Japanese cars abroad. The story was not dissimilar in the marketing businesses: a 10 per cent increase in revenue (from new ventures in Russia and the Middle East) was accompanied by a 24 per cent drop in profits, despite the divestment of several unprofitable operations during the course of the year. Services was a much more successful division, with turnover growing by 12 per cent and profits by more than 20 per cent. However, this success was not sufficient to turn around the fortunes of the group in total: while total turnover rose by 2 per cent, operating profit fell by more than half (the effect of rising costs of sales combined with significant restructuring charges). Between 1991 and 1995, operating margins have fallen from 4.4 per cent to 2.1 per cent and return on capital employed from 33.5 per cent to 19 per cent.

With (still) such a range of services and number of overseas operations, global integration and economies of scale are essential to Inchcape's long-term success. However, the sheer diversity of services and national operations poses significant challenges. While Schlumberger – as we have seen – benefits from operating in fields where technology provides a cultural and linguistic homogeneity which might otherwise be difficult to achieve, Inchcape companies do not have this glue: someone working in a shoe retailing venture in the Far East is likely to speak a very different business language to someone engaged in shipping in the Netherlands. It is not just that their native languages are likely to be different: the nature of their operations is such that they have very different requirements from language – for some, the success of their operation will be building relationships with customers, for others the focus will be more internal, such as organisational and process efficiencies. But in such an environment, communication between the different operating units becomes even more essential. If these units are comparatively independent from each other (and this is certainly the case with each of the three divisions in Inchcape, although there is more interaction within a division), then part of the function of the head office is to extract the synergy which is the group's ultimate *raison d'être*. And then, there is the fundamental problem of how – in this kind of environment – you translate the strategy of the organisation as a whole into aspects that will be meaningful for each of the local operations: the link between words and actions in this context is a remote one and there is a high degree of risk that words emanating from the centre will be interpreted very differently in the subsidiaries.

It is therefore not surprising that Inchcape is accompanying its refocused strategy with an extensive communications programme to its employees worldwide. As the company is grappling with very different problems to those of Schlumberger, the approach it has adopted to communications is naturally also very different. Rather than make words invisible, Inchcape is attempting to make them more visible. The company has its own in-house newspaper: when the

April 1995 issue appeared, entitled '*Focusing on the Future*', its cover repeated the title in more than twenty languages as varied as Chinese, Thai, Arabic, Greek and Polish. This approach is confirmed by one of the main articles which looked at internal cross-company communications and confronted head-on some of the problems raised by a diverse organisation like Inchcape:

> Information can be a bit of an animal. Like the cats of Africa, rumours can travel at lightening speed. Like the arctic fox, a story can change drastically by the time it hits the ears of employees far from Group Head Office. And, to take the metaphor dangerously close to the edge, sometimes information crawls into a hole and hides.

The fact that the problem is diagnosed in terms of a metaphor also serves to strengthen the point: language is important to Inchcape; like information, language is not something the company can afford to hide.

The article covers the launch of a group corporate affairs team aimed at addressing these issues. The team had two main objectives: to encourage people to share information at all levels and to make communication as easy as possible by 'providing managers and supervisors with the right tools for the job'. Language and strategy are seen to be two sides of the same coin: when the new strategy was announced:

> information was available to managers for team briefings as soon as it was released to the financial community. Hopefully, where possible, employees had the new strategy explained to them, face-to-face, by their managers within hours of the public announcement. And with the new communication programme, information will continue to flow to employees as it is available.

Just as the new corporate strategy is an attempt to provide a clear sense of the official direction of the company, the communications programme is intended to provide the official, structured means by which to talk about it: as a result, employees will be able to 'rely less on the rumour mill and more on the facts'.

As the first stage in this process, the group corporate affairs team sent out surveys to more than 1000 employees in the three different divisions of the business, with questions translated into Mandarin,

Spanish, Japanese, Thai and Russian, and carried out a series of interviews of senior managers. The feedback has been used to develop a view on their communication needs of employees, tailored to their specific requirements. The aim has been to ensure that, working in such diverse businesses, the common thread between employees is the need to communicate. As the group CEO, Philip Cushing, summarised it:

> No matter where they're working, every one of our employees benefits from a working environment where communication is valued.

Language has, in effect, become one of Inchcape's assets.

Part VI

The Language Business

CEOs encase their mission statement in plexiglass, hand it out, and people laugh.

(David Nadler, president of Delta Consulting Group[1])

13 Corporate Advertising in the 1990s

INTEGRITY AND CORPORATE ADVERTISING

Corporate advertising has been one of the growth markets of the 1990s. The bigger you are, the more likely you are statistically to allocate a significant proportion of your marketing budget to corporate advertising; being a service company makes you even more likely to do this.[2]

As in all cases when we are on the receiving end of advertising, we tend to be sceptical about the value of this type of corporate promotion: it is when a CEO assures us that his company is *not* going bankrupt that we really start to worry. But by and large, such attempts to deceive us are the exception rather than the rule: in practice, the objectives usually cited for corporate advertising relate – rather more prosaically – to spreading accurate information about an organisation and its services or products. The majority of corporate advertising is designed, therefore, to paint a picture which is at least close to the truth. But that 'close to the truth' is one of the reasons why corporate advertising is of interest to us here. Corporate advertising is the way in which an organisation articulates itself – in words and pictures – to its public. While this representation may be honest, it can never be either objective or neutral.

Public relations in business has always meant balancing a perceived need for confidentiality against both the necessity and the desire to communicate. For much of the nineteenth century it was secrecy which prevailed. What attempts there were to sway public opinion fell into one of two extreme categories: either they were confined to building up one-to-one relationships with individual journalists who seemed likely to produce sympathetic copy, or they involved buying newspapers in their entirety. The real impetus to concerted public relations activity came, in the USA, with the expansion of the railroads at the end of the century. Suddenly, if they were to be able to purchase the land required, the railroad companies had to solicit the support of the public at large, and it was with this objective in mind that in 1906 Alexander J. Cassatt, the president of the Pennsylvania Railroad, appointed Ivy Ledbetter Lee to manage press relations on behalf of his company. Lee's innovations were seminal: where the business community had previously chosen to draw a veil of confidentiality over their affairs, Lee's aim was to publicise them: it was – in his own words – to 'humanise' the railroad.[3] The approach of the Pennsylvannia Railroad was quickly adopted by the other railroad companies: business public relations had been born – 'American business exists at the pleasure of American public opinion. Period'[4] – and its *rasion d'être* has never been seriously questioned since: 'silence is not golden when the world wants to know where you stand or why you exist. No business today can afford the luxury of anonymity'.[5]

AT&T is one of the oldest users of corporate advertising: it ran one of its first campaigns in 1908, and notes made at the time by a representative of the advertising agency hired by AT&T, N.W. Ayer, give a fascinating insight into the intention behind the campaign:

> What we want . . . is to try a series of advertisements which will sink deep down into the hearts of all classes of people who use the telephone – giving them facts and explaining all the problems which are experienced in running a big telephone company in any part of this country. After the public have made this trip, they should have a great and more abiding faith in the good intentions of the Telephone Company.[6]

The approach is instructive. AT&T cannot prove that its intentions are 'good' – you cannot, after all, evidence intentions – but it can present the 'facts' and 'explain' the problems it encounters as an indirect means of persuading people that its intentions are good. Facts and explanation therefore become substitutes for what a company can say, but cannot demonstrate.

There are several points in this which are fundamental to understanding both the form and function of corporate advertising. AT&T's desire to reassure the public – that, despite short-term problems, its heart was effectively in the right place – is symptomatic of the objectives behind much corporate communication: many of the most important things a company wants to say about itself are things for which there is (in T.S. Eliot's words) no objective correlative. There are two reasons for this, one to do with accessibility and the other with time. A company is not like a product: we cannot go out, buy it and test it for ourselves. So, when it tells us that its production line is more efficient or its new global management structure is more effective, we can either believe it or not. It is unlikely that we will be able to visit the production line or sit in on the meetings of global managers; even if we could do either of these things, would we be in a position to judge whether they were more efficient and effective? Of course, we can take confidence from good financial results, but we will not know that if sales went up and costs went down how much of this is the result of the streamlined production process or the sharpened management. And figures help even less if we look into the future as many companies want us to: facts – any objective correlatives – are inevitably limited to past or current events.

Faced with these twin problems – that we cannot trial a company in the way that we trial soap powder, and that we cannot trial the future at all – the corporate relations manager has no alternative but to try and tell us what to think. Ceasing to communicate is not an option: 'companies communicate whether they want to or not', argues a UK public relations guru, David Bernstein, 'it is easy for a company to communicate too little. It is virtually impossible for a company to communicate too much'.[7] Research has shown that there is a relationship between the amount of information available about an organisation and the level of favourability with which it is perceived: having a low profile is often counter-productive as the public will construct their own message.[8]

And here we encounter our cultural distrust of words: saying something is not enough (as the AT&T example shows), it needs to be backed up with facts and pictures (which constitute a different type of fact). Ideally, it needs to be backed up by actions. Comments from AT&T's most recent annual report indicate the extent to which this attitude continues to persist almost a century later:

> We're re-inventing AT&T . . . again . . . But let me reassure you, neither the board of directors nor I has lost sight of the fact that Wall Street's enthusiasm is for a plan. And plans in themselves don't create value. Action does.[9]

We are caught once more on the horns of a familiar dilemma: we rely heavily on language – to allow us to say things which we cannot physically demonstrate – but we do not trust it.

All of these points are re-inforced when we turn to the conventional wisdom on business public relations. The key recommendation, which crops up repeatedly, is the need to be honest and candid: 'There is no reason', writes one expert, for the president's letter to be 'crashingly dull, wordy and confusing. What impresses the everyday shareholder is honesty, a straight-forward writing style and no fluff'.[10] It is an approach backed by David Ogilvy of Ogilvy, Mather:

> Corporate advertising should be plain-spoken, candid, adult, intelligent and specific. It should avoid preachment and self-congratulation. It should be rooted in products, or services or policies . . . It should be interesting instead of boring. You cannot bore people into admiring a company . . . Corporate advertising should avoid the verbal and visual clichés of Madison Avenue. It should use the quiet graphics and speak the language of editors – not ad men.[11]

But being candid does not just happen: it takes practice. The ways in which organizations choose to project their integrity are numerous but it is worth highlighting a handful of particularly common approaches.

The first and most important of these is invisibility. What being honest can mean is using words which are as close to the things they describe as possible. It means avoiding unfamiliar jargon, using your audience's language, substituting things for words where possible. In other words, it involves making language disappear as far as possible.

Alternatively, if you cannot make the words disappear altogether, get someone else to say them – a celebrity, an employee, or a customer. While we, the audience, know that none of these spokespeople will be entirely disinterested, our opinions can still be swayed by this illusion of independent endorsement. Or, if you cannot find someone else to read your script, make a virtue of reading it yourself: project an image of responsibility and personal accountability; talk directly and colloquially; stress your commitment by banging your metaphorical fist on the table. Another approach is to claim some sort of vicarious integrity by relating your organisation to verifiable facts, usually about the world: if what you say about the world is true, then – we are supposed to infer – what you say about yourself is also true. Give the bad news: nothing persuades us more that an organisation is being honest with us than when it tells us something we do not want to hear:

> The annual report needs more than figures and tables, or even graphs, charts, or pictures. It needs candid, specific, readable statements of objectives, of difficulties and problems and how they are being attacked, of important new products or services, and how management envisions the future of the business.[12]

And if you do not think the public will be sympathetic to your problems, talk about their problems instead and what you are doing to help resolve them.

'Honesty' is, of course, a rhetorical trick and its ingredients are simple: put a real person, like Sir Edmund Hillary recalling his ascent of Everest, into your advertisement (as BT did in 1995), add a dose of homily wisdom (be careful at 20 000 feet – 'I left my toes up there last time') and you project a reliable image that everyone can trust. That is not to say that the companies which adopt such approaches are trying to deceive us: quite the opposite in fact; it is just that – ironically – in order to convince us of the truth of what they are saying, they have to deceive us. It has been argued that one of the reasons why corporate advertising is so bland is that it makes a company vulnerable to criticism (because it effectively sets a public standard by which the company can be judged) and companies therefore tend to hedge their bets by painting a rather nondescript and uncontentious picture of itself. It would, perhaps, be more accurate to say that there is an unwitting political correctness about it.

All this would be interesting but academic if it were not for the fact that corporate advertising is designed to do more than fulfil a passive role – promoting a given image to target audience. Corporate advertising also plays an active role in making that image a reality. This appears to work in two principal ways. In the first place, the process by which organisations go about articulating their vision through advertising and other promotional events clearly helps them focus their priorities internally:

> Corporate communications programmes . . . [provide] . . . a stimulus for the company – to design a corporate strategy (or re-examine it), to decide who it is, what it does, what it believes and how the people who work there can help achieve these goals.[13]

But, second, corporate advertising – the actual articulation of the vision – makes that vision possible because it helps the organisation concentrate on it. It is easier, after all, to build a new company or change an old one when you have a game plan. Corporate communications managers have some difficulties in this area, as the dividing line between painting a picture of the future and misleading people about the present is a fine one:

> The wish must be father to the fact. We do not suggest that any corporation should go around openly bragging . . . What we have read [in order to formulate our communications strategy] is an extract from the files of a respected corporation . . . They are not necessarily absolute fact at this stage. The statement is not mere day-dreaming, but a picture of what the corporation would *like to be* and a picture it *would like* to show whenever the public looks in its direction. With such a picture in mind, actions follow automatically.[14]

A major part of the function of corporate advertising is to make things happen: to use our now familiar equation, it is to turn language into action. But, as ever, this very simple aim is complicated by our distrust of language: 'the most brilliant vision statement this side of Paraguay won't budge a culture unless it's backed up by action'.[15] A company is therefore pulled in two conflicting directions: painting a vision of the future can be a powerful way of creating that future, but as soon as it moves into this more symbolic mode, the clear link between language and action is broken and people become less willing to act on the talk because they feel they may be being deceived. What a company does and how it is perceived are seen as two linked but detached entities, and it is often this which exacerbates the problems businesses have in dealing with the public. Put another way, to realise its vision of the future, a company has to talk then act (convert language into action) but the general premise has been that a company should act then talk, if what it says is to be credible (convert action into language). Thus, a company's history (action into language) will be more meaningful than its future (language into action), and may leave it trapped by the past. This is what happened in the 1970s, when a rash of corporate advertising to promote businesses' environmental care created a public outcry:

> This time the label [of corporate advertising] is 'corporate social responsibility' . . . Needless to say, the gap between corporate claim and performance is at least as sizeable as the generation gap – and that's a whopper. And the total disregard for the role the

> corporation played in bringing about some of our major ecological problems has genuine Alice-in-Wonderland characteristics.[16]

Nowhere are these tensions more apparent than in company reports.

MAKING THE TRUTH HAPPEN – ANNUAL REPORTS

Annual reports are no longer simple summaries of an organisation's past financial performance. An increasing number of companies are treating them as a prime opportunity for corporate advertising: USA companies alone spend more than $5bn per year on the production of their annual reports.[17] And this is in spite of the fact that these are almost certainly the least read of all business publications: it has been estimated that half of the shareholders who receive them spend less than 10 minutes reading them; 15 per cent of analysts do not read them at all.

For annual reports designed in this way, the objective is no different to that of other forms of corporate advertising: the aim is to project an image which will become truthful; like other forms of corporate advertising, these annual reports are intended to precipitate those actions which will make the text of the report happen – that is, will make it truthful. Rank Xerox's 1995 annual report is a good example of this. Faced with a shrinking future market as customers switch from paper to electronic media, Rank Xerox is faced with the challenge of reinventing itself:

> We realised that to meet and anticipate market changes and to become more effective and more profitable, we had to make changes ourselves. We had to restructure our entire organisation from top to bottom and become totally customer-focused and market led. We had to communicate to the business world that no-one understands the business document better. We had to make clear that the document solutions we offer are the best, where necessary working with companies with specialist expertise and skills such as Microsoft and Novell to provide total solutions. We had to establish Rank Xerox as The Document Company.

Surveying the tens of thousands of reports produced each year, common strategies for achieving this start to emerge, each of which has a varying degree of success.

A relatively small minority of companies rely on bald statements of their objectives. The vision of General Motors, for instance is: 'to be the world leader in transportation products and related services. We will earn our customers' enthusiasm through continuous improvement driven by the integrity, teamwork, and innovation of GM people'.[18] But saying is not seeing, and it is not uncommon for statements such as these to be backed up – directly or indirectly – with visual references. Usually this takes the form of showing what the vision of the future will look like in practice: when, in 1995, Toys 'R' Us focused on the launch of its subsidiary operation – Babies 'R' Us – it put artists' impressions of the new style of store and floor plan on the cover of its annual report. The accompanying text was designed to paint a picture of what shopping in the new stores would be like:

> Expectant and new parents will be able to do all their shopping from diapers to baby furniture to clothing and have the opportunity to design their dream nursery, aided by our in-store experts, all within their budget. With a selection of products second to none, they will be able to choose from aisles and aisles of top name strollers, car seats, carriages, bumper seats . . . The store was designed with the customer in mind . . . an open, airy, customer-friendly environment with low merchandise displays in the center of the store providing a sweeping view of our entire merchandise selection from any location in the store.[19]

General Motors is not exempt, even though the strategy it is pursuing is less obviously visual than that of Toys 'R' Us. It is not immediately easy to see how concepts such as 'continuous improvement driven by . . . integrity, teamwork, and innovation' can be visualised, but, the chairman's statement assures us, 'the form and substance of the new GM is becoming clear'. We may conclude that this refers to future financial results. The implied distinction is an interesting one: we see figures, and believe them; we read words, and distrust them.

Time is another difficult concept. In theory, the annual report focuses on past performance but primarily as a guide to future trends, the assumption being: tomorrow may not be the same as yesterday, but understanding yesterday improves our ability to predict what may happen tomorrow. As with the financial results, so it is with the text of many annual reports: the future is more likely to happen in the way that we – the company – predict if we can demonstrate that what we have done and are doing is part of a single continuum: thus, Hewlett-Packard states that its 'enduring character guides the company as we both lead and adapt to the evolution of technology and markets.[20] To have a future, we need to have a history:

> Ever since its inception, Honda has placed the highest value on working for a better society through the development of unique, innovative concepts and product designs. To do this effectively, our most important task is to understand the needs of our customers and society at large. Then we set about fulfilling these needs with a verve and enthusiasm that has become Honda's defining characteristic. Over the years, this commitment to growth toward the future has resulted in a consistency of excellence that applies to every product that bears the Honda name. As markets and technology grow more complex, it is the Honda people and ideas that we look to for continued success in providing the quality, safety, comfort and convenience that have made our company great.[21]

How long the history is does not matter: Toys 'R' Us talk of having the 'true Toys 'R' Us tradition'.[22] Having it matters.

It is worth stressing at this stage that these comments and those that follow are not intended to be pejorative. There is no suggestion that Toys 'R' Us is attempting to deceive the recipients of its report into thinking that its history is longer than it is: what we are observing instead is the way in which this and other companies adopt commonly identifiable strategies for realising their vision; it should be remembered that no one vision is better – or more ethical – than another. They may be more or less effective, but this is a separate issue and one which is discussed later in this section.

But constructing an explicit history is not the only way of securing a company's future to its past. Smith & Nephew stresses its scientific credentials, founded on decades of sophisticated research and development. Strong brand leaders, such as Procter & Gamble, generally prefer to emphasise the organic evolution of their product base. P&G products will, according to the 1995 annual report, be 'bigger' and offered at 'more competitive' prices; operational improvements will be similarly incremental – cost, for instance, will be 'broader' and 'deeper'. The last things P&G appears to either want or need is some sort of paradigmatic shift which could weaken, rather than build on, its brands.

But it may be that a company cannot relate itself to its history, either because the present (and therefore the future) is altering out of all recognition or because the company itself has changed radically. The strategy here is to link the picture which the company wishes to project with the external environment in which it finds itself, on the basis that the reality of the latter gives substance to the former: as with the past–future continuum, contiguity is important. This most frequently occurs in the form of change: the world is changing and so are we. Restructuring at Philip Morris 'reflects the realities' of a world in which there have been 'seismic shifts in customer needs'.[23] Honda, like the world, is 'constantly in motion'.[24] In fact, Honda takes this approach a stage further: the company is not just the passive reflection of the world, it actively helps to shape it as well – 'a better world is our prime objective':

> Honda has continually worked to help create a better world through innovative products of quality, comfort and performance. In an increasingly diverse global business environment, Honda is bringing the world together through a network of local and regional enterprises, each representing the Honda spirit of challenge and commitment in a unique way best suited to its particular cultural and social climate.[25]

Where does Honda stop and the external world start? The annual report blurs the distinction between the two in order to make what Honda says about itself as real as the real world.

The same link was implicit in the 1995 television and print advertising campaign launched by the Dutch electronics giant, Philips. In order to raise both the awareness of its products in the market-place and the morale of its staff after a period of extensive restructuring, the catch-phrase selected by the company was 'Let's make things better'. It is a slogan which is neatly double-edged: make the world a better place by making Philips' products better.

Honda and Philips are not the only companies to employ this tactic. Many pharmaceutical companies describe their contribution to the world (Merck: 'our business is improving and preserving human life'[26]) in terms of the way in which they have changed our lives through the introduction of new drugs. In fact, the more essential the product or service being offered by a company, the more likely that organisation is to position itself as part of our individual reality. Take Unilever as an illustration which describes itself as 'one of the most international companies in the world. Its products serve people's everyday needs for foods and cleanliness'.[27]

High-tech companies can take this a stage further. Whereas the pharmaceutical companies are helping the world by reducing existing problems (disease), high-tech companies can claim to be creating the future world:

> Motorola is . . . creating whole new global industries. It is a mission without boundaries. It is not limited by geographical barriers. It is not confined to any one specific industry, such as telecommunications or electronic components. It is not limited to market segments such as industrial or consumer. It is a mission that takes us where the customers and the technologies lead us. It builds on what we learn, and ultimately it results in new industries for a new kind of world.[28]

'We're creating our future by sowing the seeds of innovation', agrees HP.[29]

In fact, it is tempting to see the stress on community programmes found in so many annual reports at the moment as at least partly influenced by this same thinking. After all, these are as much about demonstrating that an organisation can do something as they are about proving that that something constitutes a positive contribution to society at large. A statement in HP's annual report is a good instance of this:

> We continued to promote economic, intellectual and social progress wherever we did business in 1995. Our support of educational programmes helped develop talents in new generations, among whom HP will find future employees, partners and customers. Our work for the environment helped improve the quality of life, and we focused efforts to expand the diversity of our work force, enhancing HP's worldwide competitiveness.[30]

Embedding themselves in 'real life' can be more problematic for some companies. It may be, for instance, that the services (and it is usually services) they offer may be too arcane or ephemeral to be part of our daily lives. Alternatively – and for a variety of reasons – the image they wish to project may be focused on just one aspect of their organisation. Thus, Philip Morris, in its 1995 report, is a machine more than it is a manufacturer of branded goods: 'our turbo-charged tobacco business', 'one extraordinary growth machine', a 'rocket ship' which is 'revved up' is how the chairman and CEO, Geoffery C. Bible describes it. The emphasis here is on the collective infrastructure and brand power rather than the contribution of individual staff.

Another approach to the same issue is to project the company as a series of tangible products, rather than a potentially amorphous entity. When the French telecommunications company Alcatel announced a loss in 1995 of FF25.6bn, the company chose to highlight its products rather than itself in its annual report:

> Following are a few examples of Alcatel Alsthom's technological leadership: the world's largest installed switching base, one of the most complete offers on the high-speed synchronous transmission market, recognised expertise in complex satellite systems, a wide range of data transmission products designed for both the public and the private sectors, the world's most reliable high-speed trains.[31]

Perhaps the most common way of making a company seem something other than it is is to make it human: 'since nobody can belly up to a cold impersonal, faceless, thoughtless monolithic society of a company, give the company a personality with which people can relate'.[32] One of the most powerful ways of making people feel comfortable with a large organisation is to humanise it: while a remote, faceless institution can be threatening, it is hard to remain paranoid when you are presented with a bunch of ordinary people. When the Fleet Financial Group, a $48bn financial services company in the USA, wanted to increase its level of market awareness, it turned to its employees. The advertising campaign, entitled 'Hopes and Dreams', featured a handful of outstanding staff who demonstrated a commitment, not only to the goals of the company and its customers, but to the wider community as well. Taken together, their jobs represented a cross-section of the products and services offered by Fleet, but, as individuals on television, they could do what no corporate entity could do – go into their neighbours' living rooms.[33]

The company as a next-door neighbour is an image which Pepsico used in its 1995 report. 'Dear friends', begins the chairman and CEO's introductory statement; when it comes to new executives, they are introduced ('our restaurant divisions are headed by five of the best leaders you'll ever meet').[34] If a company is really a bunch of people, then a company can do things, because people do things.

But the humanisation of the corporation goes far beyond the construction of a homely and approachable public demeanour. Making it human brings an organisation to life – and an organisation which is 'alive' can do things. Humanisation is therefore one of the most potent – and most ubiquitous – means by which companies use the imagery of their annual reports to make their objectives real.

Images of humanisation abound. Working on improvements to the production process, such as training and the elimination of waste, all helped in 'breathing new ideas' into the corporate body at Toyota.[35] For Dow: 'it is our people who bring our strategy to life'.[36]

While all the above highlight the different ways in which companies choose to convince us that what they say in their annual reports is more than just talk, perhaps the single most common approach is substitution – replacing theoretical descriptions with practical examples. Take, for example, a rather bald statement from Electrolux: 'developing employee competence and stimulating new ways of thinking are important for maintaining a high rate of change within the organization'.[37] It is unconvincing because we cannot grasp what it means in practice; and, if we cannot see what it means in practice, it is effectively meaningless. We can compare this approach to that of Alcatel:

> To successfully benefit from its technological leadership and carry out internal reforms will require the full commitment and co-operation of all employees. To this end, new functional guidelines have been clearly defined: – priority is given to listening and providing customer satisfaction through meeting all of their needs; – creative individual thinking is encouraged, along with heightened interaction between flatter hierarchical levels; – co-ordinated, team-based decision making; – development of a Group-wide corporate culture to create a true internal team spirit; – intensified efforts in re-engineering, TQM and software systems management; – increased mobility between work teams to promote international and internal promotion.[38]

What Alcatel gives us is examples: it may not make for especially stimulating reading but it gives more of an impression of what is meant by the 'full commitment and co-operation of all employees'.

Justyna Pisiewicz was short of cash. That's a familiar problem for almost everyone. But Justyna was a Polish national living on her own in Bejing, China. And she was only 18.

It was 1988, and Justyna had just arrived in China, one of a select group of Polish high school graduates to have won full scholarships to study abroad. Already fluent in English and Russian, within a year she was proficient in Mandarin Chinese and was enrolled in a four-year degree programme in international relations at the prestigious Foreign Affairs College in Beijing. But money was very tight.

So Justyna and three friends started a translation service for Polish businesses investing in China. After a few months, the students realized they were capable of much more than just translating. Over the next year, their business blossomed into negotiating contracts, sourcing materials and obtaining sub-contractors. Their clientele grew steadily, and the work took them to major Chinese cities, mostly on weekends as their class schedule permitted.

Eyes sparkling as she recalls those days, Justyna, now 25 and a toiletries assistant brand manager for Gillette Poland, says, 'I loved the business and the negotiating. You had to be smart and energetic, and keep an eye on everything. It was absolutely fun.'

The business bug had bitten hard. Justyna's next move was to Boston, where she enrolled in the Simmons College evening MBA programme. She also came to the attention of Frank O'Connell, who recruited her for the Company's International Trainee Programme . . . Few Company employees have Justyna's unusual background. But in her character and early professional skills, she shows promise of achieving the world-class standard of leadership that typifies and distinguishes Gillette today.

(Gillette annual report, 1995)

Fig. 13.1

But even here the meaning of what is said is still limited: what, for instance, is actually meant by the phrase 'co-ordinated, team-based decision making'?

Gillette's approach to this problem is to give a different sort of example: 'We will attract, motivate and retain high-performing people in all areas of our business', states the company in its 1995 report, and to emphasise its point it tells the story of a Polish student, Justyna Pisiewicz (Figure 13.1). Gillette is effectively combining two strategies: giving examples and humanising the subject. But even this approach does not solve the essential problem: it does not excuse the company from saying the usual things about management policy:

> We are committed to competitive, performance-based compensation, training and personal growth based on equal career opportunity and merit. We expect integrity, civility, oneness, support for others and commitment to the highest standards of achievement. We value innovation, employee involvement, change, organizational flexibility and personal mobility. We recognize and value the benefits in the diversity of people, ideas and culture.

It is a problem Gillette itself is conscious of:

> Leadership can be difficult to define, but in a successful company, leadership begins with behaviors that are firmly grounded in a well-defined set of values that constitute the corporate culture.

Words – as always – are not enough. In fact, there is an implication here that relying on words is a sign of an unsuccessful company. Words are only important if they are meaningful, and only practice – actions – can make words meaningful: yet, to promote itself, the company has to rely on words. To one degree or another, this is a paradox which faces all organisations which use corporate advertising. The following case study looks in detail at how one company – Intel – has dealt with it.

Notes

1. Quoted in Dumaine, 1990: 55.
2. Garbett, 1981: 71.
3. Tedlow 1979: 9–13.
4. Evans, 1987: xv.
5. Galli, 1971: 20.
6. From a report from the representative who visited Theodore N. Vail, the AT&T president at the time; quoted by John H Howland, assistant vice president of AT&T, in a speech before the Association of National Advertisers in 1977, quoted in Garbett, 1981: 4.
7. Bernstein, 1985: 1–2.
8. Ibid.: 5–6.
9. AT&T annual report, 1995.
10. Bivins, 1991: 147.
11. David Ogilvy, founder of Ogilvy and Mather, 1977 address to the Dallas Advertising League, quoted in Garbett, 1981: 194.
12. Foy, 1984: 421.

13. Bernstein, 1985: 167
14. Moore, 1980: 35.
15. Dumaine, 1990: 55–6.
16. Weiss, 1970: 35.
17. Bivins, 1991: 144.
18. General Motors, 1995 annual report.
19. Toys 'R' Us annual report, 1995.
20. Hewlett–Packard annual report, 1995.
21. Honda corporate profile, 1995.
22. Toys 'R' Us annual report, 1995.
23. Philip Morris annual report, 1995.
24. Honda corporate profile, 1995.
25. Honda annual report, 1995.
26. Merck annual report, 1995.
27. Unilever annual report, 1995.
28. Motorola annual report, 1994.
29. Hewlett–Packard annual report, 1995.
30. Ibid.
31. Alcatel annual report, 1995.
32. Galli, 1971: 20.
33. *PR Newswire*, 22 June 1995.
34. Pepsico Inc. annual report, 1995.
35. Toyota annual report, 1995.
36. Dow annual report, 1995.
37. Electrolux annual report, 1995.
38. Alcatel annual report, 1995.

14 Case Study 7: Intel

'Intel Inside' is a clever line. It applies not just to the chip – hidden away in the bowels of a PC – but to our perception of the impact of the chip on our daily lives. Talk about the chip itself and most of us would be quickly lost in its technical specifications. Talk about the implications of the chip (what we can do with it) and we appreciate its significance: it is the meaning which is important, not the product.

In 1986, everything – from Intel's point of view – was still very much on the inside. A typical mention of the company in the press would be as follows:

> The Turbo Tower [is] a multi-user system from Xmark Inc of California . . . Turbo Tower supports from two to eleven users and comes with Pick, MS-DOS 2.1 and CP/M all as standard together with multi-user word processing, graphics, spreadsheet and relational database software. The system comes with a minimum of 20Mb of hard disk and an IBM Personal-compatible floppy with a low-cost tape streamer as an option. It uses Intel 8088 and 80286 processors together with a Zilog Z80A for CP/M compatibility. The master terminal on the system has 640 by 300-bit mapped graphics, managed by a 6502 processor, and 32Kb of dedicated RAM.[1]

Everything was buried: the chip was buried in the PC, its specification was buried among those of the other components, its maker's name was buried by the PC manufacturer's. The chip's significance was solely as an electronic part but – ironically – it was the jargon of electronics which deprived it of any wider significance, for instance:

> Intel is putting its Multibus II marketing campaign into top gear. The company is investing $50m in hardware and software support over the next three years as it strives to establish Multibus II as the major 32-bit industry standard bus systems architecture.[2]

It is not surprising that Andy Grove (Intel's president then and now) complained to a 1986 sales conference in Santa Clara that few people knew that the company made more than chips: 'Why the hell doesn't anybody know that?' he moaned.[3]

Since that time, the aim of Intel's advertising has been to get its image and its products out of a technological ghetto and into our everyday lives. And the way in which Intel has used language has been a critical factor in achieving this goal.

Corporate advertising in the computer industry was pioneered by Apple. As far back as 1984, it ran an advert showing a woman throwing a sledge-hammer through an Orwellian Big Brother image, in front of a mesmerised crowd. That this paean to non-conformity was directed by Ridley Scott – more famous for films such as *Blade Runner* – was a sign of things to come.

The Intel Inside campaign was launched in 1991, at a cost of more than $100m.[4] The television advertisement took the viewer on a journey into the computer, swooping and plunging through wires and circuits like a low-flying plane, to reveal not only the chip itself – the electronic heart of the machine – but the expansion slots next to it, the message being that upgrading their PCs was as simple as plugging a new chip in. 'Something's waiting inside the powerful Intel 486SX computer,' says the voice-over, 'a technology that will make it even more powerful. We call it . . . room for the future. Introducing built-in upgradability. Check into it. From Intel. The Computer Inside'.[5]

The advertisement was a collaborative effort between Intel's advertising agency Dahlin Smith White (DSW) and Industrial Light & Magic, a division of LucasArts Entertainment Co formed in 1975 to create the visual effects for *Star Wars* and an acknowledged visual effects leader in the film industry. Linking up to a company more associated with films was deliberate: 'This is a particularly exciting project for Intel and the agency,' commented Dave Boede, the group account supervisor at DSW at the time, 'working with ILM, we've been able to effectively use technology ordinarily reserved for feature films. The results are stunning.'[6] Even the music was composed by Peter Buffet who had previously composed some of the music for the film *Dances with Wolves*. The result was to draw viewers into the advertisement in the same way that they become engrossed in a film:

> Fasten your seat belt. You are embarking on a flight of discovery. Inside, the future is literally waiting. A new episode of *Star Trek*? Not quite. Rather, it's a different high-tech journey. Destination: The innards of a computer and the new, built-in upgradability Intel is offering the computer market.[7]

Intel's campaign, like of those of other high-tech companies, was in part a response to falling margins within the computer industry. The early 1990s saw the commoditisation of the PC, with manufacturers having to adopt mass-marketing techniques – primarily discounting – in an attempt to maintain sales. Compaq, for example, jumped to the industry's top sales slot by cutting the price of its PCs. But the cost was high: the company saw its gross margin plunge to 24 per cent in 1993 and barely move since[8] – they had stood at 42 per cent five years earlier. In an attempt to compensate for this, the industry took a leaf from the FMCG manufacturers' book: advertising strategies became more brand- and less product-focused, as *Computing* noted in 1993:

> US computer firms are realising they must project a specific corporate image and move away from their traditional focus on products. Advertising, public relations and top executives' public presentations must all convey a common message, building brand loyalty as much as confidence that their company's products will do the best job . . . [They] are waking up to the fact that projecting the right corporate image can help their bottom line. In the highly competitive PC market where profit margins are thin, an identifiable, positive corporate image could persuade customers to pay a little extra. It could mean the difference between survival and bankruptcy.[9]

The recent history of corporate advertising in high-tech industries is one of the flight from language to pictures. The earliest computer advertisements were highly product-specific and tried to cram a lot of technical information into short and virtually unreadable paragraphs. The growth of mass-market computing toppled the white-coated experts and industry gurus: typical consumers were more interested in whether a printer could produce images for T-shirts than in how much memory it had. This and other multimedia features were far better portrayed in pictures than in text, and 1995 in particular saw a significant shift from print to television advertising: 'You'll be seeing a lot of ads from Compaq Computer Corp. for its hot-selling Presario home PC leading up to Christmas', commented *Advertising Age*, 'but you won't read any.'[10] Moreover, the broadening range of products and services offered by companies made the description of a single product increasingly irrelevant and corporate advertising increasingly important:

> The computer business is changing. Computer firms are beginning to face the same challenges confronting firms in the consumer mass market. It's important for them to consider how customers will perceive them. With product life-cycles being measured in the order of months rather than years, as used to be the case, it's difficult to promote the products themselves. We have to try to interest people in the company itself.[11]

For Intel, the logic behind launching a corporate advertising campaign was even more remorseless. The late 1980s had seen an explosion in the number of competitors, all producing apparently indistinguishable products, from whom Intel needed to differentiate itself. While legal action kept some of the smaller, clone-like companies at bay, Intel looked to corporate advertising to strengthen its company image. 'What we want to do,' said Nairman Karanjia, manager of corporate programmes at Intel, in a 1993 interview,

> is show a direct connection between Intel and the customer's experience. We have to show that choosing an Intel product is an exciting experience. For example, Nike advertising is highly sophisticated. When you try the shoes you also experience the quality of the product. After all, why would someone pay $100 for a pair of shoes? We have to do the same. We have to demonstrate an emotional feeling to customers that will help sell our products.[12]

But if company image superseded product promotion, and pictures superseded words, words have not disappeared entirely for Intel's corporate advertising – indeed they have a crucial role to play.

The company's first step was to emerge from a sea of technical jargon onto the dry land of plain English. By 1995 this process had matured completely: the first page of the annual report gives accessible definitions for the key technical terms used, betraying almost too great a sensitivity to the terms used and making use of familiar terms for complex technology:

> Microprocessors, also called central processing units (CPUs), are frequently described as the 'brains' of the computer, because they act as the central control for the processing of data in personal computers and other computers.

However, what makes Intel's report particularly interesting is that this determinedly plain style in some areas is interspersed with sections of much more emotionally charged language. The report begins:

> In 1971, Intel introduced the world's first micro-processor and sparked a computer revolution that has changed the world. Today, Intel supplies the computing industry with chips, boards, systems and software. Intel's products are used by industry members as 'building blocks' to create advanced computer systems for PC users. Intel's mission is to be the preeminent building block supplier to the new computing industry worldwide.

That the linguistic pace should change at this point is not surprising: one of the most important functions of language for Intel is that it creates history. History is, after all, not past actions, it is the present record of past actions: where there is no record, there can be no history (hence the term 'prehistory'). And history is very important to Intel – this is a company which runs its own electronics museum in California and sponsors touring exhibits from the Smithsonian.

A 1993 report celebrating 25 years since Intel's founding shows just how important history is to Intel. It begins like a children's story – perhaps even like a modern fairy-tale:

> One weekend in the spring of 1968, Gordon Moore dropped by Bob Noyce's home, where Bob was mowing the lawn. The two men stood on the grass and commiserated about the state of affairs at Fairchild Semiconductor, which they had co-founded with six colleagues. Bob, who had co-invented the integrated circuit, was concerned about instability and bureaucracy at the top at Fairchild, and had decided to resign. Gordon suggested that semiconductor memory, an emerging technology, looked promising enough to launch a company and agreed to join Bob in a new start up. Intel was born.

As in any good story, the protagonist – Intel – is born, grows up, encounters obstacles and emerges victorious. Major commercial issues are transformed into morals: thus, lay-offs in the 1980s are a learning point for the adolescent company – 'redeployment is like always watching what you eat, rather than bingeing and going on crash diets'.

Each year in the company life-story is accompanied by highlights of the year in question (Figure 14.1). At first sight, the choice and juxtaposition of the highlights seem almost laughably bizarre – the opening of the musical *Hair* is mentioned in the same breath as the assassination of Robert Kennedy: even the inclusion of events at Intel seems to smack of arrogance. But the cumulative effect is powerful for three reasons. In the first place, it simply makes the point that Intel was there, that the company is a part of history. Revealing what is hidden is one of the common themes of the report. Take, for instance, the story of how the company's values statement was first written up by the then director of administration, Bob Reed, during the half-time of a game of football. He noted: 'the only reason I could do it so easily is because the values were already in our blood . . . I was just articulating what was already there.'

The second reason this report has such power is that the choice of highlights is highly democratic: after all, many people may have stronger personal memories of seeing *The Graduate* than they have of the assassination of Martin Luther King; to others, the gold medal winners at the Winter Olympic games in February may have meant more than the anti-Vietnam demonstrations the following August. On this basis, who can object to Intel positioning itself in history – its view of history is just as valid as a Harvard professor's. The implicit message is an empowering one: we can all make history.

Third and finally, this report is important simply because it exists. Something once said – in this case, that Intel has played a significant part in our history – is not easy to unsay. This is partly because we are all perhaps inherently lazy and, unless strongly provoked otherwise, tend not to query what we read, but it may also reflect our inability to forget what we are first told (thus, we often continue to suspect people arraigned but acquitted of crimes).

All these three themes – revealing the hidden, empowerment and simply being – lie at the heart of the way in which Intel uses language. Articulating those value statements which were already embedded within the organisation is analogous to revealing to consumers the chip at the heart of the PC – both involve turning the inside out. Similarly, by drawing out Intel's position in history, the report gives the company a meaning – it changed our lives, it was part of *our* history. Empowerment is central to Intel's position in the computing industry: the PC liberated millions of office workers from the thrall of mainframe computing which was synonymous with centralised control and bureaucracy.

1968:

Memorable Movie:
The Graduate

F E B R U A R Y

Winter olympic games held in Grenoble, France: Jean-Claude Killy and Peggy Fleming win gold medals.

A P R I L

Martin Luther King, Jr. assassinated in Memphis, Tennessee.

Hair opens on Broadway.

J U N E

Senator Robert F. Kennedy assassinated in Los Angeles, California.

J U L Y

Bob Noyce and Gordon Moore incorporate new venture as N M Electronics; purchase rights to use Intel name from company using Intelco.

Arthur Rock is chairman of the Board; Bob Noyce is president and CEO; Gordon Moore is executive vice president.

A U G U S T

Anti-Vietnam War riots mar Democratic National Convention in Chicago.

Company sets to work on Schottky TTL and silicon gate MOS technologies.

N O V E M B E R

Nixon/Agnew defeat Humphrey/Muskie in presidential election.

Fig. 14.1 *Extract from* Defining Intel: 25 Years/25 Events

But of the three themes, the third is the most important. If, by existing, this report creates history, then it also creates the future. One of the reoccurring messages from the past is that Intel could achieve the impossible: for example, on improvements made to manufacturing processes during the 1980s, it reads: 'People who were in manufacturing 10 years ago think the yields we have today should be impossible.' The same message applies going forward: if Intel can make history, then it can also create the future:

> There is more to the technology business than accounting for the money. You nurture a sense of what's possible: it's never what *is* that drives you; it's what *could* be.

Overall, Intel's corporate literature uses language in two quite distinct ways: to describe the company and its products in as clear and non-technical a way as possible, and to define the company's pivotal role in our past and future. The two styles are never confused. This means that the company never tries to link its more emotive language directly to reality – it never, for example, makes any grandiose assertions about its products or management processes. The more visionary aspects of its literature are not exposed to cynicism by being applied to present-day reality: they exist only in respect to the past and the future. Contrast this approach with that used by Hewlett-Packard:

> Ever since Bill Hewlett and Dave Packard developed the company's first product in a Palo Alto garage more than 50 years ago, innovation has been a fundamental part of what we do at HP. Today, we continue to invest in research and development because, more than ever, new products fuel our purpose – to accelerate the advancement of knowledge and improve the effectiveness of people and organizations.[13]

This approach positively invites scepticism: it is always easy to point out the actions of an organisation which do not match its public aspirations. By keeping the two forms of language separate, Intel avoids this pitfall. The moral is a simple one: keep language and reality as separate as possible, otherwise you may be in danger of showing just how far from reality your language is.

It is, perhaps, hardly surprising that Intel was ranked fifth this year in *Fortune*'s annual survey of company reputations and, as the magazine commented: 'Good name is to strong financial performance as chicken is to egg. It's not awfully clear which begets which, but it's awfully hard to have one without the other.'[14]

Notes

1. *Computergram*, 23 October 1986.
2. *Electronics Weekly*, 26 November 1986.
3. *Electronics Times*, 3 July 1986.
4. *Computing*, 6 May 1993.
5. *Business Wire*, 11 November 1991.
6. Ibid.
7. Ibid.
8. 1995 annual report.
9. *Computing*, 6 June 1993.
10. *Advertising Age*, 2 October 1995.
11. Paul Franson, head of the Silicon Valley firm Franson, Hagerty and Associates, *Computing*, 6 May 1993.
12. *Computing*, 6 May 1993.
13. Hewlett-Packard annual report, 1995.
14. *Fortune*, 4 March 1996.

15 Creating the Future: Language, Strategy and Cultural Change

This book has looked at the use of language in business from many directions – how language facilitates or hinders the introduction of new technology, the way in which we make implicit decisions about how we talk to customers – but underlying all this is the idea that the relationship between language and action is changing. We speak more and we act less. What we say – because the connection between it and action is becoming a more distant one – is open to greater misinterpretation (as our experience with IS illustrates). But, at the same time, we are finding that businesses are increasingly exploiting language for its own sake – creating vision statements, corporate advertising, talking and listening to customers: this is the essence of corporate speak.

So where does this leave that activity which is most clearly and absolutely predicated on the idea that words lead to action – creating the strategic plan? After all, it is the essence of strategy that words result in actions: why else would we write them?

In fact, we might legitimately start with the question: why write them at all? Strategic planning, like weather forecasting, has a questionable track record.

> Planning systems were expected to produce the best strategies as well as step-by-step instructions for carrying out those strategies so that the doers, the managers of businesses, could not get them wrong. As we know now, planning has not exactly worked out that way.[1]

As these comments by American academic Henry Minztberg suggest, many of the problems with strategic planning have been blamed on the fact that is has been – conventionally – carried out by planners, not managers: people of words rather than actions. In 'Planning on the Left Side and Managing on the Right', Mintzberg linked planning as an activity with the linear left-hand side of the brain and managing with the holistic right-hand side. Tellingly, he also associated the left-hand side with language[2]. If we could ensure that planning is less about writing and more about acting – the argument goes – many of these problems will evaporate. A strategy cannot be created in a hot-house environment: it emerges organically from the business; it is non-linguistic – 'a not-too-precisely articulated vision of direction':[3]

> It is a closed loop. You make the argument that in the beginning of the company, the founders wanted to make certain products, which in turn led to our way of managing, which reinforced our products. It all hangs together. It isn't the result of any intellectual process, but it evolves. The pattern of principles which emerge out of a lot of individual decisions is totally consistent, and it is a fabric which hangs together and leads to success.[4]

To stretch the analogy: formal planning is like grammar; strategy should be spontaneous (and occasionally grammatically incorrect) conversation. Managing is not dependent on strategic planning; indeed, it is in many respects an anathema to it, as operational managers tend to act spontaneously, solving problems as they emerge, being flexible: 'managers tend to favor action over reflection and the oral over the written'.[5] Those that can manage, manage; those that cannot, plan. And if operational managers are biased against language, they will necessarily be sceptical about the value of a written plan. If plans work, it is because those who are responsible for executing them 'know what is meant'. How many times have we heard people say the following:

- Don't bother reading all that, I'll tell you the most important points. . .
- It's all in the plan, but here's what we're really trying to do. . .
- We've got a formal plan, but we don't use it much because we all know what we're doing. . .
- Planning is a waste of time because we were going to do this anyway. . .

Having to use a plan is a sign of failure – the good manager simply knows what to do.

Of course, this is overstating the case – although I think there are instances of it in almost every business. But there are organisations that clearly take planning very seriously and rely heavily on their plans once completed. First, an obvious point: the amount of importance attached to planning generally rises in proportion to the size and complexity of an organisation: a small, owner–manager business will rarely need to spend much time planning because it knows what it is doing, but a multinational will typically invest a great deal of time because it has a diverse range of products and resources to coordinate. Planning is in part an exercise in control by those in charge of an organisation: it is about the people at the top saying that they want to do things (which is why it is rare for a conventional strategy to be created bottom-up). Strategy is about power.

> The more authoritarian and hierarchical the system, the more information is a secret property of select groups, and the more it can be utilized to control and punish people at lower levels. In such a system there is little horizontal communication across levels of equal rank. The department chief knows about his ten division heads and their respective divisions, but each one of them knows only about himself and his own division. Hence the department chief is in a powerful position to manipulate them as he will.[6]

Often the benefit derived from strategic planning does not come from a series of action points and budgets: it comes from the fact that those running an organisation use the opportunity to communicate their vision and values.

> The important lesson to be drawn from these attempts to develop formal statements of beliefs is that the invisible beliefs can be made more visible in this way.[7]

But even this rationale for planning is now being questioned. Remember the superstition that says that when you blow out the candles on a birthday cake and make a wish, you should not tell anyone because it will mean that your wish will not come true: we are beginning to think the same about strategy. The strength of organizational beliefs is directly related – in inverse proportions – to the amount we say about them. A powerful belief requires no articulation – everyone knows it: a weak belief needs to be constantly reinforced.

That successful organisations have visions rather than plans is at the heart of *Built to Last* by James Collins and Jerry Porras, and it is worth pausing for a moment to look at their argument: 'but *vision* has become one of the most overused and least understood words in the language, conjuring up different images for different people'.[8] For Collins and Porras, a vision comprises two elements: a core ideology and an envisioned future. The ideology is who you are, rather than where you are going (which will change); it cannot be created, only discovered. An envisaged future involves having a clear and compelling view of the impact you want to have on the world – what Collins and Porras term a 'big, hairy, audacious goal' (the 'BHAG'):

> A true BHAG . . . serves as a unifying focal point of effort, and acts as a catalyst for team spirit . . . A BHAG engages people – it reaches out and grabs them. It is tangible, energising, highly focused. People get it right away; it takes little or no explanation.[9]

It is the last point which is particularly relevant to us here: BHAGs do not need language:

> For example, NASA's 1960s moon mission didn't need a committee of wordsmiths to spend endless hours turning the goal into a verbose, impossible-to-remember mission statement. The goal itself was so easy to grasp – so compelling in its own right – that it could be said 100 different ways yet be easily understood by everyone . . . Think of it as translating the vision from words into pictures, of creating an image that people can carry around in their heads. It is a question of painting a picture with your words.[10]

What habitually goes wrong with vision statements – in Collins' and Porras's view – is that their connection to the fundamental dynamics of an organisation is tenuous at best:

> Many executives thrash about with mission statements and vision statements. Unfortunately, most of those statements turn out to be a muddled stew of values, goals, purposes, philosophies, beliefs, aspirations, norms, strategies, practices, and descriptions. They are usually a boring, confusing, structurally unsound stream of words that evoke the response 'True, but who cares?'. Even more problematic, seldom do these statements have a direct link to the fundamental dynamic of visionary companies: preserve the core and stimulate progress. That dynamic, not vision or mission statements, is the primary engine of enduring companies.[11]

The real vision of an organisation does not need to be articulated – it is continually present: 'a visitor could drop in from outer space and infer your vision from the operations and activities of the company without ever reading it on paper'.[12]

Although on a larger scale, this perspective is not so very different to that of the manager who cannot see that writing down what he is going to do into a plan adds any value. When you put something into words, you will fail: even feeling you have to put it into words is a sign of failure. We can conclude that strategy and planning are only useful to an organisation so far as they remain outside language. At a strategic level, the 'vision' should be apparent without articulation – effectively because everyone will be clearly engaged in realising it; and at an operational level, people should know what to do instinctively, not because it has been preplanned – because they act, rather than talk.

Undoubtedly a contributory factor to this situation is that many people think that when organisations talk about themselves, they are often economical with the truth – they are talking about what they want to be true, not what actually is true. We have already seen that this is certainly the case as far as corporate advertising is concerned. Contrary to its ostensible *raison d'être*, one of the main aims of the annual report is to create the future, not restate the past. However, it is important to understand that the sceptical reactions with which some of these attempts are met are less the result of an organisation setting out to be deliberately misleading than they are the effect of using language. For example, suppose you have spent the evening at a party chatting to just one or two people in the corner of the room. Your host, noticing this, asks whether you are enjoying yourself (something which he or she perhaps would not have done if you had been moving around, talking to lots of people). When you politely say you are enjoying yourself, you may either be telling the truth or diplomatically lying. These two possibilities exist as soon as you reply and irrespective of what you reply. In effect, as soon as you open our mouth, you are introducing the idea of truth and falsity.

Similarly, when an organisation starts to talk about itself, it too introduces the possibility that it could be being truthful or dishonest – it is the inevitable consequence of using language. For this reason, an organisation which does not talk about itself cannot be accused of hypocrisy: it has never articulated any values or standards and it cannot be judged against them. The idea of 'walking the talk' is less about providing concrete examples against which the truth of the 'talk' can be seen than it is about replacing words with actions. Truth and honesty are synonymous with action. When we talk more than we walk, we are being less 'truthful'; the more we act and the less we talk, the less we can be seen to be dishonest. 'Walking the talk' is about removing the distinction between language and action.

Seen from this perspective, you also have to question the value not just of strategy and planning but of any activity which involves translating the non-linguistic areas of an organisation (actions, culture, vision, and so on) into language. As soon as you do this, you create the possibility that what you write down does not match the actions of the organisation (that it is not 'truthful'). Moreover, the very act of writing it down divorces it from its practice (makes it false). It is a situation which is complicated by the flatter structure of today's businesses: people have more peers to talk to and more ways of communicating with them more quickly. There is simply more information (formal and informal) available on which people can base their judgement about the extent to which the organisation for which they work is telling the truth. And, in a world where almost every business claims to be a 'people business', disaffecting people by even unwittingly misleading them can have a significant impact on their morale and commitment.

It is catch-22: you cannot fix a problem without talking about it, but as soon as you talk about it, you cannot fix it.

Noting all these difficulties does not take us away from the practical issue. Organisations still need to get things done. For small companies, 'walking the talk' continues to offer a workable solution:

> Leadership helps make strategy a day-to-day reality. Unless top managers profess the religion of customer service, employees will view the most elegant strategy as just another easily ignored public relations campaign. Leaders of companies that produce outstanding service incessantly pronounce their beliefs and back up their words with actions.[13]

But as organisations become more and more complex, their actions need to be coordinated across different functions, different locations and different cultures, and this requires – one would suppose – better planning and more communication. Organisations also need to change: telling IBM, when it announced one of the biggest losses in corporate history, that it could not use its strategy to articulate where it wanted to go to because its staff would be cynical about it would have been a singularly unhelpful comment. How can organisations plan and change themselves if they cannot talk about it?

The conventional solution to this has been to improve communications, either by utilising the increasing number of informal links within an organisation (which can be very efficient communication networks) or by orchestrating sophisticated internal public relations campaigns. This is ironic, given that communication itself causes people to doubt the truth of what they are told: more communication can only make this situation worse. Recently, therefore, more companies have been looking at evolutionary – rather than radical – change. It seems that what the visions of successful companies have in common

> was that they took fundamentally new ideas and meshed them with some old beliefs about how to compete effectively, how to manage their employees, and about corporate finances. Such a fusion of old and new is realistic because it reflects the best assessment these executives could make about their own and their company's capabilities. Psychologically it made sense because it enabled them to retain as many beliefs from their cherished culture as possible, even as they fashioned new directions.[14]

Incremental change is easier to communicate because it relates more closely to the existing actions of an organisation: no leap of faith is required. When a change is described in terms of being a slight shift from the present state, it is more believable than a more dramatic change. This is not just because it seems realistic, but because the words used are closer to current actions: it is, effectively, a more 'truthful' statement. An alternative approach is not to talk about what you are planning to do at all, as in this example, taken from a handbook on company rescues:

> In all this communication the word *turnaround* should be avoided. What is needed is a program of action, not a promise. Turnaround talk at this stage casts the leadership in the role of would-be miracle men, and invites cynicism. *The label* turnaround *belongs on the finished product when the achievement is recognized and applauded by all.*[15]

As with so many occasions in this book, you start to wonder how this leaves consultants whose prime medium and *modus operandi* is, after all, language. When a team of consultants goes into an organisation, perhaps to review its organisational structure and suggest ways in which it can be made more efficient, their essential job is to translate what they find into language (to write a report). Unless they can do this they can neither analyse what they see nor make recommendations about it. Fundamentally, consultancy is based on the premise that you can both talk about a problem and fix it.

So how does this work? I would suggest that there are several reasons to account for this, each of which is relevant to organisations trying to grapple with the problems of creating, communicating and implementing strategic programmes of any sort.

First, it works because a consultant is an outsider: he or she cannot, and is not expected to, speak with the corporate voice. Indeed, consultancy has its own distinctive language, quite different to that used operationally by its clients. Second, when a consultant's report describes, for example, the drawbacks of an organisation's current organisational structure, it is in fact describing the consultant's view of reality, not directly reality itself. It is certainly not judged in terms of the accuracy of its description of reality, but its analysis and interpretation of the implications of that reality. A board of directors does not pay a consultant to come and tell them what is already apparent, but to tell them something new. In this context, 'newness' matters more than truth or falsity. Third and perhaps most important, a consultant's report is not intended to be immediately actionable. It is true that every self-respecting consultant will have included a final section headed 'Next Steps', but it is a rare client who would expect to go straight from these recommendations into execution: more usually, the report is followed by a validation exercise by the client's own staff to explore and plan its practical implementation.

Of course, this does not mean that every corporation should get consultants to write its strategic plan, but it does point to three useful lessons, each of which are worth considering in some detail:

- A strategy needs to be written in a language other than the organisation's own, as the latter will have an established framework for relating words to actions and which, for reasons explained above, is unlikely to be sympathetic to the relative merits of words against actions.
- It needs to be based on judgements and analysis, rather than description, as description will inevitably be judged against reality.

- Strategy and action are mutually exclusive. To have an impact on an organisation a strategic plan needs to be new – outside the organisation's existing frame of reference. If it tries to address the status quo its credibility will be judged against it. 'Having an impact' therefore involves setting an overall sense of direction: it does not include producing a detailed plan of actions which the organisation will follow.

USING A NEW LANGUAGE

Every organisation has its own language for talking about strategy: indeed it is possible to track the way in which the organisation is evolving by the words it uses to describe its strategy. If the language of strategy has any single source, it probably lies in classical warfare: our plans for expansion and competition remain heavily – if unconsciously – influenced by ideas of winning wars, beating our enemies, securing our position. However, management strategy first evolved a distinctive language of its own in the 1960s and was focused on the decisions taken by management and the types of analysis required to facilitate them: decision-making was the essential activity of management, because decisions led to actions. In keeping with this scientific perspective, a quasi-technical vocabulary appeared, with individual words or phrases acquiring specialist meanings: the division between 'strategy' and 'tactics' for instance; words like 'objectives', 'goals', 'planning horizon', 'operating policies'. What this vocabulary did was create a hierarchy: objectives came before goals, policies followed goals, and so on. Every part of the strategy – every word in the strategy dictionary – knew its place. It is hardly surprising therefore that, as this specialist vocabulary evolved, the images it incorporated reflected this rigid framework. Organisations were machines and engines: strategies were the user manual. By the mid-1980s, the analogies were architectural: strategies were the infrastructure, people the replaceable building blocks. The recognition – principally since the late 1980s – that the perimeters of organisations were no longer strong walls has given us a rather different vocabulary, drawn from biology and evolutionary theory: our strategic vocabulary is increasingly drawn from the natural, rather than the man-made, world: 'webs', 'porous boundaries', business 'ecosystems', and those words which implied a rigid framework or clear delineation are starting to fall from favour. If organisations are networked together, what relevance does the term 'industry' have, for example?

As noted above, we are also now moving into a phase of what could be termed 'conviction strategy', where beliefs and values matter more than analysis. Linked to this trend is the idea that successful organisations effectively go beyond language – they do not need to articulate their strategy because everyone already knows it. However, if we accept that strategy has its own, distinctive language, then this trend is just the most recent development in its evolution: rather than being precise and analytical, the language of strategy is becoming less specific – qualitative instead of quantitative. What matters most is that the language is different. If the language is different, then the organisation can do something different: if the language is that which the organisation already uses, then the strategy cannot change the status quo.

Clearly, the examples of a consultant submitting a report to a client or adopting the language of another profession (scientists, for example) both meet this criterion, but they are not the only way of doing so. The richest sources of new language often lie within an organisation, but among those people rarely asked to contribute to its strategy, such as people on the customer front line, new recruits, and many more. Who these people are precisely varies from organisation to organisation and is a function of the way in which an individual organisation manages language. Thus, to identify ways in which you can incorporate a new language into your own organisation's strategy, you first need to understand how language is managed across your organisation as a whole.

There are three main paradigms for the language environment.[16] First, language (in terms of both the words used and the meanings attributed to them) can be consistent and centrally controlled (usually by the founders of a business or long-serving executives). The people at the top establish the organisation's key words: the people below learn them, primarily through repetition. When it works well, this style of language management can have a visionary quality to it, inspiring rather than ordering those involved. When it works badly, it breeds a form of political correctness in which individuals try to curry favour with their superiors by mirroring the latter's language. Privatisation is, perhaps, a good illustration of both of these traits. In the second paradigm, there is no single, unified language for the organisation, but a series of sub-languages: the linguistic environment is characterised by diversity – a highly-diversified multinational corporation would be one example. Language management, so far as it exists in this context, is handled by small groups: changes emerge (often unintentionally), rather than being imposed from above. Ambiguity and chaos are the critical features of the third paradigm. Unlike the first two, each of which is based on some form of structure, the third paradigm has no static framework, but is continually changing, making it difficult to control from either the top or bottom of the organisation. Again, this state has both advantages and drawbacks: it can lead to an enormously flexible 'learning' organisation which is continually striving to change and improve what it does; less positively, it can also be an organisation in turmoil – one company being taken over by another, for instance, where many of the old cultural rules are being thrown out of the window.

Each of these paradigms presents its own challenges in terms of finding new ways to talk about strategy. The first is perhaps the easiest:

> Make no mistake: there are revolutionaries in your company . . . All too often, however, there is no process that lets those revolutionaries be heard. Their voices are muffled by the layers of cautious bureaucrats who separate them from senior managers.[17]

This is how the academic and futurologist Gary Hamel sees the process of 'strategising': 'to invite new voices into the strategy-making process, to encourage new perspectives, to start new conversations that span organizational boundaries'.[18] Language plays a key role in this process: when we think of an organisation, the model we tend to have in our minds is one in which those at the top talk, while those at the bottom do. Flatter organisations and the empowerment of those who work in them may mean that the distribution of talking and doing has changed, but I think most of us would still have difficulties in finding a company where this division has completely disappeared, especially when it is applied to internal processes such as developing a strategy. Taking the words from the bottom of your organisation, rather than from the top, reverses this state: it means that the doers start talking. The result is less suspicion about language (from the doers) and a different way of using language (for the talkers): both ways, it moves the goalposts in terms of what the strategy sounds like, making it more likely that the organisation as a whole will listen more effectively.

For the second type of organisation – where multiple corporate languages are distributed across autonomous business units – the situation is more problematic. Reversing the status quo (stressing a single, unified language) is an unworkable approach because it is already clear that no language which is perceived to be internal is capable of dominating the environment: any attempt to impose one language is doomed to failure. Similarly, writing one strategic plan for an organisation such as this will equally fail. In this environment, it is the individual team's or group's own languages which are important, as these create the framework within which any strategy will be judged: anything not written in that group's language is likely to be (at best) ignored and (at worst) rejected. The conventional solution is to get the buy-in of autonomous business units by creating a bottom-up strategy, but this approach has an inevitable cost in terms of the difficulty in going from these individual plans to an integrated plan for the organisation as a whole: anything larger in scope than a single business unit (investments, new ventures, and so on) becomes difficult, if not impossible. This is the kind of environment in which a 'new' language for strategy has to be precisely that – the organisation has to find some sort of external model, one which, because it is not 'owned' by any individual team, is less likely to be rejected by others.

Clearly, of the three language environments, the third type is by far the most difficult in which to develop a new language for strategy. In a situation where ambiguity reigns and no part of the organisation has any faith in the notion that strategy – or language – can be meaningful, there is very little in the way of a foundation on which to build. At least in the two other scenarios, strategy and language are perceived as having a role, even if a problematic one. The solution here is to start to spread the idea that strategy does not have a 'meaning' in the conventional sense. Habitually, we define 'meaning' – at least in business – as something which connects words to actions: we now need to go beyond this view, and see language as something which is not directly linked to action.

GOING BEYOND DESCRIPTION

The second problem with conventional strategies is that they spend too much time attempting – or, as we shall see, purporting – to describe reality. This takes many forms: analyses of external market conditions or internal opportunities and constraints, reviews of progress to date, or lists of action points for the near future. Either way, the basic premise remains the same, that it is possible to give an objective description of an organisation and its past or planned activities. Thus, whatever the structure of organisational language – centralised, devolved or chaotic – there remains some underlying thread of consistency in *interpreting* what that language means. After all, we traditionally distinguish an organisation from a group of independently functioning individuals by arguing that the former has some sort of collective being, whether this takes the form of shared goals or a uniform approach to interpreting data:

> A piece of data, a perception, a cognitive map is shared among managers who constitute the interpretation system. Passing a startling observation among members, or discussing a puzzling development, enables managers to converge on an approximate interpretation. Managers may not agree fully about their perceptions, but the thread of coherence among managers is what characterizes organizational interpretations.[19]

We assume that whatever the language used (it could be management jargon or specialist technical terms) we can cut through this to the reality behind. We assume that we can make the language invisible and irrelevant, and we can only do this because we also assume that there is a 'reality' to get through to and that that reality matters.

In case this is starting to sound a little existential, let us take a practical example. As a management consultant, one of the most common things you have to do on an assignment is to interview a series of people on the client's staff. You go from one office to another attempting to unravel the 'facts' behind a particular situation or problem. As you start to assemble a picture of what is happening in the organisation, you typically also identify a small number of examples which substantiate your argument. These become touchstones almost: points which you return to again and again because they encapsulate the key points you are trying to make. However, it is often the case that the descriptions your interviewees give you of these examples differ widely – and there is rarely any documentary evidence which can be brought to bear. Faced with this kind of problem, the last thing you do is describe the situation: to do so would invite people to criticise your portrayal. Instead, what you try and do is move the discussion on to a more theoretical plane where people will not be tempted to judge whether what you say is true or false.

I once had to look at the efficiency of a Customer Services department in a large utility. It was a large, centralised department run along rather old-fashioned lines: there was a long and rigid chain of command and, despite paying lip-service to ideas of employee empowerment, individual initiative was effectively frowned upon. During the course of talking to the people there, it became clear that a couple of years earlier one team had experimented with the kind of working practices I felt should be implemented more widely – more flexible working arrangements, closer cooperation with other departments (all of whom thought they had shifted responsibility for serving customers out of their areas into the official Customer Services team, even though they all dealt with customers in one way or another). It was not the stuff which revolutions are made of, but it did represent a significant change in the organisational culture – what had started as an assignment to cut costs and improve service quality was rapidly growing into a much more fundamental reassessment of the organisation's values. All of which made it particularly important that I understood why this small initiative, taken by one team of many, had not been followed up (the team leader had moved on to something else and the project effectively fizzled out). But, at the same time, it was impossible to construct a single, coherent picture of what actually happened from those involved. The views were in fact quite extreme: some people said that the experiment had been a great success, others a total failure – and of course there were no performance measurements or other information which could have been used to decide the case. To describe this incident would have been disastrous – it would simply have ended in a distracting argument about what actually happened. In fact, what actually happened was much less important than how the organisation had reacted to it, by not examining the advantages or drawbacks of the approach but consigning it to its collective mythology. In this context, describing reality would have held back the organisation because it had no single 'objective' framework for interpreting what happened: what could take it forward was taking such incidents out of the purely descriptive realm and instead analysing their implications for the organisation.

The lesson is that the more you describe something, the less likely it is that you will have any effect on your audience. Once you are into an argument about what actually happened in a particular situation the more you are essentially reinforcing the status quo. Put like this, it sounds like obvious advice, but it is extraordinary how may strategies end up being descriptive. All that happens when you do this – however tempting it is – is that you get bogged down in a discussion about whether your description is true or false, a discussion usually couched in terms of whether the strategy is 'realistic' or 'credible'. This distracts the organisation, rather than focusing it on the fundamental vision to be achieved.

The fundamental point is that we assume that a description is the nearest thing which we can do in words to action: if we can describe an action, then we are very close to doing it. This is why we tend to append lists of actions to any plan – in fact, it is our main justification for planning. This is fallacious: first, because it assumes that we can give an objective description of an action; and, second, because there is no connection between a description of an action and the action itself. No matter how objective we make our description, it does not change the probability that the action desired will take place. Objectivity does not exist, and we expend a great deal of time and money pretending that it does.

What matters is getting an organisation to go beyond its mental boundaries of what is true and false, right and wrong, credible and incredible. To stop people thinking whether a particular strategy is credible, it needs to be symbolic – visionary – rather than mundane. It may be that Collins and Porras's 'big, hairy, audacious goals' reflect this: because they are so ambitious, it is not easy to analyse them within a conventional true/false frame of reference. The aim of NASA was to put a man on the moon: the question of whether this was a credible or incredible goal did not significantly enter into the equation.

SEPARATING STRATEGY FROM ACTION

The two previous sections looked at the way in which conventional strategies and plans do not – indeed, cannot – lead directly to any action by the organisation concerned. To make a strategy more effective you need to move the goalposts either by providing a new frame of reference – a new language – or by avoiding the descriptive language in which the majority of strategies are written. However, it remains tempting – even while we bear these points in mind – still to think of a strategy as something which is designed to initiate actions: this tends to be how we measure the effectiveness of a strategy. And it is this which is the most fundamental thing that needs to change if we are to make the strategising process a really useful one – we need to change our assumption that the purpose of strategy is to lead to action. We looked earlier at all those factors which prevent this translation from words to actions taking place in practice (such as our cultural preference for doing rather than talking), but if we can move away from the starting assumption that this is what we want out of a strategy, we might find that strategies can be useful in other respects. In other words, we have created the environment in which a strategy can never be effective: to make a strategy succeed we need to redefine what 'effective' means. And the starting point to this is not seeing a strategy as a substitute for action, but as an 'action' in its own right.

I would suggest that a strategy can have a very different purpose, but one which is becoming increasingly pertinent in the business environment of the 1990s. A truly effective strategy is not concerned with initiating a detailed series of actions, it is not even concerned with being a credible way forward for an organisation: it is about creating a new language for an organisation.

Consider this problem. You are the chief executive of a large corporation. For the past two years you have been trying to implement a major cultural change programme to empower the people who work for you, devolving responsibility, promoting the idea of personal career development. While this programme has had the effect of increasing the sense of initiative and responsibility amongst many people and has reduced the numbers of people in middle management, it has been accompanied by a growing disenchantment with the collective organisation and its senior management. As you sit at your desk, you wonder why this should be: after all, you've tried to be as direct as possible about the increasingly competitive external environment and the need to remain as flexible as possible. You've stressed the need for individuals to take more control of their lives, and yet they murmur that you're being hypocritical. You do not think you could have been any more honest – so what's gone wrong?

I would suggest that it is your language which is the problem. As we saw before, when an organisation talks about itself, it itself introduces the idea that it can be hypocritical – it has created a framework in which the truth or falsity of its own statements can be judged. You, as chief executive of this fictitious corporation, have made this mistake: you have created a new business environment in which people feel more powerful as individuals but also more vulnerable (if they have to develop their own careers, then it is clear their organisation cannot be relied on to help them in this process). At the same time, nothing in the way in which your organisation communicates – or, indeed, in the substance of what it communicates – would allow your staff to have a realistic discussion about this situation. In essence, you are using an old language in a new situation, and this comes over as hypocritical to those involved:

> The new employer–employee contract boils down to this: The employer won't promise security, but it will support your individual development. If you think your company believes that, ask yourself the Hobbesian question: How comfortable would you be if you went to your boss, or if a key subordinate came to you, and candidly said, 'since lifetime employment is no more, I want to discuss how to change what I do here so that I will be more attractive to the next company that hires me'?[20]

This problem extends from the institutional (such as the example given above), to the individual:

> Take face-saving. To work, it must be unacknowledged. If you tell your subordinate Fred that you are saving his face, you have defeated your own purpose. What you do tell Fred is a fiction about the success of his own decision and a lie about your reasons for rescinding it. What's more, if Fred correctly senses the mixed message, he will almost certainly say nothing. The logic here . . . is unmistakable: send a mixed message ('Your decision was a good one, and I'm overruling it'); pretend it is not mixed ('You can be proud of your contribution'); make the mixed message and the pretence undiscussable ('I feel good about this outcome, and I'm sure that you do too'); and finally, make the undiscussability undiscussable ('Now that I've explained everything to your satisfaction, is there anything *else* you'd like to talk about?').[21]

The language which you have cannot accommodate the kind of cultural changes which you are trying to bring about: you therefore inevitably appear hypocritical – your people no longer believe what you say. To get round this, you need to find a new way of talking. For example, is one of the most common languages of strategy – that of war – really still appropriate in a world where co-evolution with other companies is superseding our conventional attitudes to competition?

Language, as we noted at the very beginning of this book, influences (some would say determines) the way in which we perceive the world. If we have to use an old word to describe a new product, then the newness of the product is automatically devalued. Our future is only what we can say it is. If our strategies are written in our existing language, then we will never do much more than we are currently doing, however much market analysis, SWOTs and performance measurements we include. Strategy is about doing things differently; and that includes talking differently.

Notes

1. Minztberg, 1994: 107.
2. Mintzberg, 1976: 49.
3. Mintzberg, 1994: 108.
4. A senior manager, quoted in Lorsch, 1986: 97.
5. Mintzberg, 1994: 112.
6. Katz and Kahn, 1966: 244–5.
7. Lorsch, 1986: 105.
8. Collins and Porras, 1996: 66.
9. Ibid.: 73.
10. Ibid.: 73–4.
11. Ibid.: 77.
12. Ibid.: 77.
13. Davidow and Uttal, 1990: 85.
14. Lorsch, 1986: 102.
15. Goodman, 1982: 35.
16. Based on the three paradigms of interpretive culture, in Meyerson and Martin, 1987.
17. Hamel, 1996: 74.
18. Ibid.: 82.
19. Daft and Weick, 1984: 285.
20. *Fortune*, 10 June 1996.
21. Argyris, 1994: 81.

16 Case Study 8: Coopers & Lybrand and Andersen Consulting

It would seem only appropriate to make management consultancy the final case study of this book. After all, these are the organisations most often blamed with coining new business jargon (and charging for it), as this comment from *The Daily Telegraph* illustrates:

> Just as there is a danger of being hoodwinked by specialist management jargon, so there is the possible hazard of being unjustly deterred when the racket of buzz-words conceals genuine benefit. A classic target for the sceptics might be corporate cultural change. What with its core values, mission statements, workshops and benchmarking, it sounds like classic consultant-speak degraded by psychobabble.[1]

Perhaps the most exciting or terrifying aspect of consultancy – depending on whether you are on the inside or the outside – is the extent to which it is possible to 'make things up', because as yet comparatively little investment is required to translate a project for one client into a methodology for several (although this may change in the future as management consultancy becomes increasingly technology-dependent). This is not to suggest that this 'making things up' is a worthless process – much of the benefit of consultancy work comes from the passing of concepts and ideas from client to client, and from industry to industry – but it does bring home the extent to which consultancy, of all service industries, is the most dependent on language. Nor should we forget that management consultancy continues to be one of the world's fastest growing industries, worth $23.2bn in 1995, up by more than 20 per cent on the previous year.[2]

LANGUAGE AND MANAGEMENT CONSULTANCY

Language has always been important in management consultancy, arguably more so than numbers, despite the fact that the majority of the leading consultancies evolved out of accountancy firms. Consultancy was, if you like, the response of those accounting firms to that shift within business from numbers to language – away from simple processes to complex relationships – described in the introduction to this book. Indeed, just as accountants could not exist without numbers, consultancies could not exist without words. When business made those evolutionary steps, in the first place, into standard accounting practices, and from there into language, it was acknowledging that it was possible to think about business in abstract terms. It was recognising that, although every business may be different and may still depend heavily on the skill of the individual who manages it, some parts of its operations are common to all commercial organisations and can be discussed independently of the specifics of the enterprise. If it were not possible to establish standard formulae for profits, or analyse the efficiency process (rather than just describe it), then accountancy and consultancy would not exist, as both are founded on this basic principle.

However, consultancies were not simply the beneficiaries of this trend: they also unquestionably contributed to it by disseminating new ways of doing and thinking, all of which were dependent on language. Consultancy services were language-based, not only because that was the nature of the market, but as a matter of survival: if consultancies could not sustain the notion that it was possible to have theories about business – that it was possible to talk about it – then consultancy itself had no future. Consultants have – quite literally – to keep talking. This explains why continental Europe has a rather different perception of consultancy than the USA and the UK, as individual skills continue to be more highly rated than business school techniques and management theory: business people in continental Europe talk about business (in abstract terms) far less and they therefore make less use of consultants.

Dependency on language brings its own opportunities and threats. Undoubtedly, it has made product development a low-cost affair: consultancies do not have to struggle with the massive investment decisions of, say, pharmaceutical companies – fortunately, given that the majority continue to be partnerships and have a poor track record in investment. Launching new services and products can be done comparatively quickly with little attendant risk; equally, it is possible to re-engineer a service which is performing badly or is poorly differentiated. The supply chain is minimal (the biggest headache being staffing of engagements) and the fixed cost base is usually low.

However, these relatively low barriers to entry mean that consultancies are continually vulnerable to being outmanoeuvred by their competitors (and it takes little capital outlay to become a competitor). In the late 1980s, much of this increasing competition came from niche consultancies; as such, it tended to be ignored by the big, established firms. That was until the recession of the early 1990s, which saw the first significant downturn in the consultancy market, certainly in the USA and Europe. More sophisticated clients, faced with an ever widening range of potential suppliers, could cherry-pick both a service and a price to suit them, and were unworried by the distinction between the big consultancy firms and their niche competitors: the playing field was suddenly level. Today, if anything, that playing field is now stacked against the big firms who tend to have higher fixed costs (and fee rates) and are often less responsive to market changes.

The situation is further complicated by the advent of the Internet which allows what in the early 1990s would have been regarded as core consulting know-how to be distributed globally at lower cost and with little if any direct contact with a traditional consultant. Such a service is offered by Ernst & Young in the USA: called ERNIE, it is intended to make consultancy ideas available to small businesses who would not typically be purchasers of traditional consulting.

The implications of these developments are enormous: as, at one end, their new services have to compete against lower-cost versions from niche consultancies and, at the other, their established services are commoditised into digital information, the established management consultancies are going to be under increasing pressure to generate more services more rapidly than ever. Put simply: they are going to have to talk more and more. We can already see signs of this in any book shop, as the number of business books proliferates at an exponential rate (this one being no exception to the general trend). The precise impact of these trends is twofold. First, management consultancies are going to need more to talk about, as the rate at which what they talk about is adopted by competitors increases; second, they are going to have to talk more effectively if they are to be able to gain and keep a client's attention long enough to sell something to them.

If these are two of the major challenges facing these organisations in the future, they are challenges with which they are poorly equipped to deal. Many of the big management consultancies have grown out of innumerable mergers of small accountancy firms: used to operating in a relatively circumscribed local environment, these organisations are poorly equipped (in terms both of technology and cultural preference) to communicate and share ideas. Historically, they relied on individual partners to grow parts of the business, building up their own teams of people and focusing on specific areas of the market. Firm-wide investment has been difficult because each partner can be pursuing his or her own agenda. Addressing the market on a sustained basis has been inhibited by a tendency for partners to 'own' clients and control access to them. The globalisation of their client base has meant that many of the biggest firms are now trying to change this situation, making substantial investments in knowledge-sharing software and engaging in extensive cultural change programmes. But the legacy persists and, in some cases, will take an entire generation of partners to eradicate. Consultancies, therefore, have tended to have no product development pipeline, as one of their manufacturing clients might have: they are unfamiliar with the process of taking ideas off the drawing board and converting them into services about which they can talk to clients.

Management consultancies have also been – at least until very recently – poor external communicators. Part of this stems from a cultural bias against advertising which, like sales, has for a long time been seen as a dirty word among the professional services community. Conventionally, the reputation of the firm would carry everything before it: information on its services would be spread by word of mouth, by personal recommendation from one client to another in some sort of late twentieth-century manifestation of an old school network. When you start to consider it, this was a fairly paradoxical stance: here were organisations whose existence was founded on talking but who refused to talk about what they did in anything other than the most low-key and informal terms. This, in fact, is the source of that paradox: what consultancies are suspicious of is 'formalised' language, whether it comes in the form of an advertising hoarding or a standard sales pitch. This is because they effectively want to have their cake and eat it: consultancies need business language to be able to analyse a client's problems in abstract, but they do not want a language which is so standardised that anyone can learn it – after all, their reputation and indeed identity as consultants would become questionable. There is, in effect, part of the consultancy service as it is generally conceived, which continues to be promoted as involving the skills and judgement of an experienced individual (and which justifies the high charge-out rates).

The need to communicate effectively with the external environment challenges this delicate ecological balance, as it requires communicating on a systematic basis rather than the traditional informal and individual model of operation. It almost certainly requires public relations campaigns; it may require advertising of some sort: what it will unavoidably require is using language on a more formal, proactive basis. It will also necessarily change the nature of that language. It will mean, for instance, that consultancy companies will have to evolve their own, distinctive images in the market-place – their own languages – partly as an entry barrier to would-be competitors, but also as a means of differentiating their services.

This case study looks at two of the world's leading management consultancies, Coopers & Lybrand and Andersen Consulting, each of whom – as we shall see – has a very different approach to these challenges and to language in general.

COOPERS & LYBRAND (UK)

Coopers & Lybrand is one of the world's largest professional services firm offering a comprehensive range of services including accountancy, business assurances, insolvency and corporate finance, as well as management consultancy.

Its organisational structure owes much to its history as a series of small accountancy firms in that many of its services continue to be run as quasi-autonomous businesses with the managing partners allowed considerable freedom and autonomy. More than a multi-dimensional matrix, the firm operates what can only be described as a very complex internal market. This goes far beyond the idea of assigning an internal account charge to professional staff working outside their own cost-centres, but is fundamentally based on the idea that all staff have to 'sell' their services to internal 'clients' (other, usually more senior, consultants): a good consultant is someone who keeps him or herself occupied on chargeable work by networking within the firm. At its best, like any market, this could be extraordinarily efficient. Among the consultants, all but the rawest new recruits know what their 'value-added' is to any assignment: in order to survive, everyone has had to learn what skills they bring to any particular party.

The advantages of this approach is that it promotes entrepreneurialism and flexibility among its staff: if a significant gap exists (clients who want a particular skill which the firm does not have), individuals will gravitate towards it, re-configuring their own skills to match what is required: this shift happens almost unplanned and very rapidly (because the market is efficient). However, this kind of structure also has its weaknesses. It creates an environment in which the internal language is always in danger of being sacrificed to external market forces, simply because people are more used to acting independently.

The language used by staff at Coopers & Lybrand reflects all of these things. One cannot call it a 'corporate language', because it is client-driven: indeed, if it did, it would be anathema to the firm's individualistic culture. Everyone has their own words for things; even where you find pockets of consistency – a team which provides a very specific service to a very homogeneous market sector, for example – these are almost always isolated from the mainstream firm. In fact, one might be tempted to argue that where such teams do evolve, the firm prefers to marginalise them because their 'monolingualism' threatens what is essentially a multilingual environment.

Once again, there are positive and negative implications to this. The upside is that new ideas and words can be adopted by individuals and relayed to clients very quickly. Indeed, as many of these new words and ideas originate with clients, the firm's linguistic flexibility (it learns to speak its clients' language) reinforces its desired market positioning – working, not just as another supplier, but in productive partnership with clients. But the downside is that it can be difficult to get ideas – words – more generally adopted.

The Coopers & Lybrand model, therefore, is one of linguistic heterogeneity. The challenge is how to marry the very successful side of this culture to an environment which is demanding more effective dialogue, internally and externally. How, for instance, could Coopers launch an advertising campaign, when it has not yet evolved a distinct language of its own (and can see good commercial justification not to)? How can it launch products which take more than the investment of a few individuals' time and energy, if it does not share a common language with which to describe and develop them? Moreover, how could it do either of these things, while still retaining what it values most – being able to respond quickly and effectively to the needs of individual clients? How can it learn a language of its own, while also being able to speak that of its clients?

ANDERSEN CONSULTING

The approach adopted by Andersen Consulting is almost the complete opposite to that of Coopers & Lybrand, although it too has its own strengths and weaknesses.

Like its rival, Andersen Consulting is a global practice: it has more than 30 000 employees operating in about fifty countries. But unlike Coopers & Lybrand, the parent firm, Arthur Andersen, has always pursued what it terms a 'one-firm concept'. The mere fact that it can sum up its strategy in a single term like this tells us a great deal about its linguistic homogeneity. Comments made by Martin Vandersteen (who was responsible for running the London office's consulting business between 1973 and 1986) in a 1991 interview confirms this sense of a single origin:

> our consultancy work grew out of the Arthur Andersen blue book which was a management letter which we did as part of our accountancy service. It was operational recommendations. The consultancy business was originally called Administrative service.[3]

The 'one-firm' idea has been reinforced by Andersen's positioning and the markets it has chosen to address: much of its consulting work has been focused around information technology, allowing it to concentrate on certain types of clients and to standardise some aspects of its staff training. It has been further reinforced by the firm's move into the outsourcing market (whether in the more traditional form of IS services or, more recently, the financial departments of organisations such as Sears): taking on similar work for a variety of clients also has reinforced the relative homogeneity of the firm's services.

It is therefore unsurprising that Andersen Consulting feels more comfortable with systematic communication than many of its competitors. Accustomed to the need for integration, it has invested heavily and over a long period in the technology and culture which promotes knowledge-sharing (it has, for instance, for some time been a major user of Lotus Notes). And it is equally unsurprising that it is the only consultancy in the UK to have initiated a sustained external communications campaign, including advertising hoardings, with the straplines 'Metamorphosis in a world of change' and latterly 'What shape is your business in?', and television advertisements.

But these advertisements also illustrate how the firm uses language and the trade-offs this approach necessarily involves. The words in the advertisements have a symbolic rather than literal meaning. Taken at face value, neither of the straplines actually mean anything, and this – I would suggest – is part of the point. The impact of the advertisements comes in two ways: first, from the repetition of these phrases in all the advertising literature over a sustained period of time; and second, from the fact that a consultancy company is advertising on this unprecedented basis. It does not come from the meaning of the words used, as it might have done if, for example, the firm had been detailing a particular service. These words are not intended to be descriptive, nor are they designed to make anyone – even clients – do anything specific. They are not even really aimed at raising market awareness of Andersen Consulting: hoarding advertisements by the sides of roads would be a rather indiscriminate means of achieving this. What they do achieve is to position Andersen Consulting as being in control of the language environment. Because it has been the first consultancy firm to advertise in this fashion, Andersen Consulting has set the pace for its competitors: the use of the word 'change' for instance, helps to establish the firm's preeminence in change management for businesses.

But taking the high ground in this way does have a cost. Once it has established such strong associations in the mind of clients, it can be difficult to alter them. Once change management slipped off the corporate agenda, Andersen Consulting was in danger of being linked to an outmoded service (and the switch to 'What shape is your business in?' can be seen as a response both to this specific problem and as a means of moving the firm's positioning on to an even more strategic plain).

A monolithic language culture can also inhibit innovation and flexibility: that new words, like new ideas, have to be officially sanctioned to gain acceptance inevitably means that fewer new words appear than in Coopers & Lybrand, although those that do become assimilated into the organisation more comprehensively.

Notes

1. 19 December 1994: p. 28.
2. The Gartner Group; *Management Consultant International*, June 1996.
3. Quoted in Rassam and Oates, 1991: 76.

Part VII

Conclusion

17 Managing Language for Competitive Advantage

The aim of this book has been to raise awareness of the important and complex role which language plays in business. Its primary focus, therefore, has been to analyse that role – showing where it creates opportunities or throws up threats – and to look at how individual companies have recognised and responded to these challenges. While it has been possible, as part of this, to draw together some conclusions about the practical implications for business, it would be unsatisfactory to stop there without bringing together these thoughts on how organisations can understand the part that language plays in their own environments and how they can manage it to their advantage.

Developing a blueprint for effective language management has three essential steps, each of which we will consider in detail.

- analysing the external language environment;
- analysing the internal language environment; and
- using language for competitive advantage.

ANALYSING THE EXTERNAL LANGUAGE ENVIRONMENT

The starting point for any organisation has to be to evaluate the role that language plays in its external environment.

We have already seen that it is possible to think about customer service in terms of the decisions taken (usually unconsciously) by an organisation about the kind of dialogue it wants to have with its customers, based on the economics of delivering the service to a customer (scheduling the appointments of a washing machine repairman or a doctor), placed against the marginal benefit gained from changing the nature of that dialogue (explaining to a customer why something has broken down is unlikely to improve the relationship between the washing machine company and a customer, but it may improve that between a doctor and a patient). However, it is equally important to take other aspects of the external environment – notably market structure and competition – into account, and it is perfectly possible – indeed, wholly appropriate – to analyse the language environment just as we would analyse any other external market.

First of all, what do we mean by the 'language environment'?

Every organisation operates in a language environment: engineering companies inhabit a world where engineering terms are common; high-tech companies use high-tech languages. Challenging or crossing the boundaries between such languages can be difficult, as the experience of privatised companies shows. At any given time certain words are likely to be dominant. 'Quality', for example, was one of the watchwords of the 1980s and it was rare to find an advertisement for a product or a company which did not make some reference to it then, although it now seems to be fading from view.

Not all language environments are the same; nor does an individual environment necessarily stay the same over time. As with any other form of market, the structure of the language market may be dominated by just one or a small number of organisations, or it may be highly fragmented with no single organisation dominant. Where one or a small number of organisations dominates, language can act like a brand. The phrase 'It's the real thing', for instance, implies not just that Coca-Cola is the original product of this type, but also that other products can only ever be imitations (because they are not 'real'): no other words (taste, price, and so on) are relevant here, the term 'the real thing' is being used to control the language environment.

However, such language environments can be very unpredictable. Because language requires no substantial or long-term investment (although the Coca-Cola example shows that the language environment is not completely without barriers to entry), market dominance can change rapidly. Having the biggest share in your market today does not guarantee that you will still have it tomorrow. Indeed, once you have started to lose this control, it can be immensely difficult to regain it.

Recent competition between supermarket chains in the UK provides an excellent illustration of a language environment in practice. Unlike many continental European countries, a small number of chains (J. Sainsbury, Tesco, Safeway and Asda) dominate the grocery sales market. Recent government tightening of planning regulations has meant that the traditional expansion strategy of these companies

– opening large out-of-town stores to encourage consumers away from the relatively few remaining high-street grocery stores – is no longer an option. The only way of maintaining the growth to which their shareholders have become accustomed has been to steal customers from each other, for instance through loyalty schemes. In 1995, the long-standing leader in terms of market share, J. Sainsbury, slipped to the number two position behind its arch-rival, Tesco. Surveying the language used both about and by these two companies over the past five years tells a similar story.

Back in 1992, the words associated with J. Sainsbury were mainly positive: the press referred to the chain's 'staggering statistics', its 'inexorable' growth and its 'pre-eminent' position'. Its financial performance was attributed to the fact that it had remained close to its core competencies and historical roots: it was 'a model of consistency' and 'stable'. The qualities it exhibited as an organisation reinforced this image: it 'concentrated', and was 'committed' and 'unremitting'. 'Everything we do at J. Sainsbury is evolutionary', summed up one director in an interview.[1] By contrast, its rivals Tesco and Asda were described respectively as 'trying to close the gap' and 'ageing'. But not all the press was good: there was a hint that J. Sainsbury's single-mindedness equated to 'blandness' in some areas.

By 1995, the language environment had changed markedly. Words which had had positive connotations three years earlier now had negative implications. The key change was that all the terms relating to J. Sainsbury's stability, commitment and consistency now implied that the company was 'jammed', 'bureaucratic' and 'unwilling to change'. It was now Tesco's turn to set the linguistic pace: 'fast', 'flair' and 'experimenting' were just some of the words associated with it. Similarly, Asda was seen as 'fast' and 'active'. Many of the words connected with Tesco and Asda imply speed and movement, in contrast to J. Sainsbury which was 'too slow', but what is important to notice about this is not that the values ascribed to the latter had changed fundamentally, but that they were no longer the 'right' values: thus, consistency had become rigidity. J. Sainsbury was still using the same words in 1995 as it had in 1992, but they were no longer the right words: they had been superseded by Tesco's new vocabulary. Indicative of its new position as second in terms of market share, many of the words connected with J. Sainsbury imply some degree of secondary relationship as though the company is measured against standards other than its own ('reassert', 'copied', 'catching up', 'wrest back', 'lacked', 'clawed back'). By contrast, those associated with Tesco included 'first', 'top', 'initiative' and 'pushing'.

This example shows just how quickly the language environment can change. Controlling that environment is all about ensuring that the words which describe your organisation are those which become the standards for the market in which you operate. It is not much good excelling at something – as J. Sainsbury excelled at being consistent – if that which is excellent is no longer seen as important (and, again, the word 'quality' in advertisements is another example of this). To dominate the environment, you need to get other people to use your language, not be forced to use another's.

Therefore, to take advantage of language in your markets, you need to understand two issues:

- how important is language in your market?
- who controls it?

The role played by language varies from market to market. It grows in significance as the service component grows, because we need to interact with customers more. It also grows as competition intensifies, because we have to work harder internally and externally to respond. But across the world, the importance of language is also generally increasing because business itself is changing: manufacturing plants are spread further; customers are more knowledgeable and demanding; processes are increasingly carried out by computers. In effect, people need to talk more and do less.

To evaluate how important language is in your market and who controls it, you need to look at the four main interfaces between your organisation and the outside world: your customers, your stakeholders, your suppliers and your competitors. For each of these groups you need to look at not just the means and frequency of communication, but also the type of language used:

- How often do you communicate with each group (i.e. customer, stakeholder, supplier or competitor)? In each case, what is the medium of communication and how long does it last?

- What information do you give each group? What do they give you? Do you encourage these groups to respond and, if so, how do you do this?
- What are the most common words and phrases with which these groups describe your products or services? Are they the same across all four groups, or do they vary? Do they match those that you use?

The most effective way of illustrating this is to take a hypothetical example.

Suppose you are a sizeable clearing bank. Changes in your market over the past few years mean that you have to communicate more than in the past: you are probably selling a much wider range of financial products; your customers have become more exacting in terms of the service they want; you may have outsourced a host of administrative functions which you no longer regard as your core activities; you are probably at the receiving end of increasingly extensive and complex regulation. Plotting the relative frequency of communication and its information content would start to highlight differences across these four interfaces, especially when we start to compare the extent and type of communication *from* the bank with that *to* the bank. What this might show – to take a very simple illustration – is that the bank's relationship with its customers is heavily information-dependent, but that the overwhelming proportion of information flow is from the bank. It might also show that communication to and from the bank's suppliers was imbalanced: receiving more information from its suppliers than it is sending to them might imply that the bank was not getting the most from its supplier relationships (Figures 17.1 and 17.2 overleaf).

These findings indicate the bank's own understanding of communication within its immediate environment, but to be truly useful they need to be compared to the language used with each of the four groups, in order to identify inconsistencies between how communication is perceived and the way in which language is actually used. Scanning press-cuttings and competitors' advertising over a period of time will reveal the public language environment: reviewing correspondence with customers and suppliers and market research will reveal the private. You should be looking for several things:

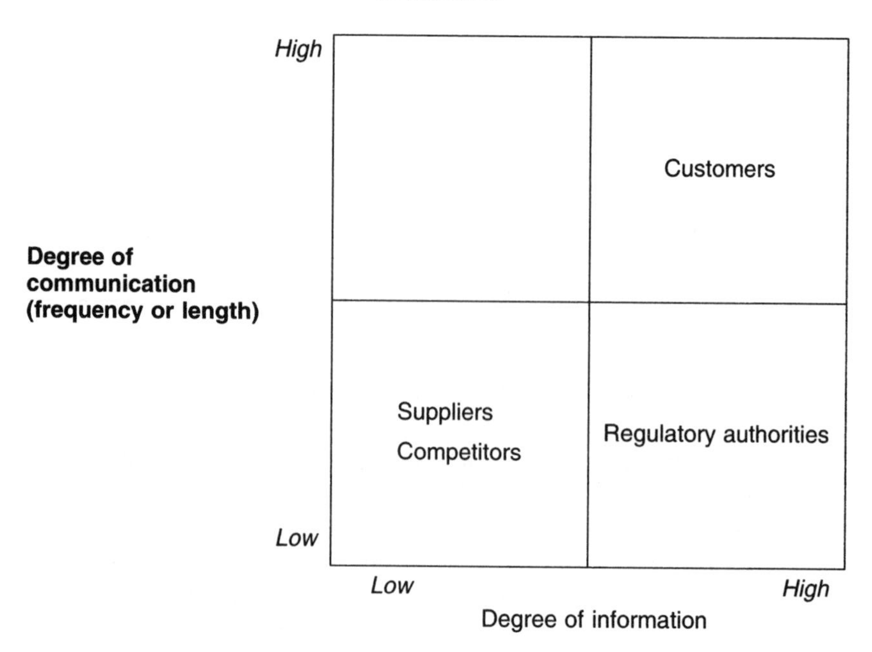

Fig. 17.1 *Communication and information from the bank*

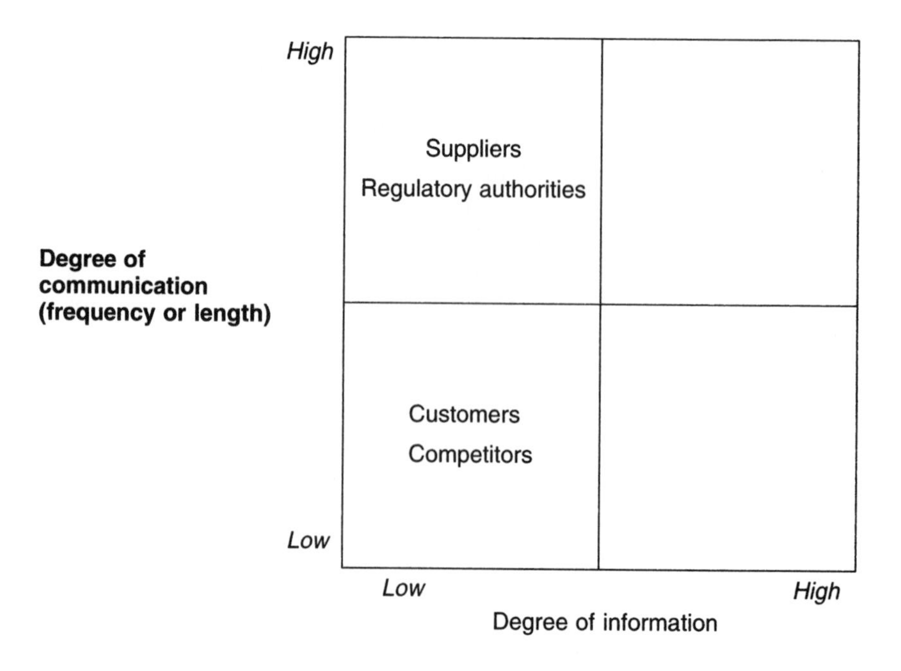

Fig. 17.2 *Communication and information to the bank*

- Are there any words which occur particularly frequently? What kind of words are these (do they describe something or are they active words (e.g. verbs); are they technical terms or common words; do they appear 'traditional' or are they new words)?
- How are these words defined (that is, is there any consistent definition or is it likely that everyone who uses them has a slightly different interpretation; are they defined by reference to their opposite qualities, rather than as themselves)?
- Who uses these words – your competitors or your customers? If you look at this over the past couple of years, can you see any trends (for example, do your competitors use words after your customers have used them, or is the reverse true)?
- Can you calculate how quickly customers or competitors adopt a particular word? If so, can you pinpoint those factors which either increase or decrease the take-up rate?
- Still looking retrospectively, can you identify any sources for the words which have become prominent (most importantly, do they come from within your industry or from outside sources?)

Let us again take banks as a simple illustration.

In the 1970s, banks were still associated with the image they had built up over the previous decades of financial propriety and stability: they were symbols of paternalistic authority, telling their customers what to do for their own good. A combination of many factors since then (from increased competition to new technology) has meant that this traditional image has been discarded in favour of one which is more accessible and street-wise. In the first place, this was expressed in terms of flexibility (telephone banking, access to a wider range of complementary financial services not historically offered by banks), but latterly this has metamorphosed into realising their customers' dreams (recent advertisements focus on individuals setting up their own companies or moving to a better quality of life outside the city).

Apparently, the banks have performed a complete U-turn: from telling their customers what to do, they have become – in the words of their own advertising – 'the listening bank' and 'the bank which likes to say "yes"'. The role of language therefore seems to have changed radically in this sector since the 1970s: the language of the banks has been replaced by that of their customers. In the 1970s, asking the kinds of questions listed above would have shown the banks to be very much in control of their language environment: they were defining the kind of service people wanted – and this was both explicit and quite deliberate: it was the banks, not their customers, who were best qualified to judge what services were required. The language of customers was important only in so far as it indicated the extent to which customers subscribed to the banks' agendas – that is, they did what they were told. Nowadays, the banks would probably argue that it is the language of customers which is most important – that is why so much air-time in advertisements is given over to what customers – not the bank – think and say.

Of course, we should not accept this shift totally at face value: the 'customers' are actors, and what they say is prescripted by the banks and their advertising agents. To that extent, the banks have chosen not to relinquish control of their operations. To some degree, they are still telling their customers what to do (and, indeed, say): for example, they want their customers to have aspirations and ambitions which the bank can service (and charge for). But despite this, the point remains that the words now being used in relation to banking are less authoritarian than used to be the case: even in the late 1980s, when 'flexibility' was top of the corporate agenda, this was a word which was defined by the banks (for instance, in terms of longer opening hours, telephone banking, different types of loan arrangements). The fact that the vocabulary now being used is that of the ordinary person, not the bank, remains a significant change, not least because it opens up the possibility that customers will have a more genuine 'say' in the future.

By looking at the questions listed above, a bank – or any other company – could begin to explore these ideas and perhaps challenge some of its basic assumptions. Exploring in detail how it uses language – for instance, the tension between empowering its customers and retaining operational control – would allow the bank to understand where it is making trade-offs and where it may be missing opportunities. It could also show the bank how to segment its use of language most effectively: there are likely to be some areas where – to take an example – the language of customers matters more than others; for some types of service (the high-risk or the very technical), the bank's experienced voice may far outweigh that of its inexperienced customers.

However, this kind of analysis represents only one side of the equation. Understanding the external language environment and increasing the effectiveness with which you exploit it will not succeed unless you have also understood your internal language environment.

ANALYSING YOUR INTERNAL LANGUAGE ENVIRONMENT

Analysing your internal language has one overriding benefit: it allows you to understand the relationship between language and action in your organisation.

This is important for two reasons. First, it is fundamental to understanding how you manage effectively. After all – at the most simplistic level – how can you get people (whether they are colleagues, employees or customers) to do the things you want without talking or writing to them at some point? Second, as has been noted several times in this book, business is becoming increasingly language-dependent. The direct link between language and action (on which management is predicated) is becoming longer and more circuitous: more and more, the distinction between the two is starting to dissolve as language becomes an action in its own right.

In the historic model of business, the boss told the workers what to do: trouble only occurred when the workers did not do what was asked. It was to this way of working that Frederick Taylor addressed his 'science of shovelling': the role of the manager was to work out the optimum model of shovelling and to tell the workers (who could not work this out for themselves) what to do. Indeed, this style has always been the Achilles heel of management given that we are culturally biased against language; associating management with talking rather than action inevitably raised the question of what managers actually do. What managers did was control the organisation. Language was about giving orders: business was run along semi-military lines; seniority was defined in terms of distance from action. The chief executive would tell someone who would tell someone who would tell someone. . . . Only the most junior people actually did things.

This paradigm has changed. Control has given way to coordination; hierarchies have flattened; routine clerical work has been automated. What we are left with is more people having to talk more to get their work done. Take, for example, the idea of matrix management. A multinational manufacturing company might choose to complement its established country-based reporting system with a transnational product-based structure which would ensure, say, that global resources are managed more effectively. In the old, vertical structure, the link between language and action was straightforward – the local managing director told someone to do something and this message was communicated down the line until somebody actually did it. Assuming that the local company was a reasonably effective and cohesive business unit, there was little danger that this message would be mistranslated: people tended to get what they asked for. But with the new structure, this changes: there are two lines down which messages can be sent or interpreted and it is relatively easy for them to get out of step. What this means in practice is that what gets done is not always what was supposed to be done. As organisations grow in size and complexity, this problem intensifies. Hence the extent to which such companies are increasingly stressing internal and external communications programmes.

So how do you understand how language fits into your organisation? A starting point is anecdotal evidence. The next time you come to the end of a meeting, you might like to tick off the items on the following mental checklist.

- What proportion of the discussion was spent talking about what (relaying information formally or informally, analysing the information, deciding what to do)?
- Did people repeat words used generally throughout your organisation, or were they using either new words or words which were specific to the particular meeting or subject?
- Did any words (and, if so, which?) become prominent in the discussion – in the sense that they seemed to touch a general nerve or sum up a particular point or mood?
- When common words appeared, did everyone appear to have the same definition or was there some potential for confusion?
- Who used what words? Did the people who led the discussion also set the agenda in terms of the language used?

Clearly, you need to be cautious with this. This checklist is not an evaluation (under the guise of something else) of how effectively the meeting was managed: none of the above items are positive or negative. Some organisations – and newly formed, entrepreneurial companies are especially prone to this – will spend a high proportion of the meeting time on gossip. Gossip may be the way in which the people involved work out what is important: no one may ever say 'do that', but they may come out of the meeting knowing what they should be doing next. An example would be a group of people chatting about a colleague who has recently been promoted: it is likely that everyone would have their own thoughts on why he or she succeeded. Many of the thoughts will be adopted by those present because they are likely to see it – consciously or unconsciously – as a pattern for advancing their own careers: gossip, as much as straight-talking, can lead to action.

Rather, the purpose of this checklist is to determine how language is used within your organisation and whether there is potential to use it more effectively.

In thinking about the words used, you should try and categorise them. Were they, for example, formal or informal words? Was the conversation dominated by verbs (words of action) or adjectives (words of description)? Were any of the words new (implying that a new idea was being tabled) or imported from another company (a possible sign of competitive pressure and a 'me too' culture)? Does the company have any special words which it uses for its own purposes? We have seen before how naval rankings and other related terms create a 'language' which is specific to the navy, but the same trait is evident in many organisations. Such words may be part of an organisation-wide language (repeated, for instance, in official communications) or part of a subculture – a team within a team which uses language both to make itself more effective and to establish boundaries between itself and outsiders. Do you have a corporate language, or are you all speaking your own individual 'dialects'? Are your colleagues ever – literally – lost for words? Or what concepts does your organisation have problems articulating: can you talk about one subject more easily than another? Do 'dominant' words emerge during a discussion – that is, a word spoken by one person which somehow seems to sum up the feelings of those present or the key points of a particular issue, and which is then repeated by the other people present? And how quickly are such words picked up? Finally, you need to understand how important language is in your organisation. Some organisations rely on images, rather than words, to communicate: their presentations are mostly graphics and charts – text is kept to a minimum. Others use key words to create a framework – the way that British Airways repeats words like 'serve' and 'service' or American Express uses 'deserve', and the way that Xerox has chosen to rename itself 'The Document Company'. What is yours?

MANAGING LANGUAGE FOR COMPETITIVE ADVANTAGE

Understanding and comparing your internal and external language environments are necessary precursors to being able to exploit them. But how, then, do you set out to take control of your language environment?

Let us take a hypothetical scenario in which the market is dominated by a small number of big companies. The first thing you have to do is learn your competitors' language, not because you want to use it, but because doing this will highlight its most important aspects and demonstrate how your rivals have built and now maintain their advantage.

Let us suppose that you are a small law partnership operating in a market dominated by a handful of very large firms. Let us also suppose that your competitors have recently consolidated their hold by building up their strengths around the idea of 'knowledge'. Knowledge is a term which first achieved prominence in the 1980s when it became clear that one of the major challenges facing organisations was transforming the wealth of data produced by the expensive computer systems installed over the previous two decades into usable information. With such volumes of data now available, a key source of competitive advantage was seen to be the way in which organisations changed processes and lowered internal barriers in order to make the best use of this opportunity: by sharing information, organisations could convert it into knowledge. 'Knowledge' is in effect the gold which organisations – rather like sixteenth-century alchemists – are trying to distil from the raw material of their organisation. And there are an increasing number of examples of companies which have succeeded in putting it to good use. McDonald's, for example, can print out the number of calories of a specific meal on the till receipt, as information for the health-conscious among its customers.

Thus, to use 'knowledge' as the focal point for legal services carries a lot of associations with it: as the concept is still relatively new, it positions an organisation as innovative and leading-edge. Moreover, it implies that knowledge is the key component of any legal service provided, that is, that it is the expertise and collective skills of the firm which matter, not other factors (long-term relationships with clients, efficiency of service, a regional network, and so on). We could call this approach 'high-concept' marketing – a term more usually associated with Hollywood blockbusters in which style and special effects are everything and plot and character are comparatively irrelevant. In language terms, the word 'knowledge' represents the high ground, the point of strategic differentiation between the leading law firms and the rest: but it is also a relatively new word (in its business usage) which is therefore difficult to define. Meaning (like character and plot) is less important than the image it projects and the associations it carries.

But what appears to be a sign of strength may also be a point of weakness. Precisely because the application of knowledge in business is still in its infancy and because examples of its practical use, although growing, are comparatively scarce, using knowledge as a point of differentiation is vulnerable to a variety of counter-attacks. Of these, perhaps the most obvious would be to invent a concept which would supersede knowledge – because there is as yet little substance behind the idea of knowledge, it would be fairly easy to develop and launch on to the market another concept (with no more substance than knowledge itself). In fact, this is already happening: 'knowledge' is just one step on an evolutionary path which began (in the 1970s) with 'data', metamorphosed into 'information' in the 1980s, became 'knowledge' in the early 1990s and looks set to change again (into 'wisdom') by 2000. All one needs to do to compete with the legal firm which differentiates itself around the concept of knowledge is to use the idea of wisdom as the key point of differentiation as this, because it is alleged to be higher up on an evolutionary scale, makes knowledge appear obsolete, even as the latter becomes fully established (indeed, *before* it is fully established).

And in case we are tempted to think that a strategy like this is pure fantasy, we should remember how CSC Index, a US-based management consultancy, spent about $200 000 a week buying (via an intermediary) copies of its own book, *The Discipline of Market Leaders*, to keep it in the *New York Times* best-seller lists in 1995.

Another management book, *Re-engineering the Corporation*, had previously helped the company double in size.[2]

Of course, saying 'all one needs to do' implies that competing in this fashion is a simple and straightforward process. In practice, there are two fundamental (and potentially complex) parts to this.

First, you have to select the right 'high-concept' term with which to compete. In our example, 'wisdom' has the advantage that it has already been positioned as a more sophisticated version of knowledge – it is supposedly the nirvana to which leading-edge organisations are aspiring. Using 'wisdom', therefore, has the advantage of adopting a relatively established term and idea. However, in many cases the next evolutionary step will be less obvious and therefore needs to be chosen with care: the scrap-heaps of business are littered with concepts which went – to use the Boston Group matrix – from being question marks to dogs, without the intervening periods of star and cash cow status. Concepts succeed when the words used to describe them have strong positive associations (often with science rather than management theory, or with highly-thought-of-organisations). This is because concepts are most effective when they are symbolic rather than literal. The word 'knowledge' has no precise meaning in business but it sums up a whole host of ideas which businesses find attractive. Its power in business comes from the word itself (and these associations), not because it is designed to initiate a specific action. This is not to argue that 'knowledge' – or indeed any high-concept business term – is content-free (that it is all image and no substance MBA-speak), as many would: it is instead to argue that our old ideas of language (that it has a meaning and is aimed at making something happen, or someone do something) have no relevance here. 'Knowledge' is an action in its own right.

But identifying a high-concept idea like this would be pointless if you did not also follow it through. Thus, the second part to competing on this basis is to ensure that you promote the concept consistently and continuously. You need to repeat your words over and over again until it becomes impossible to talk about the services you offer – or, indeed, your industry as a whole – without using this same terminology. Ultimately, you have to reach the point at which the words you use become the way the customer describes the service. This is, after all, only the extension of something which companies have been doing for decades: the fact that we can use 'xerox' when we talk about photocopying, or 'hoover' when we mean vacuum, are some testimony to the way in which words can be used by companies to try and take control of a new idea or market. Hence, the importance of brand names – ground beef in a bun is a McDonald's as much as a hamburger: the only difference is that you cannot eat a McDonald's at Burger King. And it is consistency which matters here – not any notion of backing up words with actions, 'walking the talk'. In a world where the relationship between action and language is becoming more remote – we can buy goods from factories we never see, sold in shopping malls we never go to, sold by people we never meet – the old idea that actions speak louder than words is fast becoming irrelevant. Consistency is our substitute for action: if any organisation is consistent in what it says publicly, then it cannot be being deceptive because we have nothing to judge it against except its own words.

The commercial battles of the future will not be won on the drawing board or in the customer focus group, or even in the boardroom. In a business environment which we thought was just uncertain, but which we now increasingly recognise is profoundly complex and chaotic, that much we know. What we also know is that we will need new ways to compete, new strategies and new skills. In such a world, it does not seem too far-fetched to assert that one of the ways in which those battles may be won is through high-concept ideas which bear little relation to what we think of as marketing today.

The battles of the future will be won by the way we use language.

Notes

1. Interview with Ian Coull, quoted in *Chartered Surveyor Weekly*, May 1992.
2. Exposed in *Business Week*, 7 August 1995.

Bibliography

Allen, Thomas J. (1977) *Managing the Flow of Technology*, Cambridge, Mass: MIT Press.

Anthony, Peter and Mike Reed (1995) 'Public Service and Private Profit: The Managerial Limits to Enterprise', in *Privatisation and the Welfare State*, edited by Philip Morgan, Aldershot: Dartmouth, 45–59.

Argyle, Michael (1981) 'Inter-Cultural Communication', in *Social Skills and Work*, edited by Michael Argyle, London: Methuen, 172–94.

Argyris, Chris (1994) 'Good Communication that Blocks Learning', *Harvard Business Review*, 72, 77–85.

Bagdikian, Ben H. (1975) *The Information Machines: Their Impact on Men and the Media*, New York: Harper.

Baker, Michael J. (ed.) (1991) *The Marketing Book*, Oxford: Butterworth-Heinemann.

Barsoux, Jean-Louis. (1993) *Funny Business: Humour, Management and Business Culture*, London: Cassell.

Bartlett, Christoper A. and Sumantra Ghoshal (1989) *Managing Across Borders: The Transnational Solution*, London: Century.

Bates, A. (1977) 'Ahead – The Retrenchant Era', *Journal of Retailing*, 29–45.

Benlow, David and Ian Scott (1983) *Fighting Privatisation: The Struggle for Wandsworth*, NUPE/IWC Pamphlet.

Berger, Pete and Thomas Luckmann (1967) *The Social Construction of Reality*, Harmondsworth: Penguin.

Bernstein, David (1985) *Company Image and Reality: A Critique of Corporate Communications*, London: Holt, Rinehart & Winston.

Bickley, Verner C. (1982) 'Language as the Bridge', in *Cultures in Contact*, edited by Stephen Bochner, Oxford: Pergamon, 99–125.

Birkle, John R. and Ronald Yearsley (1976) *Computer Applications in Management*, London: Associated Business Programmes.

Bivins, Thomas (1991) *Handbook for Public Relations Writing*, Lincolnwood, Ill.: NTC Business Books.

Boguslaw, Robert (1965) *The New Utopians*, Englewood Cliffs, NJ: Prentice-Hall.

Bono, E. de (1979) *Wordpower*, Harmondsworth: Penguin.

Brooke, Michael Z. (1984) *Centralization and Autonomy*, London: Holt, Rinehart & Winston.

—— (1986) *International Management: A Review of Strategies and Operations*, London: Hutchinson.

—— and H. Lee Remmers (1977) *The International Firm: A Study of Management across Frontiers – Trade and Investment*, London: Pitman.

Brown, Andrew (1989) *Customer Care Management*, London: Heinemann.

Brunsson, Nils (1989) *The Organization of Hypocrisy: Talk, Decisions and Actions in Organizations*, Chichester: John Wiley.

Bryson, G. D. (1961) *American Management Abroad*, New York: Harper.

Burns, A. (1984) *New Information Technology*, Chichester: Horwood.

Chandra, Jeff and Andrew Kakabadse (1985) *Privatisation of the NHS*, Aldershot: Gower.

Chapman, C. (1990) *Selling the Family Silver: Has Privatization Worked?*, London: Hutchinson.

Chisholm, Cecil (1955) *Communications in Industry*, London: Business Publications.

Clegg, Stewart R. (1974) *Power, Rule and Domination*, London: Routledge.

—— (1987) 'The Language of Power and the Power of Language', *Organization Studies*, 8/1, 60–70.

—— (1989) *Frameworks of Power*, London: Sage.

Cleveland, Harlan G., Gerard J. Mangone and John Adams (1960) *The Overseas Americans*, New York: McGraw-Hill.

Clutterbuck, David, Susan Kernaghan and Deborah Snow (1991) *Going Private: Privatisation Around the World*, London: Mercury Books.

Collet, Peter (1982) 'Meetings and Misunderstandings', in *Cultures in Contact*, edited by Stephen Bochner, Oxford: Pergamon, 81–98.

Collins, James C. and Jerry I. Porras (1996) 'Building Your Company's Vision', *Harvard Business Review*, 74, 65–77.

Condon, J.C. (1966) *Semantics and Communication*, New York: Macmillan.

Daft, Richard L. and Karl E. Weick (1984) 'Toward a Model of Organizations as Interpretation Systems', *Academy of Management Review*, Vol. 9, Issue 2, 284–95.

Davidow, William H. and Bro Uttal (1990) *Total Customer Service: The Ultimate Weapon*, New York: Harper & Row.

Davis, G. B. (1974) *Management Information Systems*, New York: McGraw-Hill.

Davis, Keith (1968) 'Success of Chain-of-Command Oral Communication in a Manufacturing Management Group', *Academy of Management Journal*, 11, 379–87.

Dizard, Wilson P. (1985) *The Coming Information Age: An Overview of Technology, Economics and Politics*, New York: Longman.

Drucker, Peter (1969) *The Age of Discontinuity*, London: Heinemann.

Dumaine, Brian (1990) 'Creating a New Company Culture', *Fortune*, 15 January N/70A, 55–8.

Dunlop, Charles and Rob Kling (1991) 'The Dreams of Technological Utopianism', in *Computerization and Controversy: Value Conflicts and Social Choices*, edited by Charles Dunlop and Rob Kling, Boston, Mass: Academic Press, 14–30.

Evans, Fred J. (1987) *Managing the Media*, New York: Quorum.

Evered, Roger (1980) 'The Language of Organizations: The Case of the Navy', in *Organizational Symbolism*, edited by Louis R. Pondy, Peter J. Frost, Gareth Morgan and Thomas C. Dandridge, Greenwich, Conn.: JAI, 123–43.

Fayerweather, J. (1960) *Management of International Operations*, New York: McGraw-Hill.

Finnegan, Ruth (1988) *Literacy and Orality: Studies in the Technology of Communication*, Oxford: Blackwell.

Fisk, Raymond P. and Stephen J. Grove (1995) 'Service Performances and Drama: Quality Implications and Measurement', in *Managing Service Quality*, edited by Paul Kunst and Jos Lemmink, London: Pane Chapman, 107–19.

Forsyth, Michael (1983) *The Myths of Privatisation*, London: Adam Smith Institute.

Foster, Richard N. (1986) *Innovation: The Attacker's Advantage*, London: Macmillan.

Foy, Fred C. (1984) 'Annual Reports Don't Have to be Dull', in *Business and its Public*, edited by Douglas Dickson, New York: John Wiley, 415–27.

Freedman, David H. (1992) 'Is Management Still a Science?', *Harvard Business Review*, 70, 26–38.

Friedman, Andrew L. and Dominic S. Cornford (1989) *Computer Systems Development: History, Organization and Implementation*, New York: John Wiley.

Galbraith, John Kenneth (1967) *The New Industrial Estate*, London: Hamish Hamilton.

Galli, Anthony (1971) 'Corporate Advertising: More Than Just a Nice Warm Feeling All Over', *Public Relations Journal*, 27, 19–77.

Garbett, Thomas F. (1981) *Corporate Advertising: The What, The Why and The How*, New York: McGraw-Hill.

Ghent, W. J. (1902) *Our Benevolent Feudalism*, New York: Macmillan.

Goldzimer, Linda S. (1990) *Customer-Driven*, London: Hutchinson.

Goodman, Stanley, J. (1982) *How to Manage a Turnaround*, New York: Free Press.

Hall, Edmund T. (1966) *The Hidden Dimension: Man's Use of Space in Public and Private*, New York: Doubleday.

Hall, Stuart (1983) 'The Problem of Ideology: Marxism without Guarantees', in *Marx: A Hundred Years On*, edited by B. Matthews, London: Lawrence & Wishart, 57–86.

Hamel, Gary (1996) 'Strategy as Revolution', *Harvard Business Review*, 74, 69–82.

Hammer, Michael (1990) 'Reengineering Work: Don't Automate: Obliterate', *Harvard Business Review*, 68, 104–12.

Hampden-Turner, Charles and Fons Trompenaars (1993) *The Seven Cultures of Capitalism*, New York: Doubleday.

Handy, C. (1996) *Beyond Certainty: The Changing World of Organisations*, London: Arrow.

Heenan, David A. and Howard V. Perlmutter (1979) *Multinational Organizational Development*, Reading, Mass.: Addison-Wesley.

Hildebrandt, H.W. (1973) 'Communication Barriers between German Subsidiaries and Parent American Companies', *Michigan Business Review*, 9, 7–14.

Hirsch, Paul M. and John A. Y. Andrews (1983) 'Ambushes, Shootouts, and Knights of the Roundtable: The Language of Corporate Takeovers', in *Organizational Symbolism*, edited by Louis R. Pondy, Peter J. Frost, Gareth Morgan and Thomas D. Dandridge, Greenwich, Conn.: JAI, 145–55.

Hodgetts, Richard and Fred Luthans (1994) *International Management*, New York: McGraw-Hill.

Hofstede, Geert (1991) *Cultures and Organizations: Software of the Mind*, New York: McGraw Hill.

Hymer, Stephen H. (1979) *The Multinational Corporation: A Radical Approach*, Cambridge: CUP.

Jenkins, Clive and Barrie Sherman (1979) *The Collapse of Work*, London: Eyre Methuen.

Kameda, Naoki (1992) '"Englishes" in Cross-Cultural Business Communication', *The Bulletin*, March, 3–8.

Katz, Bernard (1987) *How to Manage Customer Service*, Aldershot: Gower.

Katz, Daniel and Robert L. Kahn (1966) *The Social Psychology of Organizations*, London: John Wiley.

Kerr, Clark, John T. Dunlop, Frederick H. Harbison and Charles A. Myers (1964) *Industrialism and Industrial Man: The Problems of Labor and Management of Economic Growth*, Cambridge, Mass.: Harvard University Press.

Kidder, Tracy (1981) *The Soul of the New Machine*, New York: Allen Lane.

Kling, Rob and Suzanne Iacono (1991) 'Making a Computer Revolution', reprinted in *Value Conflicts and Social Choices*, edited by Charles Dunlop and Rob Kling, Boston, Mass.: Academic Press, 63–75.

Labour Research Unit (1982) *Privatisation: Public or Private?*

—— (1983) *Privatisation: Who Loses? Who Profits*?

—— (1985) *Privatisation The Great Sell-Out.*

—— (1987) *Privatisation: Paying the Price.*

Laurant, A. (1985) 'The Cultural Diversity of Western Conceptions of Management', in *Managing in Different Cultures*, edited by Pat Joynt and Malcolm Warner, Oslo: Oslo Universitet Forlaget, 41–56.

London, Keith (1976) *The People Side of Systems: The Human Aspects of Computer Systems*, London: McGraw-Hill.

Lorsch, Jay W. (1986) 'Managing Culture: The Invisible Barrier to Strategic Change', *California Management Review*, Vol. 28, No. 2, 95–109.

Lyytinen, Kalle (1987) 'A Taxonomic Perspective of Information Systems Development: Theoretical Constructs and Recommendations', in *Critical Issues in Information.*

McMaster, Michael D. (1996) *The Intelligence Advantage: Organising for Complexity*, Boston, Mass.: Butterworth-Heinemann.

Martin, William B. (1991) *Managing Quality Customer Service*, London: Kogan Page.

Mattelart, Armand (1979) *Multinational Corporations and the Control of Culture: The Ideological Apparatus of Imperialism*, London: Harvester.

Mayo, Elton (1945) *The Social Problems of an Industrial Civilization*, Boston, Mass.: Harvard University Press.

Meyerson, Debra and Joanne Martin (1987) 'Cultural Change: An Integration of Three Different Views', *Journal of Management Studies*, 24: 6, 623–47.

Michelmann, Hans, J. (1978) *Organisational Effectiveness in a Multinational Bureaucracy*, London: Saxon House.

Mickelthwait, John and Adrian Wooldridge (1996) *The Witch Doctors: What the Management Gurus are Saying, Why it Matters and How to Make Sense of It*, London: Heinemann.

Mintzberg, Henry (1976) 'Planning on the Left Side and Managing on the Right', *Harvard Business Review*, 54, 49–58.

—— (1994) 'The Fall and Rise of Strategic Planning', *Harvard Business Review*, 72, 107–14.

—— (1996) 'Managing Government: Governing Management', *Harvard Business Review*, 74, 75–83.

Mirtoff, I. I. and R. H. Kilmann (1976) 'On Organization Stories: An Approach to the Design and Analysis of Organisations Through Myths and Stores', in *The Management of Organization Design*, edited by R. H. Kilmann, L. R. Pondy and D. P. Slevin, New York: North Holland.

Moore, George S. (1980) *Managing Corporate Relations: A Practical Guide to Business Survival*, Aldershot: Gower.

Moore, James F. (1996) *The Death of Competition: Leadership and Strategy in the Age of Business Ecosystems*, Chichester: John Wiley.

Moore, John (1992a) 'British Privatization – Taking Capitalism to the People', *Harvard Business Review*, 70, 115–24.

—— (1992b) *Privatisation Everywhere: The World's Adoption of the British Experience*, London: Centre for Policy Studies.

Mumford, Enid and Olive Banks (1967) *The Computer and the Clerk*, London: RKP.

Mumford, Enid and T. B. Ward (1968) *Computers: Planning for People*, London: Batsford.

Negandhi, A. R. (1990) 'External and Internal Functioning of American, German and Japanese Mutlinational Corporations: Decision Making and Policy Issues', in *Multinational Corporations*, edited by Mark Casson, Aldershot: Edward Edgar, 557–77.

Newman, R. (1975) 'The Use of Computers in Department Stores', *Retail and Distribution Management*, 6–10.

Noble, David F. (1984) *Forces of Production: A Social History of Industrial Automation*, Oxford: Oxford University Press.

Nyquist, Jody D., Mary J. Bitner and Bernard H. Booms (1985) 'Identifying Communication Difficulties in the Service Encounter: A Critical Incident Approach', in *The Service Encounter*, edited by John A. Czepiel, Michael R. Solomon and Carol F. Surprenant, Lexington, Mass.: Lexington Books, 195–212.

Ogden, W. F. (1964), *On Culture and Social Change*, edited by Otis Dudley Duncan, Chicago, Ill.: University of Chicago Press.

Ohmae, Kenichi (1994) *The Borderless World: Power and Strategy in the Global Marketplace*, London: HarperCollins.

Ong, Walter J. (1982) *Rhetoric, Romance and Technology*, London: Cornell University Press.

Peet, John (1987) *Healthy Competition: How to Improve the NHS*, London: Centre for Policy Studies.

Peters, Thomas J. (1980) 'Management Systems: The Language of Organizational Character and Competence', *Organizational Dynamics*, 9, 3–26.

Pfeffer, Jeffrey (1995) *Competitive Advantage Through People: Unleashing the Power of the Work Force*, Boston, Mass.: Harvard University Press.

Pondy, Louis R., Richard J. Boland and Howard Thomas (1984) *Managing Ambiguity and Change*, Chichester: John Wiley.

Porter, L. W. and K. Roberts (1977) *Communication in Organizations*, Harmondsworth: Penguin.

Prokesch, Steven E. (1995) 'Competing on Customer Service: An Interview with British Airways 'Sir Colin Marshall', *Harvard Business Review*, 73, 101–12.

Rassam, Clive and David Oates (1991) *Management Consultancy: The Inside Story*, London: Mercury.

Redwood, John (1994) *Looking over the Jargon Wall: The Way to Better Public Service*, London: Centre for Policy Studies.

Rogers, Everett M. (1983) *Diffusion of Innovations*, New York: Free Press.

Rose, Michael (1969) *Computers, Managers and Society*, Harmondsworth: Penguin.

Rothery, Brian (1971) *The Myth of the Computer*, London: Business Books.

Salama, Alzira (1995) *Privatization: Implications for Corporate Culture Change*, Aldershot: Avebury.

Sanderson, Harold (1976) 'How Mothercare Captures Sales Data', *Retail and Distribution Management*, 4, 34–7.

Scarbrough, Harry and J. Martin Corbett (1992) *Technology and Organization: Power, Meaning and Design*, London: Routledge.

Schein, Edgar H. (1985) *Organization, Culture and Leadership*, San Francisco: Jossey Bass.

Senge, Peter M. (1990) *The Fifth Discipline: The Art and Practice of the Learning Organization*, London: Century.

Shapero, Albert (1976) 'What Management Says and What Managers Do', *Fortune*, May, 275–6.

Shipman, A. (1992) 'Talking the Same Languages', *International Management*, June, 68–71.

Stanley, Manfred (1978) *The Technological Conscience: Survival and Dignity in an Age of Expertise*, New York: Free Press.

Stopford, John M. and Susan Strange (1991) *Rival States, Rival Firms: Competition for World Market Shares*, Cambridge: Cambridge University Press.

Stopford, John M. and Louis T. Wells (1972) *Managing the Multinational Enterprise: Organization of the Firm and Ownership of the Subsidiaries, London: Longman.*

Tannen, Deborah (1995) *Talking from Nine to Five*, London: Virago.

Tedlow, Richard S. (1979) *Keeping the Corporate Image: Public Relations in Business 1900–1950*, Greenwich, Conn.: JAI.

Terpstra, Vern (1978) The Cultural Environment of International Business, Cincinnati, Ohio: Southwestern.

Thackery, J. (1986) 'The Corporate Culture Rage', *Management Today.*

Toffler, Alvin (1980) *The Third Wave*, London: Collins.

Weisenbaum, Joseph (1976) *Computer Power and Human Reason: From Judgement to Calculation*, San Francisco: Freeman.

Weiser, Charles R. (1995) 'Championing the Customer', *Harvard Business Review*, 73, 113–16.

Weiss, E. B. (1970) 'Management: Don't Kid the Public with Those Noble Anti-Pollution Ads', *Advertising Age*, 3 August, Vol. 33, No. 4, 35–8.

Whisler, Thomas L. (1970) *The Impact of Computers on Organizations*, London: Praeger.

Wilson, David C. (1992) *A Strategy of Change: Concepts and Controversies in the Management of Change*, London: Routledge.

Wiltshire, Kenneth (1987) *Privatisation: The British Experience*, Melbourne: Longman Cheshire.

Winner, L. (1983) 'Mythinformation in the High-Tech Era' *IEEE Spectrum,* 90–6.

Yoshino M. Y. (1976) *Japan's Multinational Enterprises*, Cambridge, Mass.: Harvard University Press.

Yousef, Fathi S. (1974) 'Cross-Cultural Communication: Aspects of Contrastive Social Values between North Americans and Middle Easterners', *Human Organization*, 3: 4, 383–7.

Index